Trade Unions and the Economic Crisis of the 1980s

Edited by
WILLIAM BRIERLEY
School of Languages and Area Studies,
Portsmouth Polytechnic

Gower

Published by
Gower Publishing Company Limited,
Gower House, Croft Road, Aldershot, Hants GU11 3HR,
England.

Gower Publishing Company,
Old Post Road, Brookfield, Vermont 05036,
United States of America.

British Library Cataloguing in Publication Data

Trade unions and the economic crisis of
    the 1980s.
    1. Trade-unions
    I. Brierley, William
    331.88   HD6483

    ISBN 0-566-05245-8

Printed and bound in Great Britain by
Biddles Limited, Guildford and King's Lynn

Contents

PART II EASTERN EUROPE

PART III DEVELOPING COUNTRIES

Editor's foreword

This collection of essays examines the responses of trade unions in several countries in Western Europe, Eastern Europe and the developing world to the effects of the international economic crisis particularly over the last ten years.

The economic crisis has affected national economies in different ways, and the institutional arrangements and industrial relations systems of the countries studied have clearly developed in different ways, especially with regard to the degree of involvement of the representatives of organised labour in the development and implementation of economic policy at the national level and in management decisions at the level of the enterprise. In all of the countries studied, however, the experience has been the same: the gains obtained principally in the 1970s in the areas of the extension of workers' rights, the protection of their living and working conditions and their increased involvement in political and economic decision-making have all been rolled back as neoliberal monetarist economic policies have generally replaced Keynesian interventionism. The tendency has been to attempt to return the control of the labour market and industrial relations systems to market forces.

This is not to argue, however, that trade unions have become redundant and have no role to play in contemporary society. Nowhere has the recession hit so hard as to suggest a move towards a completely unmediated relationship between capital and labour. Labour unions have not conceded defeat - indeed they have shown a great deal of flexibility and invention in their responses to the crisis. But the dilemma remains: in the defence of workers' interests, is the best strategy to concentrate effort on the defence of employed labour in the work place or can the general objective only be achieved by defending all sections of the working and non-working (unemployed) class through cooperation with management and government in economic decision-making at the enterprise, sectoral, regional or national level? Within this broad concern, a second problem is whether these objectives are best achieved through legal structures regulating the relationships between capital, labour and government, or through more traditional collective bargaining structures which preserve the independence of the bargaining agents.

It is not intended to suggest in this book that there is a common resolution to these dilemmas, nor even that there are common determiners which make the dilemmas more or less difficult to resolve. Our purpose is to examine the ways in which labour movements in very different social, political and economic circumstances have grappled with the problem and to examine the extent to which their efforts have been successful within their national socio-political confines. The feature which unifies these experiences is the need for unions increasingly since the mid-1970s to take cognisance of the worsening economic climate and to take the crisis into account when formulating their demands or responding to the retrenchment of management. Some unions have been more successful than others, but everywhere, and no more so than where the economic crisis is at its most profound, trade unionism is in crisis.

Contributors

ROB ATKINSON is Lecturer in Politics and History in the School of Social and Historical Studies, Portsmouth Polytechnic.

JEFF BRIDGFORD is Senior Lecturer in French Studies in the School of Modern Languages, Newcastle upon Tyne Polytechnic

BILL BRIERLEY is Senior Lecturer in Italian Studies in the School of Languages and Area Studies, Portsmouth Polytechnic.

DAVID CORKILL is Senior Lecturer in History in the Department of English and History, Manchester Polytechnic.

LLUIS FINA is Lecturer in Economics at the Universidad Autónoma de Barcelona and the Escuela Superior de Aministración y Dirección de Empresas, Barcelona.

RICHARD HAWKESWORTH is Principal Lecturer in Contemporary European Studies (Economics) in the School of Languages and European Studies, Wolverhampton Polytechnic.

JOHN HUMPHREY is Senior Lecturer in Sociology and Latin American Studies at the University of Liverpool.

GAIL MARTIN is Senior Lecturer in Latin American History in the School of Languages and Area Studies, Portsmouth Polytechnic.

FRANCES MILLARD is Principal Lecturer in Politics in the School of Social and Historical Studies, Portsmouth Polytechnic.

MARK MITCHELL is Principal Lecturer in Sociology in the School of Social and Historical Studies, Portsmouth Polytechnic.

PETER MORRIS is Lecturer in Politics at the University of Nottingham.

HÜSEYIN RAMAZANOGLU is Senior Lecturer in Third World Politics in the School of Social and Historical Studies, Portsmouth Polytechnic.

DAVE RUSSELL is Senior Lecturer in Sociology in the School of Social and Historical Studies, Portsmouth Polytechnic.

MICA YOVANOVIC is Senior Lecturer in Industrial Sociology at the University of Belgrade, Yugoslavia.

The chapters by Atkinson, Bridgford and Morris, Brierley, Corkill, Humphrey, Martin and Millard appeared in somewhat different form in the Journal of Area Studies, no. 13, Spring 1986. They appear here by kind permission of the Editors.

The editor would like to thank Mrs Ann Lindsay for her kind and patient help in preparing the typescript.

PART I
WESTERN EUROPE

1 Trade unions, industrial change and the effects of recession in West Germany and the United Kingdom

ROB ATKINSON

INTRODUCTION

The assumption underlying this chapter is that the current world recession will have important implications for trade unions in all countries. However, it is also argued that the extent and nature of these 'implications' cannot simply be derived from an abstract analysis, nor will they be uniform even within the 'advanced' capitalist core of Western Europe and North America. Thus the effects of the recession on unions in each social formation will be mediated by a series of factors such as the 'strength' of the national economy, its position in the international economy, its political and economic institutions and the forms of hegemony established. In order to illustrate these differential effects we will examine the trade union movements in West Germany and the United Kingdom.

The first section of the paper will analyse the current recession and the changes implicit in recent developments before moving on in sections two and three to an analysis of its effects on trade unions within the wider political, economic and ideological relations of each social formation as we argue these relations play a major role in defining the problems encountered by unions and, to an extent, their response.

THE CURRENT RECESSION: ORIGINS AND IMPLICATIONS

It is commonplace to locate the origins of the current recession in the mid-1970s, beginning initially as a result of the oil crisis in 1973 and then being exacerbated by the second oil crisis of the late 1970s. Such factors alone do not, however, constitute a rigorous basis for an

3

understanding of the recession; in a sense they are exogenous factors which, despite being important conjunctural variables, cannot form the basis of a coherent explanation.

For such an explanation, we must turn to the theory of long waves which in recent years has been associated with the work of Mandel (1). In Mandel's work, a long wave lasts approximately fifty years and is divided into two periods each of about 20-25 years duration. During the long wave, the traditional business cycle continues to operate but each period is dominated by either accelerated or decelerated accumulation, each following on from the other in successive waves.

The key question is 'what causes periods of accelerated accumulation to begin, and why do they come to an end?'. Mandel explains these developments by recourse to concepts such as the 'tendency of the rate of profit to fall', class struggle and the generation of technological revolutions which open up qualitatively new opportunities for capital accumulation. There are undoubtedly problems with Mandel's theorisation of long waves and their causes, mechanisms of decline, and so on (2), but his general point is that when one of these 'technological rev- olutions' is exhausted, a period of decelerated accumulation begins in the world economy which requires a fundamental reorganisation of pro- duction and demand before a new period of accelerated accumulation can begin. The implication is that the current recession cannot be traced back to 1973. Following Mandel, the current recession can be dated as beginning in the second half of the 1960s (3) and it is this whole period which has structured developments in the national economy (4) and provides important pointers for our analysis.

ot would be a major error, however, to conclude our more general analysis at this point. Quite simply, the concept of long waves in itself is insufficient. In addition we need to develop concepts of analysis more directly applicable to the post-1945 era. Here we must turn to the concepts of fordism (5) and in particular to the work of Aglietta (6).

The concept of fordism has its origins in the work of Gramsci (7) where it is used to denote a form of mass production which displaces Taylorism by the use of production line techniques and attempts to regulate workers' lives. In essence the concept refers to the artic- ulation of mass production with mass consumption. On the one hand, it refers to the methods of production and organisation to be found in mass production industries which developed the semi-automatic assembly line. This involves the structuring of the production process around machines rather than people in order massively to increase production. On the other hand, it also refers to the development of a 'social consumption norm' which allows for the realisation of surplus value created (8). These two closely related aspects entail major changes in the organ- isation of the capitalist enterprise and relations between enterprises. We refer here not simply to new forms of concentration and central- isation, but also to new forms of control within the production process and capitalist hierarchy (9).

The decay of fordism is at the same time the decay of the post-war period of accelerated accumulation, and it is this which has produced the current recession. As a consequence of this decay, we have witness- ed the massive destruction of constant capital (devalorisation) along

4

with an equally massive expulsion of variable capital (labour) from the production process. The extent of devalorisation and expulsion will depend upon a number of factors such as the extent to which fordism has been established, the ability of the economy to restructure in response to changing conditions of accumulation and the role of the state. An economy which is strong and dynamic will be more likely to develop the new forms of production necessary to cope with the recession and emerge strengthened when (if?) a new period of expansion occurs. What we are suggesting here is that just as there is no inevitable final crisis of capitalism, nor is there inevitably going to be a new period of expansive capital accumulation. The transition to neofordism is therefore not inevitable.

What we have tried to emphasise is the importance of each social formation's institutional and organisational arrangements in its economy and polity as important factors determining an economy's ability to respond to the changing conditions (10) and restructuring (11). Of course, this means that these processes are not automatic; different social formations will respond in different ways according to their perceptions and definitions of the crisis, and the balance of class and political forces. Thus, any process of restructuring will not simply be limited to economic institutions but will, in some cases, also involve fundamental changes in the industrial culture and forms of hegemony. It is in this context that trade unions must be considered.

Since the 1880s, capital has increasingly taken on an international form. In the post-war period, however, and especially since the 1960s, this has taken new forms. Capital no longer remains tied to particular social formations but has acquired a considerable degree of mobility not simply in terms of the movement of money capital but also in relation to the production process itself. In its new form, production has increasingly been internationalised. Trade unions, on the other hand, have remained tied to particular social formations and consequently levels of international cooperation are low. This gives capital a major advantage over labour as it is now able to search for conditions which best suit particular aspects of the production process and locate them where profitability is optimum (12).

The crisis of fordism cannot, in our view, be characterised by a single factor explanation - such as overproduction. It has occurred on a number of levels, each of which has a different temporality and dynamic of its own. However, since the mid-1970s, these different levels have increasingly begun to reinforce one another thus greatly exacerbating the crisis (13).

In relation to trade unions, the single major area of the crisis which concerns us is changes within the production process, arguably the ultimate source of the crisis. Fordism requires a constant increase in profitability which in turn requires constant new investment to increase productivity. Towards the end of the 1960s, however, this increase began to falter and wages began to rise at the expense of profits. In essence, we are back to the problem of conflict within the production process, i.e. workers and trade unions have become a barrier to further accumulation, which requires a radical reorganisation of the labour process and a further intensification of mechanisation and capitalist control of the production process - it goes under the title of neofordism (14). Neofordism is still in its early stages and its future

5

development is difficult to predict, but it would appear that the hall-mark of neofordism will be greater flexibility: greater flexibility in the production process, in the products produced (15) and in the spatial location of production (16). All of which entails a greater flexibility in the use of labour both in terms of the tasks carried out and numbers employed.

WEST GERMANY

Economic and political background (17)

The so-called economic miracle ('Wirtschaftswunder') which has occurred in West Germany since 1945 is widely assumed to have been based on a prolonged period of industrial peace and widespread use of capital intensive production techniques. If developments are examined more closely, however, it soon becomes apparent that neither of these factors is true of the period as a whole. Several authors (18) have pointed out that in the immediate post-war years, and even during the 1950s, there was considerable worker unrest and that industry was not capital inten-sive. Furthermore, whilst the destruction of capital during the war was extensive, it was nowhere near as high as is often assumed, thus provid-ing a solid base for expansion. Industry in fact was highly labour intensive, and profitability was based on the extraction of absolute surplus value. Nor was the economy a high wage, mass consumption econ-omy in the classic fordist sense. Figures provided by Semmler (19) suggest that only at the end of the 1950s, when full employment was approaching, were workers able significantly to improve their wage share. Prior to the 1960s, consumption as a share of GNP fell from 64.1 per cent in 1950 to 56.6 per cent in 1960.

How did the economic miracle take place? Firstly, fascism not only destroyed most of the labour movement's organisation but it also consid-erably reduced workers' standards of living, thereby significantly cheapening the reproduction of labour power (20). Secondly, the massive influx of refugees from the East, until 1961, constantly topped up the reserve army of labour and in combination with unemployment helped keep down the cost of labour power (21). Thirdly, the presence of the allies plus the refugees created a strongly anti-communist climate which also affected the unions and discredited any alternatives to the social market economy. Fourthly, the state intervened massively in favour of capital, helping to create the conditions which favoured high rates of exploitation and profit. Later it would also play a major role by encouraging the move from an extensive to an intensive regime of capital accumulation (22). These four factors alone, however, are not suffi-cient to explain the economic miracle. A fifth factor was crucial: an expanding world market on which surplus value could be realised. Thus was especially important given the lack of a mass consumption domestic market in the 1950s.

By the late 1950s, several of these conditions were beginning to change: unemployment was beginning to fall and by 1960 was below one per cent, and by 1958 unit wage costs had caught up with international levels. By the late 1950s, the limits of an extensive regime of capital accumulation were being approached and during the 1960s moves were made in the direction of an intensive regime of accumulation based on capital intensive production and the extraction of relative surplus value. The

1966-67 recession persuaded key sectors of capital and the state of the need to increase the tempo of change and greater emphasis was placed on restructuring and rationalisation.

Altvater et al. argue that this required accumulation to be based on a massive export surplus which in turn drew West Germany more closely into the world economy. This integration was further enhanced by the increasing export of money capital, largely to developed nations, as West German capital became increasingly internationalised. This accumulation strategy (23) came to be known as known as 'Modell Deutschland'.

The period since the late 1960s has seen the intensification of this strategy as the recession has intensified, first via the 1973 oil crisis, then via the second oil shock of the late 1970s and increasingly via the circuit of international credit. With regard to West Germany, Semmler argues that:

> ... especially since the beginning of the 1970s, the terms of trade have tended to rise, and input costs have tended to increase. On the whole, one can see a declining profitability of investments and a slowing down of capital accumulation ... In sum, the initially quite favourable conditions for rapid capital accumulation and high growth rates have deteriorated since the 1950s and 1960s (24).

West German capital reacted by firstly intensifying the process of modernisation and rationalisation, and secondly by increasing overseas investments. In the first instance, this has involved not only a process of rationalisation and modernisation within sectors of the economy, but also between sectors. We have witnessed, with the assistance of the state, the managed decline of sectors which are uncompetitive on the world market, plus the active fostering of sectors which allow West Germany to retain its leading position in key capital goods areas (25). In the second instance, it has involved the intensification of internationalisation to avoid protective barriers and increasing West German hegemony within the European Community (26).

The relative success of these two strategies has meant that West Germany has become increasingly concerned with the crisis of unemployment - note not of de-industrialisation as in the UK - caused by structural changes in the economy consequent upon the aggressive pursuit of this dual strategy plus an increasing emphasis on supply side economics. West German unions have been particularly concerned with these developments. Before going on to discuss their reaction, however, a further digression into the arena of politics is necessary as political arrangements have played a key role in mediating the effects of the world crisis, in defining the nature of the crisis and 'legitimate' strategies for dealing with it.

Until 1966, the social democratic SPD remained outside the federal government; post-war politics were shaped largely by the conservative CDU/CSU. It was they and the political forces they represented that forged the basis of the 'social market economy', the central feature of the post-war consensus. During the late 1940s and early 1950s, politics closely followed class lines (27), but as the 1950s progressed, the CDU/CSU increasingly pursued policies designed to appeal to working class voters thus threatening to undermine the SPD's vote. As a result the CDU/CSU moved in the direction of a catch-all party ('Volkspartei') which forced the SPD to move in a similar direction. This it did with the 1959 Bad Godesberg Programme. Both parties now accepted the social market economy. Such a compromise was always likely during a period of rising living standards and industrial expansion. As Minnerup has accurately observed:

> The demoralising impact of Stalinism in the GDR, the intimidation and persecution of socialist militants suspected of 'treacherous' Communist contacts, and the depoliticisation and social pacification in the wake of the 'economic miracle' forced the labour movement onto the defensive until, with the adoption of the Godesberg Programme in 1959, the SPD surrendered on the CDU's terms ... (28).

This bought the SPD electoral respectability and entry into government via the Grand Coalition of 1966-69 and then as governing party (in a coalition) from 1969-82. During this period, class voting appeared to decline and the 'New Politics' (29) emerged, with greater emphasis being placed on the capture of the 'new middle class' vote. The effect of recession, however, appears to have led to a reassertion of economic cleavages in the 1980s.

Trade unions: the context and response

In the early post-war years, the union movement found it difficult to establish itself. The DGB (Deutsche Gewerkschaftsbund) saw its demands for codetermination throughout German industry rejected; only in the coal and iron and steel industries, and only then after strikes, did they win codetermination under the law of 1951. Elsewhere, they found themselves banished from the shop floor by the 1952 Works Constitution Act which set up the Works Councils, which were responsible for all matters relating to individual plants while unions were restricted to the national and regional level where pay and hours were negotiated (30). This dual system of industrial relations has been reinforced by the reforms of the 1972 Works Constitution Act and the 1976 Codetermination Act.

The 1951 Act gave workers parity of representation on the supervisory boards of firms and the 1976 Act extended this to all firms with 2,000 or more employees, though representation on the supervisory boards was limited to one-third of its members. Both codetermination and the works council system are embedded in a legal framework which closely regulates and limits what each element in the industrial relations system can do. For instance, works councils are charged with the obligation of 'maintaining social peace' and it is illegal for them to call a strike; workers who sit on these councils do not do so as mandated representatives of the work force (even though they are elected) but are charged by law to act in the best interests of the enterprise - in other words, they are not legally speaking workers at all (31). In the case of the unions, bargaining takes place on industrial lines with the relevant employers federation at the regional or national level. The effect of this is that compared to the UK there are far fewer unions: the DGB with a membership of over 7 million has only 17 constituent unions, each of which covers one industry. This removes the possibility of inter-union competition over jobs. All of the unions, including the DGB itself, are highly centralised and professionalised with their own expert negotiators and economists. Such a set-up allows the unions to exercise a considerable degree of control over the membership.

The concept of industrial unionism also serves another purpose as it allows the unions to pursue a 'solidaristic wage policy', i.e. one in which negotiators working at national or regional level for a whole industry negotiate a deal which does not reflect the position of workers employed either in the most profitable firms or in the least profitable firms. A settlement will be somewhere between the two, thus benefiting the workers in the weaker firms. It might be thought that this would cause dissension among workers in stronger firms, but this is overcome by an unofficial second round of negotiations at the plant level carried out by the works council. This allows additional payments (wage drift) to be related to the profitablity of individual plants or firms. It may also allow works councils to demonstrate their usefulness to workers. All in all this dual system plays a major role in the maintenance of social peace, giving the system an important degree of flexibility. Once agreement has been reached it is legally binding and when renego- tiation occurs it does so within a strictly defined legal framework which regulates both the nature of the negotiations (i.e. demands must be capable of being met through collective bargaining and conducted in 'good will') and the level of sanctions which may be used by either party at each stage of the negotiations (32). The term 'juridification' is frequently used when describing this system, acknowledging the extent to which the law is built into it.

Unlike the UK, where the experience of law by trade unions usually takes a negative form, the West German system endows upon unions a series of 'positive rights' - such as the right to strike under strictly defined circumstances, codetermination, access to information, and so on. This system contains most conflicts within a strict institutional framework which arguably reduces most conflicts to a process of ritual- ised confrontation in which the rules of the game mean that at any particular point in the negotiation each side knows what the other's next move will be and what it has to do to convince the opposition of its seriousness. Thus we have a highly functional system which aids the maintenance of 'social peace' and played an important part in the econ- omic miracle.

Despite the relatively hostile atmosphere in the late 1940s and 1950s, trade unions accommodated themselves to the new Bonn republic. Mark- ovits argues that in part this was because they have always been major supporters of liberal democracy, but he also argues that they have been 'Staatsstragend' bodies (i.e. state-supporting or state-carrying) during the two periods of liberal democracy in German history. Thus they were unlikely to adopt outright opposition to the new regime. Markovits also contends that historically the unions have had a 'state fixation' ('Staatsfixierung') which has led them to look to the state for concrete reforms and to reflect in their own internal organisation the state's own structural characteristics and outlook (33). In this sense, they have always been closely identified with the state and their willingness to accept juridification must be seen partly in this context (34).

Despite these problems, unions and their members prospered during the 1950s and with the advent of full employment began gradually to increase the wage share (35) and brought with it the possibility of inflation. These developments coincided with the changing economic conditions des- cribed above and the move of the SPD into the political mainstream. The economic crisis of 1966-67 was to be the catalyst which formalised the notion of 'social partnership' already implicit in works councils and codetermination into a form of neocorporatism.

Neocorporatism became an important part of the 'Modell Deutschland' strategy and the unions played a key role in maintaining the 'magic square' (price stability, full employment, balance of foreign trade and economic growth). Inherent within the 'Modell Deutschland' strategy, however, was a contradiction for the unions: the unions were committed to the growth of the economy via a continuous process of modernisation and rationalisation. In some instances this would mean loss of jobs which would be replaced by growth elsewhere in the economy. Part of this strategy, however, required that in some cases production was located overseas in order to maintain the firm's market share and profitability. Given the commitment of workers and unions to this general strategy, they were also committed to overseas investment. During the period of economic growth, jobs lost could easily be replaced and the contradiction lay dormant, but if growth were to drop or cease the contradiction might become real rather then implicit and major problems could arise.

When neocorporatist arrangements were formalised through the tripartism of 'concerted action' in 1967 (36) these problems were potential rather than actual. The form of neocorporatism developed utilised and built upon the dual structure of worker representation to insulate trade union leadership from membership and thus enable them to participate more easily (37), while the highly centralised nature of the DGB and its constituent unions enabled them to participate in an authoritative manner (38). Thus the DGB was able to cooperate with state macro-economic policy in the aftermath of 1966-67 and persuade its members to accept moderate wage settlements in order to allow West German capital's profitability to be partially restored and the modernisation and rationalisation process to continue.

It would be wrong, however, to give the impression that workers were simply passive objects who followed the union's line obediently. By 1969, a series of unofficial (and illegal) strikes had broken out as a response to the quick recovery by individual firms and the economy as a whole (39). This forced union leaders to initiate official strikes in 1970 and 1971. Thus, even where institutional structures exist to dissipate and institutionalise conflict, there is no guarantee that they will prevent industrial disruption by workers at the point of production if they feel that their living standards are under threat. This is particularly the case in a 'growth conscious' economy where the work force is strongly aware of the importance of growth and of their right to participate in the benefits as one of the conditions of the 'social partnership'. Clearly, then, the whole process was underwritten by economic growth and rising living standards.

As the 1970s progressed, however, the increasing pressure to accelerate and intensify modernisation and rationalisation reached a new peak in the aftermath of the 1974-75 crisis. The depth of the crisis (40) plus West Germany's increased integration into the world market, greatly exacerbated the situation, convincing capital and the state of the need for more radical changes.

Sengenberger (41) has argued that prior to 1974-75, a covert form of labour market segmentation had developed during the period of full employment. Segmentation differed from industry to industry but generally speaking we can draw a distinction between a permanent core of male, skilled, unionised workers and a secondary or marginal group of weakly unionised, semi- or unskilled, foreign and female workers. During the period of full employment, this secondary group was unaffected, but as the world economy moved deeper into recession it caused considerable problems even for the most profitable sectors of the West German economy. Unemployment increased from 1.2 per cent in 1973 to 4.7 per cent in 1975, dropping to 3.8 per cent by 1979 but then increasing steadily from 5.5 per cent in 1981 to 10.4 per cent in February 1986. With the first rapid increase in unemployment the lines between the core and the secondary work forces became much sharper. As the mass of trade union members were concentrated in the core work force, unemployment did not present itself as a major problem to the unions, especially as much of the reduction was borne by foreign workers (42). At the same time, firms began increasingly to develop their own internal labour markets partly as a way of retaining skilled workers but also to create flexibility in the use of labour within plants.

Segmentation should also be related to another development. Gabriel and Holzapfl (43) argue that in the post-1975 situation, firms had to be able to adjust the volume of production to meet an increasingly uncertain demand which meant a greater emphasis was placed on flexibility. As we mentioned in the previous paragraph, this led to the development of internal labour markets with a stable, skilled and highly productive core work force and a more flexible secondary work force. Doshe (44) found that foreign workers in particular took on the role of a mobile reserve at plant level, buffering the core work force from unemployment. In addition, there is also some evidence that management used the recession to 'weed out' the core work force, getting rid of elderly workers via early retirement and only employing young, skilled and highly productive workers. Throughout this process works councils actively cooperated, which should not come as a surprise given the over representation of the core work force on the councils (45). Thus the core work force was able, through the works councils, to protect itself and shift the burden of unemployment onto the secondary or marginal sectors of the work force.

With the further intensification of the recession in 1979, unemployment began to rise once again, and has continued to rise up to the present. In such conditions the works councils may come to identify themselves so closely with the needs of their individual firms that solidarity with the rest of the union could be undermined. We shall return to this point later.

How have the unions reacted to this increase in unemployment? Clearly they have been worried by its rise as it has probably been the most important single factor undermining their strength since 1975. Particularly worrying for them has been the employers' use of these conditions to increase flexibility as part of the modernisation and rationalisation process. The difference between the 1980s and the 1970s is the lack of jobs being created to replace those destroyed. In a sense, a key aspect of the material basis of the unions' commitment to 'Modell Deutschland' is under threat.

With regard to the federal government's attitude, there have been strong indications that over the last six or seven years it has abandoned its previously 'neutral' position between labour and capital.

While still attempting to treat economic policy decisions as objective and technical, it is increasingly supporting capital's aim of increasing flexibility and overseas investment. Even the SPD-led government was strongly criticised by unions for its increasing support of capital's strategy and the abandonment of its own social base (46), while the CDU/CSU-led government formed in autumn 1982 has increasingly identified with capital, even describing the metal workers' strike in 1984 as "stupid". Both governments also reflected this shift in an increasingly supply side oriented economic policy (47).

The above factors have combined to play a major role in the gradual weakening of organised labour's position (48), but this weakening of the trade union movement has potentially threatening consequences, as Sengenberger argues:

> There are signs that the productivity and modernisation pact between capital and labour is crumbling, as workers no longer receive a reasonable share of productivity gains and as social security arrangements are dismantled. The productivity pact depends on the effective exchange of workers cooperation in rationalisation policies in return for their shelter from the hazards and risks which tend to result from rationalisation ... If organised labour is weakened both in its political and organisational ability, it is highly doubtful if it can continue to play the requisite role in the productivity and modernisation bargain ... (49).

There are signs that sections of capital and the CDU/CSU government have concluded that the discipline of the market is the best way of continuing modernisation rather than relying on the cooperation of the unions. Recent changes in the law relating to the right of workers laid off because of strike action to unemployment benefit would appear to be a move in this direction. This move is a direct result of the tactics used by IG Metall (the metal workers' union) during their 1984 strike over the 35 hour week (50). Such a move implies that the government is determined to tip the balance of power further in capital's favour.

Before going on one should ask: what effect has the recession had on trade union membership and wages? Until 1982, DGB membership was increasing and there was no indication of any overall increase in strike activity. The fact that DGB membership did not decrease should come as no surprise, given that most of the union membership is concentrated in the protected core work force. More recent reports, however, suggest that unemployment has begun to affect this core membership. It was recently reported that in 1985 the DGB lost 100,000 members and that since the advent of the Kohl government membership has fallen by 200,000 (51). Clearly there are problems here, and while the loss is nowhere near as high as in the UK, it is still serious.

An even more important indication of a trade union's strength is the yearly wage increases it achieves. As can be clearly seen from Table 1.1, there have been major changes over the last fifteen years, each coinciding with major intensifications of the recession, first in 1974, and then again in 1980. This suggests that wage settlements tend to be fairly closely tied to the economy and its performance.

These developments would appear to be the result of West German capital's attempts to deal with the effects of the intensification of the

Table 1.1
Negotiated wage and salary increases
% increase from previous year, 1970-85

1970	15.3	1976	7.0	1981	4.9
1971	11.3	1977	6.9	1982	4.1
1972	9.2	1978	5.4	1983	3.2
1973	11.2	1979	5.7	1984	2.9
1974	10.9	1980	6.7	1985	2.9
1975	6.4				

Source: Deutsche Bundesbank Monthly Reports

crisis of fordism. As a result, workers appear to have benefited much less in terms of wage increases and levels of employment as the recession has intensified, lending some support to Sengenberger's contention that the 'productivity pact' may be in danger.

Unions find themselves in a difficult position because, as we suggested above, they have become so closely identified with 'Modell Deutschland', particularly its growth strategy. This situation is accentuated, as Bruce (52) has pointed out, because unions and workers have identified themselves too closely with management and with its definitions of the growth strategy and the solutions required to maintain the West German economy's international competitiveness. Thus, unions and works councils have tended to administer rather than fight redundancies.

At the level of the works council, this aspect has become even more pronounced because of the close identification of each works council with its own plant's interests and the consequent danger of 'plant egoism' opening up divisions between workers within the unions, i.e. a split between those employed in profitable firms and those in unprofitable ones, a split which the 'solidaristic wage policy' of unions has sought to suppress. Works councils are often seen as the 'hidden hand of the union', about 80 per cent of the representatives are union members; the government has recently suggested that the election procedures should be reformed to give white collar, particularly senior, staff a greater presence on the councils, thereby diluting union influence.

In a general sense, however, there seems to be an underlying feeling among the unions that the West German economy will emerge from the recession as one of the winners and that, rather than digging in their feet and resisting the process of restructuring, it is better to go along with it on the assumption that losses can be made up later.

The unions' major opposition has come through the demand for the shorter working week, which began to emerge in the late 1970s from several unions (especially IG Druck - the print workers, and IG Metall) in order to create more jobs. IG Metall have taken a leading role and in 1978 went on strike in the steel industry for six weeks. The result was a compromise: no reduction in the working week, but an extension of annual holidays up to 30 days. In addition, the agreement reached meant that no further action could be taken until 1983-84. In 1984, IG Metall once again took up the issue and went on strike, with the support of the DGB and of IG Druck in particular. A seven week strike resulted - the biggest and longest in post-war German history, involving some 430,000 workers directly and indirectly. The resulting settlement of a 38.5

hour week was a classic compromise. · At the same time, however, it does represent an important concession by the employers. The settlement itself was not implemented until 1985 and then by the works council and management within the limits of a 37-40 hour week. It seems likely that many firms will be able to exploit this fact and adopt more flexible working practices as works councils try to protect jobs.

IG Metall adopted tactics which aimed to bring the motor industry to a standstill by bringing out key groups of workers in the components industry. As a result, the government has changed the rules governing eligibility for unemployment benefit so that workers laid off because of strike action from which they stand to gain cannot claim benefit.

Does this herald a major offensive against the unions? This seems highly unlikely, given the already high degree of juridification of the industrial relations system and its adaptability. What seems most likely is that wage negotiations will tend to move away from national and regional levels towards the plant level, thus threatening to by-pass the unions. Such a move would allow wage settlements to be tied more closely to the profitability of individual firms and encourage the growth of 'plant egoism'.

Despite this, all is not gloomy for the unions. The attempts by the Kohl government to fine-tune the industrial relations system may actually help create greater unity. Changes in the strike law pushed the DGB into balloting its members on these changes and 7.1 million members voted against, while only 327,837 voted in favour. As Bruce has put it:

> Almost every leader in the DGB, including its vice-president, Mr Gustav Ferenbach, a member of Chancellor Kohl's CDU, has warned that a change in the strike law would represent a fundamental attack on trade union rights (53).

So, on the one hand, while it appears that divisions may be opening within the DGB, on the other, greater unity may be created as a result of the actions of the government. Despite these developments, unions are faced with a difficult choice because of their identification with the growth strategy and implicitly their commitment to West German capital's transition to neofordist forms of production. The likelihood that on the whole they will continue to support the growth strategy is predicated on their belief that an SPD-led government will be elected in the near future which will be much more sympathetic to the needs of unions.

UNITED KINGDOM

Economic and political background

It is widely recognised that the UK economy is one of the weakest in the advanced capitalist world and there is general agreement that this is most clearly demonstrated in the area of manufacturing industry (54). Various authors refer to different aspects of the 'crisis' such as over-manning, low productivity, lack of investment, restrictive practices, resistance of management to new techniques, and so on. One factor which most authors agree on is that the crisis has not suddenly developed, but it has been present, in various forms, for many years. Basically, we would contend that the origins of the present crisis can be traced back to the end of the nineteenth century when Britain was presumed to be the workshop of the world (55). This is not to suggest, however, that the present situation of de-industrialisation was inevitable: in the intervening years the economy could have been turned round and the current crisis avoided (56).

During the inter-war period, British industry largely stagnated, though one can detect the beginnings of fordist mass production industries in the south and Midlands, but there was never an adequate demand to provide the mass consumption required as an essential element of this mode of regulation. Even in the post-war period, the UK economy could still have been fundamentally restructured during the period of accelerated accumulation from 1945 to the mid-1960s. Many sectors of British society were well aware of the need to instigate such a fundamental restructuring, but despite various initiatives there was a failure to implement and adopt fordism adequately in the UK.

There are a number of reasons for this failure, but briefly one can suggest the following: a) a lack of investment by capital; b) the weakness of industrial capital vis-a-vis financial capital - the latter's position as the hegemonic fraction in the power bloc (57) meant that policies favourable to it and often disadvantageous to industrial capital were followed by government; c) the defensive strength of the trade union movement and the control which workers exercised over the labour process; d) management unable to see the advantages of new production and marketing techniques.

Every government since the late 1950s has had as a central aim the restructuring of industry; in a rather crude sense it might be said that they aimed to 'fordise' it. From 1964 to 1979, every government's attempt involved some form of corporatism as they attempted to gain the cooperation of labour and capital. As each attempt failed, the crisis deepened and was further accentuated by the international decay of fordism as a mode of regulation and the consequent transition to a period of decelerated accumulation. At each point in the developing crisis of the world economy, the UK's weak industrial structure and dysfunctional political and economic institutions magnified the scale of the crisis. What Jessop (58) calls the dual crisis of representation developed to intensify even further the crisis of the UK's political system. This in turn interacted with the economic crisis to further accelerate decline. As a result of this political and economic instability, the post-war social democratic consensus began to crumble and by the mid-1970s it was approaching a state of advanced decay leaving a political vacuum as the traditional political and economic techniques of Butskellism appeared unable to halt Britain's decline. Into this vacuum stepped the forces of the new right, led by Margaret Thatcher (59), welding monetarism, the free market, libertarianism and moral outrage into a populist electoral appeal which has since become known as Thatcherism. The object of attack was social democracy in all its forms, whether through the welfare state, 'wasteful' public expenditure or the unions.

In this context the Thatcher government set about restructuring not only British industry but also society, to create an industry sensitive to and structured by the market but also a 'market culture' which was supportive of entrepreneurial initiative and a restructured industry.

15

The Thatcher government came to power armed with general ideas but few clear notions of exactly how to achieve them (60). Thus, while making radical noises, it found itself floundering in the political institutions and organisations which had been developed largely during the period of social democratic consensus. After an initial period of consolidation, Thatcher finally gained control of her cabinet in late 1981 when the remaining Tory wets were either butchered or marginalised. Since then, a more gradual but arguably more coherent and effective strategy has developed which, because of its apparent gradualism, has had some success. The Conservatives have also been aided by the rise of the Liberal-SDP Alliance which has split the opposition to Thatcherism and seems likely to give her a third electoral victory, though on a much reduced scale, in 1987 or 1988.

Trade unions: the context and response

The trade unions hold a high place in the priorities of Thatcherism; they are major targets for reform because they are seen not only as an obstacle to the development of neofordist production structures but also as a source of collectivist values which must be transformed.

The current government's attempt to reform the industrial relations system through legal intervention is not the first. In 1969, the Labour government introduced the White Paper In Place of Strife and in 1971, the Conservative government passed the Industrial Relations Act. Both were attempts to curb shop floor militancy and both suffered ignominious defeats. Both attempts, however, may be seen as attempts to follow the West German example and impose a legal framework on industrial relations as part of a move towards more fully fledged corporatism.

In the UK the question of shop floor militancy has preoccupied several governments. Edwards has highlighted the importance of this factor:

> In countries such as Sweden and Germany the problem of shop floor militancy has been relatively slight and it has been possible to fashion a political order to cope with the tensions of capitalist development. In Britain, these tensions have emerged in a particularly acute form (61).

Edwards highlights the importance of the compromise reached between labour and capital and the institutional forms which this takes. As we have seen in West Germany, labour has been much more closely integrated into the political order, in the factory and hence into the process of change. In the UK no such accommodation has been reached: unions, particularly at the local level, have tended to be excluded from the process of change and have vigorously reacted to management's attempts to encroach upon the traditional areas of control over the labour process.

As part of its attempt to come to terms with these problems, the Labour government of 1974-79 developed what became known as the social contract (62), which produced a policy of negotiated wage restraint as a method of reducing inflation. Unfortunately it also succeeded in alienating large sectors of the union movement and from 1975 onwards there was growing disenchantment with the government. At the same time, unemployment was approaching 1.5 million and workers began to question the value of their sacrifices on the wages front. The build up of wages pressure finally exploded in the winter of 1978-79, helping the Conservatives to victory.

The Thatcher government was well aware of the problems it would encounter should it try to impose legal regulation on the industrial relations system. Rather than engage in a frontal assault on the unions, it chose to move along a more cautious path, utilising the unions' commitment to collective bargaining and only introducing new forms of legal intervention slowly and by the amendment of existing legislation. It thereby avoided providing a single focus for the unions to rally round.

The government was aided in this by the fragmented nature of British trade unionism. Unlike the West German case where unionisation is on industrial lines, in the UK there is a multiplicity of unions in each industry often in direct competition with each other for members and jobs. By allowing individual groups of workers to exercise their industrial muscle, the already existing divisions were automatically widened. In addition, up until 1981 the government also treated the public and private sectors very differently: in the public sector a series of large wage claims were agreed, while in the private sector unemployment was allowed to make its effects felt (63). As a result, public and private sector unions were unable to unite to oppose trade union legislation

It is interesting to note how the legislation has been spread over three Acts (1980, 1982 and 1984) which have gradually attempted to undermine key aspects of the unions' collective strength without creating the conditions which would have provided a focus for a concerted campaign against the government. This was partly because of the effects of unemployment, but partly because the legislation had wide support among both the general public and trade union members. Typical issues were the closed shop, secondary picketing and the use of ballots before strikes, to elect leaders and to determine contributions to political funds. In cases such as the closed shop and secondary picketing, the government had very astutely left it up to individual workers or management to take the initiative thus making it appear that the state was not involved - the law was only being invoked to protect individual rights and freedoms against 'oppressive' collectivities. Changes since 1979 must be seen as representing a widening of individual rights at the expense of collective rights (64).

While the legislation has been used infrequently, it is perhaps more important to recognise that it represents part of a wider attempt to change the political and industrial climate. The government aims to make it easier for management to assert the 'right to manage', but will leave it up to management, under economic pressure, to assert this right (65).

Yet it would be wrong to focus purely on legal changes as they are only the most obvious developments facing trade unions. There are other developments, some of which have been under way since the early 1960s, which have been accentuated over the last ten years and which threaten to alter the very nature and composition of trade unionism in the UK.

Recent research has suggested that there has been a dramatic centralisation and concentration of capital in the UK during the post-war era (66). As part of this change, firms have increasingly moved in the direction of single company wage agreements (67), the effect of which has been to tie wage settlements more closely to the performance of individual firms. During a period of sharply rising unemployment, it is likely that workers will be more concerned with keeping their jobs than with achieving substantial wage rises. In the case of profitable firms, there will be less need for a trade off between wages and jobs but this will only serve to exacerbate the existing divisions between profitable and unprofitable firms.

In addition, research has also suggested that the growth and spread of shop stewards during the 1970s was to a large extent sponsored and supported by management. Management favoured shop stewards because they provided a regular forum for consultation with the work force. If, however, management should feel it no longer needs shop stewards, serious problems could emerge if they withdraw their support and leave an exposed shop stewards organisation with no organic basis in the work force.

Perhaps the process which has most implications for the work force is de-industrialisation. This to a large extent represents a process of 'automatic' restructuring of the British economy which has been aided and encouraged by governments since the early 1960s (68). Since 1979, the Thatcher government's policies have greatly accelerated this process, but rather than government selectively intervening, its attitude has been to encourage the market to play the deciding role in the form restructuring will take. Increasingly, restructuring in the UK has taken the form of closures and massive job losses. Nor has it simply been restricted to the nineteenth century industries (textiles, ship building, iron and steel, engineering), but it has also spread to the 1930s and post-war industries such as motor cars and electronics. This has led to the decimation of these industries in the areas where they are traditionally based (North West and North East England, the Midlands, Scotland and Wales). As industry has been decimated, so too has union membership and as these areas form the heartland of British trade unionism (69) it has important implications for the nature of unionism in the UK.

Equally important is the shift away from manufacturing industry which has been taking place at the same time. Between June 1974 and June 1984 some 2.2 million jobs have been lost in manufacturing (70), to be replaced mainly by jobs in services and the public sector. In a sense, the whole structure of the working population is changing as the traditional nineteenth century industrial working class, which formed the core of the union movement, has been destroyed. The effects on unions is illustrated by the 17 per cent drop in membership from the 1979 high point of 13.28 million to 11.08 million in 1984, a drop heavily concentrated in areas where traditional industries are based.

Not only has there been a massive restructuring of the work force, but this restructuring has been accompanied by fundamental changes in the way people work (71). By this we refer mainly to the growth in part-time work, which can be traced back to the 1950s. Robinson has pointed out that:

Between 1951 and 1981 there has been a fall in the number of full-time employees of 2.3 million (1.9 million men and 0.4 million women) while the number of part-timers has risen by 3.7 million (0.7

18

million men and 3 million women) (72).

Given that unions generally have a rather poor record as regards unionising part-timers and representing women, these changes have major implications for trade unionism at a time when its traditional base is being decimated. Arguably these changes have also increased capital's ability to utilise its labour force in a more flexible manner (73), a development which is likely to become increasingly important in the 1980s (74).

This latter point leads us to another observation about the ability of unions to organise workers. The increasing use of part-time workers since the 1950s indicates how sections of capital can restructure the work force to meet its needs even during a period of relative union strength. In the current climate, there is some evidence that firms are also engaged in a more extensive restructuring of their work forces. It would appear that some firms, particularly expanding ones, are moving in a similar direction to that taken by West German firms in the 1970s, i.e. towards a segmented labour market, in search of greater flexibility (75). In these situations, firms are retaining a core work force of highly skilled workers and utilising a secondary labour force of part-timers, self-employed and sub-contracted workers. The resulting division may make it even more difficult for unions to unionise workers or create any sense of collective solidarity.

Further complications arise because several unions, notably the EEPTU and the AUEW, have recognised that major changes are under way and have decided to swim with the tide, thus they have entered into single union agreements and in some cases no-strike agreements with employers. These moves have threatened to open up serious divisions within the TUC making it almost impossible for the movement as a whole to oppose these developments. The most notable example has been the dispute involving the EEPTU, the NGA, SOGAT 82 and News International. Here Rupert Murdoch and News International with the aid (conscious or unconscious) of the EEPTU and other unions has been able to move the printing of Murdoch's titles from Fleet Street to a new computerised plant at Wapping. Such a move would have been unthinkable without the changes in the law and the balance of political forces which have occurred since 1979. But once again it has opened up serious divisions within the union movement and brought the threat of the EEPTU's expulsion from the TUC (76).

Similar divisions have opened up over the attitude adopted towards the trade union legislation, particularly that relating to secret ballots for strikes and elections. Some unions, such as the EEPTU, have always held secret ballots and therefore felt able to accept government money for them in future. Thus they came into conflict with TUC policy. As a result the EEPTU and the AUEW have been threatened with expulsion from the TUC, something which has only been avoided by the TUC's ability to fudge issues and thereby allow unions to pursue their own policies.

A third group of unions also recognises that quite fundamental and largely irreversible changes have occurred. This group does not expect a future Labour government (assuming there is one) to repeal all the changes in trade union law. It recognises that many of these changes have been genuinely popular with the public and among trade unionists. Suggestions emerging from this group are that a future Labour government should redress the balance by recognising collective rights in law over individual rights. Positive legal rights for trade unionists should be provided, according to this group. They aim to make the secret ballot a source of trade union strength and its outcome legally binding on employers and workers. Doubtless unions have been encouraged to take this attitude by recent successes in the ballots over political funds.

Such a tactic seems more likely to take the UK closer to the West German model, i.e. juridification, while at the same time utilising the traditional defensive qualities of British trade unionism. Clearly there is much to be said for a well defined legal framework, especially if it can prevent the judiciary intervening on the basis of their own preference for individual over collective rights. As this path seems to be the one currently favoured by the Labour Party, it may well be that much more will be heard of it in the future.

The current world recession, in combination with the nature of economic and political institutions, plus the Thatcher government, have had major effects on the trade union movement. Together these changes have forced the unions to rethink their attitudes, and in some cases fundamentally alter them. Whatever the result of the next election, Thatcherism has fundamentally changed British society and, in combination with the recession, it has fundamentally changed British trade unionism.

CONCLUSION

The comparative study of trade unions offers us the possibility of not only identifying common points of reference, but also of recognising the peculiarities which might otherwise go unnoticed if we focus on one country. Such an approach must, however, be comparative in both an historical and institutional sense if we are to understand the ways in which the effects of the current recession are mediated by the existing political and economic systems. It is in this context that the actions of trade unions must be placed if we are to understand the effects of the recession on them.

In the case of both West Germany and the UK, the history and structure of the existing economic and political institutions have played a key role in the ability/inability to adapt. In both the UK and West Germany the recession has accelerated already existing tendencies in the economy and presented unions with new problems. The relationship established between organised labour, organised capital and the state during the 1960s and 1970s has determined the adaptability of the system as a whole. This has been much less painful in West Germany than in the UK precisely because of the nature of this relationship and the institutions developed to regulate conflict. To a certain extent this has been true because of the West German trade unions' closer integration into the process of growth and change (77), but also because union members have benefited from this process through increased standards of living.

Adaptation has also been assisted by a labour market already structured to aid flexibility before the worst of the recession developed. As a result, there has been no need for capital to press for a major restructuring of industrial relations; it simply needs to devolve collective bargaining from the national/regional level to the works councils where flexibility can be further enhanced as rising unemployment ties workers ever more closely to their firms.

A major side effect of this process has been a considerable increase in structural unemployment (2.6 million in February 1986). Unions have responded by demanding a cut in the working week and IG Metall's 'success' in 1984 clearly marks a major, though not unambiguous, break-through (78). As a result of this success, sections of capital have pressed a sympathetic government for changes in the law which will place the full financial burdens of industrial action upon unions, their members and even workers only indirectly involved in disputes. In response the unions appear to be presenting a united front in demanding that the law return to the status quo. Despite this conflict and the strains placed on what Sengenberger has called the 'productivity pact', it remains unlikely that the 'social peace' of West German industry will be shattered.

In the UK, on the other hand, unions are facing major changes not only in economic and industrial terms but also socially and politically. With the real rate of unemployment running at over four million (as against the government's claimed 3.2 million), unions face a difficult future, but when faced with the changes we have described the very nature of traditional trade unionism must be in question. The government's attempts to undermine trade union power by legal changes must be placed in its political and ideological context (79): in a sense the government has tried to make unions superfluous to members' needs and has attempted to by-pass the leadership by appealing over their heads directly to the membership. Thus, unlike previous governments, there has been no attempt to strengthen the leadership: in the current government's view, the membership are moderates led by militants (a rather interesting redefinition of the 'trade union problem' compared to the late 1960s and early 1970s). To date the unions have been rather slow to respond to 'juridification' but they are now increasingly aware that there is little prospect of a return to the status quo ante. Evidence of this can be seen in recent requests that a future Labour government should provide positive legal rights for trade unionists.

If the above changes were the only threat, the situation facing the unions would be serious enough, but further problems have arisen from the different attitudes that individual unions have adopted towards the legal and industrial changes we have described. This reached a peak when the TUC threatened to expel both the AUEW and the EEPTU. Thus the spectre of an 'alternative TUC', involving either or both of these unions plus the break-away miners' unions and possibly dissident members of the NUJ, should not be ruled out entirely.

Finally there is the vexing question of the changing composition of the work force. The implications of these changes for the trade union movement are still unclear, but their combination with the development of a more segmented labour market suggests a difficult time ahead during which traditional trade unionism in the UK will have to reconcile itself to a declining role while these new social forces try to create a source of collective identity and solidarity.

In combination these factors mean that trade unions in the UK face a much more difficult and uncertain future than their West German counter-parts, a future in which the very values and attitudes upon which trade unionism has been based for over a century are increasingly being questioned, and in some cases undermined.

21

NOTES

(1) See E. Mandel, Late Capitalism, London, Verso, 1978; The Second
     Slump, London, NLB, 1978; Long Waves of Capitalist Development,
     Cambridge University Press, 1980; and 'Explaining long waves of
     capitalist development' in C. Freeman (ed.), Long Waves in the
     World Economy, London, Frances Pinter, 1984.
(2) For criticisms see R. Day, 'The theory of the long cycle -
     Kondratiev, Trotsky, Mandel' in New Left Review, no. 99, 1978;
     B. Rowthorn, Capitalism, Conflict and Inflation, London, Lawrence
     and Wishart, 1980; A. Kleinknecht, 'Innovation, accumulation and
     crises' in Review, IV, 1981; P. Mattick, Economic Crisis and Crisis
     Theory, London, Merlin, 1981.
(3) As well as Mandel's work, see I. Saprio and J. Kane, 'Stagfaltion
     and the new right' in Telos, no. 56, 1983.
(4) While we continue to use the term national economy, we recognise
     that the increasing internationalisation of capital throughout
     the twentieth century has made this something of an artificial
     concept. See H. Radice, 'The national economy - a Keynesian myth'
     in Capital and Class, no. 22, 1984.
(5) A similar recognition of the inadequacy of long wave theory and the
     need to combine it with fordism may be found in P. Blackburn,
     R. Cooms and K. Green, Technology, Economic Growth and the Labour
     Process, London, Macmillan, 1985.
(6) M. Aglietta, A Theory of Capitalist Regulation, London, NLB, 1979;
     and 'World capitalism in the eighties' in New Left Review, no. 136,
     1982; see also A. Lipietz, 'Towards global fordism' in New Left
     Review, no. 132, 1982; and 'Imperialism or the beast of the
     Apocalypse' in Capital and Class, no. 22, 1982. For an interesting
     review and critique of Aglietta, see M. Davis, 'Fordism in crisis:
     a review of Michel Aglietta's Régulation et Crises: l'Expérience
     des États-Unis', in Review, II, 1978.
(7) See Gramsci, Prison Notebooks, London, Lawrence and Wishart, 1973,
     pp. 277-318.
(8) Aglietta, op. cit., chapters 2 and 3.
(9) Ibid., chapters 4 and 5.
(10) On these points, see K. Dyson, 'The cultural, ideological and
     structural context' in K. Dyson and S. Wilks (eds.), Industrial
     Crisis, Oxford, Martin Robertson, 1983; F. Scharpf, 'Economic and
     institutional constraints of full employment strategies: Sweden,
     Austria and West Germany' in J. Goldthorpe (ed.), Order and
     Conflict in Contemporary Capitalism, Oxford University Press, 1984;
     B. Jessop, O. Jacobi and H. Kastendiek, 'Corporatist and liberal
     responses the the crisis of post-war capitalism' in O. Jacobi
     et al. (eds.), Economic Crisis, Trade Unions and the State, London,
     Croom Helm, 1986.
(11) On restructuring, see B. Fine and L. Harris, 'The British economy:
     May 1975 - January 1976' in Bulletin of the Conference of Socialist
     Economists, 14, 1976; and Rereading Capital, London, Macmillan,
     1979; J. Grahl, 'Restructuring in West European industry' in
     Capital and Class, no. 19, 1983.
(12) See F. Robel, J. Heinrichs and O. Kreye, The New International
     Division of Labour, Cambridge University Press, 1980; and
     D. Massey, op. cit., for an illustration and analysis of how capi-
     tal uses space to structure the production process and increase
     profitability.
(13) On the crisis of fordism, see the references in note 6. Aglietta

in particular seems to place much more emphasis on the role of international monetary crises, i.e. the relationship between productive and monetary accumulation, while Lipietz focuses more on the problems of realising an adequate rate of return on investment and inter-imperialist competition plus the problems created by fordism's expansion to peripheral social formations.

(14) See Aglietta, op. cit., esp. pp. 122-130 and the last chapter; C. Palloix, 'The labour process: from fordism to neofordism' in Conference of Socialist Economists (eds.), The Labour Process and Class Strategies, London, CSE, 1976.; Blackburn, et al., op. cit., chapters 5-8.
(15) See Blackburn et al., op. cit., chapters 5 and 6.
(16) See Massey, op. cit., and Frobel et al., op. cit.
(17) This section draws particularly heavily on E. Altvater et al., 'On the analysis of imperialism in the metropolitan countries: the West German experience' in Bulletin of the Conference of Socialist Economists, no 8, 1974; and A. S. Markovits (ed.), The Political Economy of West Germany: Modell Deutschland, New York, Praeger, 1982, esp. the paper by W. Semmler, 'Economic aspects of Model Germany'. See also G. Minnerup, 'West Germany since the war' in New Left Review, no. 99, 1976; W. Olle and W. Shoeller, 'Direct investment and monopoly theories of imperialism' in Capital and Class, no. 16, 1982; J. Hirsch, 'Developments in the political system of West Germany since 1945' in D. Scase (ed.), The State in Western Europe, London, Croom Helm, 1980, and 'The fordist security state' in Kapitalistate, no. 10-11, 1983.
(18) See Altvater et al., art. cit., pp. 6-13; W. Muller-Jentsch and H. J. Sperling. 'Economic development, labour conflicts and the industrial relations system in West Germany' in C. Crouch and A. Pizzorno (eds.), The Resurgence of Class Conflict in Western Europe since 1968, vol. 1, London, Macmillan, 1978, p. 261; A. S. Markovits and C. S. Allen, 'Power and dissent: the trade unions in the Federal Republic of Germany re-examined' in J. Haywood (ed.), Trade Unions and Politics in Western Europe, London, Cass, 1980, p. 69; and Semmler, art. cit.
(19) Semmler, art. cit., pp. 31 and 28.
(20) Altvater et al., op. cit., p.p. 6-7.
(21) Ibid., pp. 10-11; Markovits and Allen, art. cit., p. 70.
(22) For further discussion of these terms, taken from Aglietta, op. cit., see the previous chapter in this book.
(23) B. Jessop, 'Accumulation strategies, state forms and hegemonic projects' in Kapitalistate, no. 10-11, 1983.
(24) Semmler, art. cit., p. 32.
(25) J. Esser and W. Fach with K. Dyson, 'Social market and modernisation policy in West Germany' in Dyson and Wilks, op. cit.
(26) C. F. Lankowski, 'Modell Deutschland and the international regionalisation of the West German State' in Markovits op. cit.; and R. Parboni, The Dollar and its Rivals, London, Verso, 1981.
(27) K. Hildebrandt and R. J. Dalton, 'The new politics: political change or sunshine politics?' in M. Kaase and K. von Beyme (eds.), Elections and Parties, London, Sage, 1983; and U. Feist, M. Gullner and K. Liepelt, 'Structural assimilation versus ideological polarisation: on changing profiles of political parties in West Germany' in ibid.; see also K. Baker, R. Dalton and K. Hildebrandt, Germany Transformed. Political Culture and the New Politics, London, Harvard University Press, 1981.
(28) Minnerup, art. cit.

(29) Hildebrandt and Dalton, art. cit.
(30) Useful discussions may be found in R. Adams and C. Rummel, 'Workers' participation in West Germany: impact on the worker, the enterprise and the trade union' in Industrial Relations Journal, vol. 8, 1977; E. Jacobs et al., The Approach to Industrial Relations in Britain and West Germany, London, Anglo-German Foundation, 1978; A. Marsh, et al., Workplace Relations in the Engineering Industry in the United Kingdom and the Federal Republic of Germany, London, Anglo-German Foundation, 1981; D. Miller, 'Social partnership and the determinants of workplace independence in West Germany' in British Journal of Industrial Relations, vol. 20, 1982; and W. Streek, Industrial Relations in West Germany, London, Heinemann, 1984.
(31) In fact about 80 per cent of workers sitting in works councils are members of a trade union (usually the DGB) so there is a considerable overlap between unions and works councils.
(32) See U. Muekenberger, 'Labour law and industrial relations', in Jakobi, et al., op. cit.
(33) Markovits, art. cit.
(34) One also needs to recognise that certain societies are more willing to accept state intervention because historically the boundary between public and private has not been drawn in so sharp a fashion. In such societies the legal system is not based purely on the primacy of individual rights as in the UK or the USA. See K. Dyson, The State Tradition in Western Europe, Oxford, Martin Robertson, 1980.
(35) J. H. Riemer, 'Alterations in the design of Model Germany: critical innovations in the policy machinery for economic steering' in Markovits (ed.), op. cit.
(36) See J. Clark, 'Concerted action in the Federal Republic of Germany' in British Journal of Industrial Relations, vol. 17, 1979.
(37) M. Alexis, 'Neocorporatism and industrial relations: the case of German trade unions', in West European Politics, vol. 6, 1983.
(38) Arguably a major preconditon for a successful system of corporatist arrangements is a highly centralised trade union movement whose leaders are able to enter into binding negotiations on their members' behalf, plus an institutional system which allows pressures from the membership to be diffused via mediating structures. Some of these points have been discussed in R. Atkinson, 'Trade unions, collective action and liberal corporatism' in Journal of Area Studies, no. 13, 1986.
(39) See Muller-Jentsch and Sperling, art. cit., pp. 262-256; Markovits and Allen, art. cit., pp. 74-76; and Semmler, art. cit., p. 31.
(40) E. Mandel, The Second Slump, London, NLB, 1978; and Semmler, art. cit.
(41) W. Sengenberger, 'Labour market segmentation and the business cycle' in F. Wilkinson (ed.), The Dynamics of Labour Market Segmentation, London, Academic Press, 1981.
(42) See K. Dohse, 'Foreign workers and workforce management in West Germany', in Economic and Industrial Democracy, vol. 5, 1984.
(43) J. Gabriel and F. Holzapfl, 'Entrepreneurial strategies of adjustment and internal labour markets' in Wilkinson, op. cit.
(44) Doshe, art. cit., pp. 500-501.
(45) Adams and Rummel, art. cit.
(46) See D. Webber, 'A relationship of "critical partnership"? Capital and the social-liberal coalition in West Germany' in West European Politics, vol. 6, 1983; and G. Schmid, 'Labour market policy under

the social-liberal coalition' in K. von Beyme and M. G. Schmidt (eds.), Policy and Politics in the Federal Republic of Germany, Aldershot, Gower, 1985.

(47) Supply-side policies have been utilised by the Federal government since 1949 and are nothing new. Keynesian policy only became influential between the late 1960s and mid-1970s. See Scharpf, art. cit.

(48) See W. Sengenberger, 'West German employment policy: restoring worker competition' in Industrial Relations, vol. 23, 1984.

(49) Ibid., pp. 341-2; on the attitude of workers and management to change, see T. Lane, 'Industrial efficiency and the West German worker' in Industrial Relations Journal, vol. 15, 1984.

(50) See O. Jacobi, 'Economic development and trade union collective bargaining policy since the middle of the 1970s' in Jacobi et al., op. cit.

(51) P. Bruce, 'Why the strains are beginning to tell' in Financial Times, 15/1/86.

(52) Ibid.

(53) Idem.

(54) This section draws on the following books and articles: R. Guttman, 'State intervention and the economic crisis: the Labour government's policy, 1974-75' in Kapitalistate, no. 4-5, 1976; S. Pollard, The Wasting of the British Economy, London, Croom Helm, 1982; B. Fine and L. Harris, 'The British economy since March 1974' in Bulletin of the Conference of Socialist Economists, no. 12, 1975; R Jessop, 'The transformation of the state in post-war Britain' in A. Stewart (ed.), Contemporary Britain, London, RKP, 1983; D. Coates, 'Britain in the 1970s: economic crisis and the resurgence of radicalism' in A. Cox (ed.), Politics, Policy and the European Recession, London, Macmillan, 1982.

(55) For a general discussion of the British economy in this period see R. Samuel, 'Workshop of the world' in History Workshop, vol. 3, 1977.

(56) Various explanations have been advanced for this continued decline but the arguments advanced by Dyson, art. cit., concerning the nature of 'industrial culture' in the UK are surely worthy of further consideration.

(57) C. Leys, 'Thatcherism and British manufacturing' in New Left Review, no. 151, 1985.

(58) Jessop, art. cit.

(59) It would be wrong to give the impression that the 'new right' only appeared in the 1970s. It has a long history in Conservatism and variants can be found throughout the post-war period. See D. Edgar, 'The free or the good' in R. Levitas (ed.), The Ideology of the New Right, Cambridge, Polity Press, 1986.

(60) See P. Ridell, The Thatcher Government, Oxford, Martin Robertson, 1983; and B. Jessop, 'Prospects for the corporatisation of monetarism in Britain' in Jacobi et al. (eds), op. cit.

(61) P. Edwards, 'The political economy of industrial conflict: Britain and the United States' in Economic and Industrial Democracy, vol. 4, 1983, p. 488.

(62) See D. Barnes and E. Reid, Government and Trade Unions: the British Experience 1964-79, London, Heinemann, 1980; and R. Taylor, 'The trade union "problem" since 1960' in B. Pimlott and C. Cook (eds.), Trade Unions and British Politics, London, Longman, 1982.

(63) See D. Soskice, 'Industrial relations and the British economy, 1979-83', in Industrial Relations, vol. 23, 1983.

(64) The relationship between trade unions and the law in the UK has hardly been easy or happy. The law, and in particular the judiciary, have always placed individual rights above collective rights. See R. Lewis and B. Simpson, Striking a Balance? Employment Law after the 1980 Act, Oxford, Martin Robertson, 1981.; P. Kahn et al., Picketing: Industrial Disputes, Tactics and the Law, London, RKP, 1983; J. A. G. Grifith, 'The Politics of the Judiciary, Glasgow, Fontana, 1981, chapters 3 and 7; Justice Peter Pain, 'Contract and contract: the trade unionist and the lawyer' in Industrial Law Journal, vol. 14, 1985.

(65) See D. Newell, The New Employemnt Legislation, London, Kogan Page, 1983.

(66) S. J. Paris, The Evolution of Giant Firms in Britain, Cambridge University Press, 1976.

(67) See W. Brown (ed.), The Changing Contours of British Industrial Relations, Oxford, Blackwell, 1981; though as W. W. Daniel and N. Millward in Workplace Industrial Relations in Britain, London, Heinemann, 1983, point out, this is only true of manufacturing industry employing 50 or more full time workers.

(68) The decline of the British economy has been uneven and its consequences have tended to be spatially concentrated in particular areas, especially the industrial heartlands of the nineteenth century. See R. Dennis, 'The decline of manufacturing employment in Greater London 1966-74' in Urban Studies, vol. 15, 1978, pp. 63-75; P. Dicken and P. Lloyd, 'Inner metropolitan change, enterprise structures and policy issues: case studies of Manchester and Merseyside' in Regional Studies, vol. 12, 1978, pp. 181-197; D. Massey and R. Meegan, 'Industrial restructuring versus the cities', in Urban Studies, vol. 15, 1978, pp. 273-288; P. Lloyd, 'The components of industrial change for Merseyside inner area: 1966-75' in Urban Studies, vol. 16, 1979, pp. 45-60; C. Mason, 'Industrial decline in Greater Manchester 1966-75: a components of change approach' in Urban Studies, vol. 17, 1980, pp. 173-184; and P. Elias and G. Keogh, 'Industrial decline and unemployment in the inner city areas of Great Britain: a review of the evidence', in Urban Studies, vol. 19, 1982.

(69) D. Massey and N. Miles, 'Mapping out the unions' in Marxism Today, May 1984.

(70) A. Britton, 'Unemployment and the structure of labour demand' in National Westminster Bank Quarterly Review, May 1985.

(71) O. Robinson, 'The changing labour market: the phenomenon of part-time employment in Britain' in National Westminster Bank Quarterly Review, November 1985; N. Meager, 'Temporary work in Britain' in Employment Gazette, January 1986.

(72) Robinson, art. cit., p. 19.

(73) Ibid., pp. 20, 22-3, 25.

(74) Meager, art. cit., and J. Atkinson and D. Gregory, 'A flexible future' in Marxism Today, April 1986.

(75) Idem.

(76) See J. Lloyd, 'The sparks are flying' in Marxism Today, March 1986.

(77) Jacobs et al., op. cit., esp. pp. 47-112.

(78) Economists have suggested that unless the reduction to a 35 hour week takes place in one go it will have no major effects on unemployment.

(79) See Karn et al., op. cit esp. chapter 2 for a useful discussion.

2 Italian trade unions: from unity to disunity

BILL BRIERLEY

INTRODUCTION

The problem of relations between trade unions, employers and governments has become a central issue throughout Western Europe. Increasingly in the post-war period, governments have taken on the role of balancing the rights, demands and expectations of the other two groups, and of ensuring a rate of economic growth that will satisfy the expectations of workers and employers by keeping unemployment low and enabling a reasonable rate of profit to be earned, whilst preventing inflation. At the same time, they must reconcile demands from the one sector for a radical redistribution of income and wealth, whilst assuring the other of an adequate reward for effort and initiative. Within this general framework, there is a second issue: the relative importance of collective bargaining in the context of the market economy, and the extent to which collective bargaining is replaced by the corporatist processes of tripartism at the national level and bipartism at the factory level (1).

Many countries in Western Europe have experimented at various times with different industrial relations systems based on 'cooperation' or 'concertation' between the 'social partners' - trade unions, governments and employers. The system involving the institutionalised participation of trade unions in the formation and management of political and economic policies will be referred to here as 'neocorporatism' (2). The system has two basic but essential characteristics: the participation of trade unions in political choices, especially in decisions on economic and social policy. This in turn implies the adoption of different attitudes to the bargaining process on the part of the contracting bodies from those shown in more traditional conflict bargaining. Secondly, and most importantly, the participation of the various social forces must be institutionalised. Such arrangements are based on the assumption that the functional organisations participating can control their members: a failure to do so will reproduce in the state conflicts within and between producer groups, creating a structural instability within neocorporatist forms. However, the resulting 'social contract' models depended on uninterrupted economic growth as the foundation for the harmonisation of the interests of the 'social partners', and as economic growth has slowed down and been replaced by crisis neocorporatist experiments have generally failed (3). Neocorporatism (whose essential feature is centralised political bargaining) led to a detachment of the trade union leadership from the grass roots and as the crisis deepened and accumulation began to predominate over consensus, the union became a less important social partner (4). The alternative to neocorporatism, more recently preferred by both the employers and the state, has been a return to the market as the appropriate forum for the regulation of industrial relations.

Trade unions in the 1980s are therefore faced with a series of choices. They can seek refuge in centralised bargaining, but this would be at the expense of their continued alienation from large sections of workers in the salaried classes. They can retreat to the factories to await a new cycle, but the European economy shows no signs that there will be an upturn in the near future. They can return to the neocorporatist arrangements of the late 1970s, but with little prospect of success because neocorporatism failed then in a less hostile economic environment, and indeed it has been argued that in some cases it aggravated tensions between trade unions and the state by multiplying the disaggregating effects of the crisis (5). More to the point, neocorporatism is in crisis not so much because of the detachment of trade union leadership from its grass roots, or because of governments' decreasing desires to consult trade unions, but rather because of the aggressive desires of industrialists to break the limitations imposed by concertation and codetermination on their managerial powers and independence (6). The growth of neocorporatism in the 1960s and 1970s reflected a growth in trade union power and the need for industrialists to control that power by institutional means. Trade unions were only allowed to participate in the management of firms and the economy because (and so long as) management would have been impossible without their cooperation. In the changed economic circumstances of the 1980s, the management of the work force can be left to the market and capitalists have a strong incentive to return to neoliberalism to recapture their traditional managerial prerogatives. This has often deprived the unions of an interlocutor and has encouraged the depoliticisation of union activity. Not all the achievements of the 1960s and 1970s have been swept away, but where forms of neocorporative unionism survive (sometimes in large factories but generally not in the economy as a whole), labour representatives have been forced to accept the international competitiveness of the company as the main criterion in the defence of their members' interests.

This view contradicts a generally held view on the left that neocorporatism must involve incorporation, where the state entices the unions to operate within a system which deprives them of their autonomy and their class connotations simply in order to obtain wage moderation (hence the importance of incomes policies). In reality, however, the situation is more complex since many neocorporatist arrangements have been arrived at within social democratic political regimes, and the victories of the new right (Reagan and Thatcher in particular) are based on a clearly anti-corporatist strategy. Perhaps, then, neocorporatism is the most 'left' solution available to trade unions to the problems of advanced capitalism.

The proposition, then, cannot be accepted in these general terms. It is necessary to differentiate among different types of neocorporatist arrangement. Regini (7) argues that stable neocorporatism may be said to exist where a strong and combative labour movement has forced a political change as part of its own strategy and produced the more advanced social democracies, as in Sweden, Norway and, to a lesser extent, Austria. The example of Sweden shows how the arena for the resolution of class conflict can be shifted from industrial relations to the political system - and to what advantage in terms of the redistribution of income and of low levels of conflict indicated by low strike figures. Where the labour movement is strong and where there is a chance for it to cooperate with a pro-labour government party, it pays the unions to moderate their demands and to institutionalise their presence within the political system because by so doing they obtain long term advantages with regard to employment and redistribution. The dominant class accepts this solution as the lesser evil in a situation where the organisational and political strength of the labour movement precludes other solutions.

Unstable neocorporatism, on the other hand, may be said to exist where there is a strong working class, but relations with the state are difficult because pro-labour parties are not always in power, or because industrial relations are highly decentralised and the unions' ability to deliver in a long term social contract is open to doubt. This has been the case in the UK, Denmark and to a large extent (especially after 1977) in Italy - strong labour movements have been unable to deliver labour cooperation in social contracts on a long term basis, and the result has been high levels of industrial conflict.

Regini confines the use of 'incorporation' to describe situations in which the working class is weak and not mobilised in the formation of economic policy. In the Netherlands, Switzerland and, to a lesser extent, West Germany, the labour movement is weaker, both in the industrial relations system (indicated by the much lower levels of unionisation) and in the political system. Parties of the left have been in government, often for long periods, but the unions have been prevented from developing a clear and consistent pattern with regard to government policy and to their own strategy because of their weakness and inability to organise workers.

As well as these political and institutional considerations, due attention must also be given to economic circumstances. In their attempts to reconcile 'industrial needs' and 'general interest', governments have also had to face the fact that their ability to regulate their own economies has gradually been undermined by the growing interdependence of western economies. This has come about as a result of the internationalisation of large companies and the generalisation of neoliberal economic strategies, and this now means that 'economic nationalism' as the favoured context for reflation, and therefore as the basis for national anti-crisis social contracts, has become more and more irrelevant. Even so, in the current crisis, the capitalist orientation of the economy has been reinforced, not undermined. Unions, therefore, especially on the left, have attempted to cling on to collective bargaining, which is perceived as an integral part of the class struggle, and which can only end when the capitalist system itself is overthrown. This often leads to a contradiction: on the one hand these unions demand a curbing of inflation and the reduction of unemployment, economic and social policies which demand centralised coordination and control, but on the other hand, these unions refuse to compromise their freedom to bargain or their right to strike (which in effect is their right to frustrate at a local level, nationally implemented policies) simply because it is the only thing which appears to stand between them and 'market forces'.

If the trend towards the re-establishment of the market as the dominant force in the regulation of industrial relations is to be resisted, it is clear that the unions must develop a new relationship with the state which must take fully into account such issues as the representativeness and democratic nature of the unions, and also the relationship between macroeconomic and microeconomic structures and their effect on the bargaining process (8).

We have already noted that the experimental partnership between unions, the employers and the state, attempted in many West European countries in the 1970s, have been increasingly undermined in the 1980s. Trade unions have shown an increasing tendency to develop new forms of action and expression compared to their traditional platforms and previous solutions based on the social compromise which had focused on the expansion of welfare and the redistribution of income. In some unions, and with differing emphases, two new themes have come to be stressed much more than in the past: firstly, the question of changing the conditions of production and controlling technological change and secondly, the demand for the qualitative extension of rights leading to 'economic democracy', that is towards social control over investment and the model of development (9). These unions, however, having widened their horizons, now face a new difficulty in satisfying at one and the same time, the immediate demands of organised labour and strategic objectives for the whole working (and temporarily non-working) class. They are faced with a choice between strategic objectives and tactical considerations, between the promotion of solidarity and the defence of the short term interests of employed labour, between political activity and economic activity; and these choices are often mutually exclusive. To many European unionists, former models of unionism - the neoliberal/pluralist, the neocorporative or the neomarxist - no longer seem plausible. They feel they must search for a new model if they are not to be condemned to corporative support for authoritarian government, subordination to market forces in a neoliberal market economy, or fragmentation into American-style business unionism.

On what premises might this new model be built? One section of the union movement would argue that trade unions have to represent both the interests of the working class in employment and wider social and political demands such as the extension of welfare, employment policies and the promotion of economic growth. This is because the technological revolution is forcing changes not only in the organisation of work, but also in social stratification, and these changes are operating against the traditional working class and in favour of new groups traditionally outside union organisation. Under this sort of pressure, many of the reference points for the values of European trade unions have begun to shift (the structure of industry and production, the pattern of urban development, organisational centralisation, even the credibility of the socialist perspective). Normal bargaining strategies are no longer appropriate to the new organisation of labour or to the economic crisis.

If the choice now is between a retreat to the factories and the absorption of new social and political demands, the dilemma is not a new one. Conflicts raged in the 1930s in the British trade union movement, for example, about the choice between the defence of real wages and the expansion of employment. What has changed in the 1980s, is firstly the trade unions' unchallenged right to represent the interests of workers; and secondly, the post-war consensus about Keynesian policies which allowed trade unions to negotiate gradual economic redistribution in exchange for political subordination.

What are the possibilities? Firstly, to join with 'single issue' social movements and thus to socialise the content of both forms of organisation. This shift would represent a rejection of the idea of the 'workers' union', established in the defence of employed workers, and a belief that it is possible to identify 'workers' interests' as distinct from the general issues of the balance between production and consumption. As unions absorb new social and political demands they will inevitably come into conflict with the political branch of the workers' movement.

A second possibility would be the development of a reformed neo-corporative model, which would aim to take away from the market its function as exclusive regulator of resources and exclusive allocator of income. This solution has been called neointerventionist (10), and it would aim to take away from the entrepreneur decisions about the provision or allocation of investment. Such a strategy might also include a form of incomes policy which would direct a proportion of profits and incomes towards socially controlled investment.

A third possibility would be the realignment of the relationship between the union and party components of the labour movement, with the control of accumulation as its objective, and thus going far beyond the Swedish model.

A fourth possibility, and by far the least radical, would be for bargaining to give way to some form of institutionalised participation with forms of representation of the work force in the workplace integrated into the firms decision-making process (such as the West German system of 'Mitbestimmung' or the various systems proposed by the European Commission in the Draft Fifth Directive) (11).

These systems are not mutually exclusive, and the adoption of one or other or a combination of systems will depend on at least three variables: firstly, the amount and type of legal support for trade unions as representatives of labour; secondly, the attitudes of employers (are they determined to smash trade unions?); and thirdly, the political variable - will the unions be smothered by the right and the Thatcher/ Reagan offensive or fostered by the gradual left revival (Sweden, Spain, Greece, France)?

If industrialised countries have shown a convergence in their political and economic structures and a similarity in their attempts to

31

resolve social and political problems, nevertheless there is still a pronounced divergence between countries as regards the ability of trade unions to negotiate at the political level, and hence their prospects of success. Each country has a peculiar mix of economic, political and institutional resources with which to confront the (common) crisis: the structure of production and the labour market, the nature of the political and administrative system, the characteristics of the trade unions themselves, but also the modes of organisation and the nature of conflicts and social tensions. If the political and economic environment is different, then the nature of the union (its capacity to act, the fields of its endeavours, its expectations) will also be different. It is against this background that I now propose to examine the trade unions in the Italian context.

ITALIAN TRADE UNIONS: FROM UNITY TO DISUNITY 1972-1986

The Italian General Confederation of Labour (CGIL) was set up by the political parties in the aftermath of the Second World War. It was a single confederation embracing all democratic political views, but it was dominated by the Communist Party (PCI). In 1948, as a result of strategic differences about the political function of trade unions, the union was torn into three factions: the CGIL (consisting of Communists and Socialists), the CISL (dominated by the Christian Democrats (DC) and the church) and the UIL (mainly Social Democrats and Republicans, but with a significant Socialist minority). Throughout the 1950s, the labour movement was weak and ineffective, and deeply lacerated by internecine conflict (12). At the same time, the close linkages between the unions and the parties which had spawned them began to show signs of weakening (13), especially with regard to the links between the CGIL and the PCI. The CGIL had briefly taken a more positive view of the EEC than had the PCI (1957-58), and it had been gradually disengaging from the Moscow orientated World Federation of Trade Unions (WFTU), and the PCI had abandoned the concept of the trade union as the 'transmission belt' of the party. In the late 1950s but more especially in the 1960s and 1970s, the CISL saw the development of new cadres who promoted a kind of unionism which has been antagonistic both to social conservation and to DC predominance over the union. Nevertheless, at this stage, labour was totally isolated within the political system. The early 1960s saw an attempt at a neocorporatist re-insertion into the political system, but this failed and was followed by a return to isolation.

The late 1960s saw a resurgence of shop floor militancy which resulted in the explosion of the 'hot autumn' of 1969 which forced the unions (led by the metal workers) to move towards unity, the better to articulate shop floor demands. 1968-1975 was a period of growth and of decentralisation of union activity. Labour demands were promoted through conflict bargaining. Neocorporatism was firmly rejected.

A unified federation (CGIL-CISL-UIL) was formed in 1972 and negotiations in all subsequent wage rounds were conducted by this federation. At the same time, however, conflict has been centred in the factory, producing a growth of union power and collective bargaining at this level without precedent in Italian history. The pattern to emerge is a highly dynamic system of plant and enterprise agreements which are largely independent of the bargaining which takes place at the other levels - industry-wide and between the confederations (14).

This development constitutes the unique characteristic of Italian trade unionism in the 1970s (15). After the hot autumn, the union leadership sought to develop a strategy that would overcome the tensions and fluctuations of the past, combining action in both the market and the political arenas for the creation of a global strategy for social, economic and political change. This attempt to merge market and political action to obtain contractual advantages for the work force and progressive political change for the benefit of large strata of the population is the source of many of the innovations made by the unions in the 1970s, and also of many of the strategic dilemmas they faced in the decade.

The strategy achieved many significant advances, notably the Law on Workers' Rights ('Statuto dei diritti dei lavoratori') (1972) and the extension of the wage indexation system ('scala mobile') (1975). Other gains include unprecedented wage increases, the forty hour week, the reduction of wage differentials (partly the result of the indexation of wages), the establishment of a common job classification system, and the setting up of the 'Cassa integrazione guadagni' (CIG - a national government fund to make up the wages of workers who were temporarily laid off). The political role of the unions was also extended by the inclusion of provisions in some important contracts from 1975 onwards giving the unions the right to have access to information about the firm's economic condition and investment programmes. The unions also won clauses in the FIAT and Montedison contracts in 1975 binding these companies to invest in the South. These latter political gains have, however, remained very much a dead letter. In fact, many of these demands differed very little from the CGIL's Labour Plan, published in 1950, which consisted of a programme of public works, public housing, land reclamation and indicative industrial planning, but at least in the process of their articulation the CISL and the UIL began to develop a strategic outlook which included socio-economic reform through action in the political arena (16).

At the same time, in the years between 1973 and 1978, there was a gradual shift to a defensive posture with regard to shop floor issues and an attempt to define a more precise set of priorities and proposals than the previous generic set of reforms (17). Unemployment, the defence of real wages and reform of the structure of the economy assumed priority; the expansion and reorganisation of the social services tended to recede. In the unions' view, a new model of economic development was required consisting of a sectoral policy, favouring investment in the South, a strategy for industrial reconversion, a plan for the development of agriculture and a new programme of investment favouring public rather than private consumption. To implement this model, the state was to assume a more active role in directing the economy (through the state holding companies), new investment was to be provided by a reform of the taxation and credit systems and a new planning initiative was demanded (18).

Italy's economic difficulties in the wake of the first oil crisis in 1973-74, however, placed increasing pressures on the social partners to revise their attitudes towards industrial relations. Contributing factors included the structural weakness of the industrial system, the endemic agricultural crisis, the inefficiency of public administration and the gap between the products of the education system and the demands of the labour market. Endemic political instability and the ensuing social tensions have not been alleviated by the gradual polarisation of votes between the PCI and the DC (19). If previous patterns of ebb and flow had been repeated, one would have expected the gains of 1969-1972 to have been quickly rolled back as labour lost and capital regained the upper hand. But thanks largely to the Law on Workers' Rights, which provided the bulwark for labour in the 1970s, the gains of the hot autumn were not all lost. The 1972 law provided the framework for the consolidation and enhancement of labour rights and the basis for much of the continued shop floor militancy throughout the 1970s (20).

Nevertheless, by the end of the 1970s, the attitudes of the government and of employers had changed. Among them, the prevailing view was that only lower wages would provide the accumulation which would provide the investment which would create new employment. In the deepening economic crisis, the wage indexation system was increasingly identified by government and industry as a major cause of inflation and unemployment. The unions' slogan right up to 1981 was "La scala mobile non si tocca" (Hands off wage indexation), but it was becoming clear that in the context of the crisis, the unions could not claim to play a responsible role in the running of the economy if the wage indexation system could not be reformed. In this context, and given the close links between the PCI and the CGIL, the inclusion of the PCI calling for austerity and wage restraint in the government majority from 1976 to 1979 posed a serious threat to trade union unity. A sudden turn around by the united federation in their position on the wage indexation would look too much like CGIL subordination to the PCI, and CISL and UIL subordination to the CGIL, and would in any case meet large scale opposition from the grass roots. Nevertheless, it was quite clear that the PCI could not enter government except in exchange for trade union moderation and the abandonment of the innovative fervour of the hot autumn and a return to their more traditional functions (21).

By 1977-1978, it was clear that the strength of the unions and their disruptive power remained impressive, but the exercise of that strength in the market arena was beginning to be perceived as counter-productive and contributing to, if not a major cause of, the crisis. The unions had been less effective in exercising their power in the political arena, and this led to an increasing threat of division within the federation (22).

The dilemmas that the unions faced and the potential lines of division are clearly seen in a study of the positions they expressed at their confederal congresses in 1977. The CISL recognised that the crucial problem which the union must resolve is that of the relationship between the immediate needs and interests of the workers (living and working conditions) and collective aspirations of wider social change. The political role of the union is based on the balancing of these objectives and the avoidance of dramatic shifts towards corporatism or blinkered defensive posturing on the one hand, and flights of paralysing globalism on the other. Collective bargaining remains the union's natural instrument of action. For the CISL, the political expansion of the role of the trade union, the extension of its areas of intervention beyond the bargaining sphere, the problems posed by the need to achieve new forms of intervention and control over investment strategies and the process of accumulation, and more generally over the direction of economic policy, should not lead either to a shift away from the traditional bargaining role of the union or even less to a post-bargaining or post-conflictual phase of union activity (23). For the CISL, the priority is for action in the work place, related to the immediate demands of the shop floor.

The CGIL gave a different weight to its political objectives and expressed its view of the dual role of the trade union as follows:

> To establish a real alternative at the economic and social level the union must be able to assert itself in its dual role: as a bargaining organisation and as a political actor whose objective is a policy which aims to create a new political and social system which will be achieved through the democratic programming of economic development, which is the premise for the defeat of social inequality and for the affirmation of new values of progress and the quality of life (24).

The way forward for the CGIL is the democratisation of the economy through factory plans, sectoral, intersectoral and territorial programmes, self-management and control over the content and progress of state decisions on economic policy. The democratisation of the economy has an ideological and political value and provides the foundation for the transformation of society and constitutes the social and institutional framework necessary to escape from the crisis of stagnation and inflation and to expand the productive base of the country in relation to the new international division of labour (25).

Lange characterises these divisions identifying two strategic models as being co-present in the Italian trade union movement (26): the conflictual model, typified by the CISL and the UIL, which stresses internal democracy, organisational decentralisation and active worker participation; and the participative model, often typified by the CGIL, which seeks to participate actively in decision-making about macroeconomic policies and which is willing to adapt its strategy and demands to its interpretation of the requirements of the broader national and international economy. Since 1972, the Italian unions have sought to reconcile these two models within an uneasy, tension-laden unitary strategy which consisted of:

> the attempt to combine the achievement of both transformative classist political objectives and of associational defensive, shop floor objectives by acting simultaneously in the political and market arenas (27).

The CISL and the UIL were forced to learn in the early 1970s that they had to develop a strategic outlook which included socio-economic reform through action in the political arena, but the CGIL was also forced to recognise that it could not continue to ask the work force to sacrifice immediate welfare gains in exchange for politico-economic pie in the sky (28). In pursuit of their unitary strategy, the unions had to achieve and maintain a high degree of autonomy from the political parties and also sustain a high level of working class mobilisation. Both of these are fraught with difficulty, and to reduce the areas of conflict all the unions have been clearly if grudgingly willing to accept the ground rules of capitalism and to act accordingly.

The EUR shift ('svolta dell'EUR') of 1978 (29), therefore, represents a significant move in that it is the first indication, on the part of the united federation, of an acceptance of the need for a policy of austerity and sacrifices in which the working class and other strata of society would have to participate - though it was also made clear that these sacrifices would only be made in return for the protection and creation of jobs especially in the South and for women and young people. The unions proposed that economic programming should be an articulated and participative process and a "rigorous instrument of the dynamic compatibility between demands and real resources" (30). The federation wanted to see expansion and growth so as to assure full employment, the development of the South, a new model of development and improvements in the environment and the quality of life. Once this had been done it would be possible for Italy to redefine its position within the shifting international division of labour. The tools to achieve these objectives are increased public expenditure, increased investment in the South, increased mobility of the factors of production including labour, reform of working time and financial reform in both the state and private sectors. The unions thus indicated an end to their traditional official agnosticism on matters relating to the management of the economy as a whole and a new realism with regard to the relationship between reform objectives and shop floor contractual demands.

The EUR shift was an important one, but it was not a defeat. The unions made a series of specific demands which were to be met in return for their moderation. The resources released as a result of the workers' sacrifices were to be used more effectively to stimulate investment. The unions offered to participate in bargaining at the firm and sectoral level over investment plans; they demanded a more efficient and rational implementation of existing government instruments for economic intervention; they demanded that the government should reduce waste and rationalise the patronage ridden public sector. This offer of moderation was not taken up by the government, however. The three year plan published in 1978 did make some attempt at medium term planning, but only in the context of a neoliberal attack on the 'excessive guarantees' supposedly enjoyed by employed labour (the main target was the wage indexation system). The plan was sunk when the Andreotti government (1976-1978) was brought down by a national strike of metal workers and the threat of a general strike against the government's economic policy. Although the unions continued to display their considerable disruptive power, they did not abandon the EUR strategy.

There was no formal revision of the EUR position up to the crisis of trade union unity over the issue of the revision and possible dismantling of the wage indexation system in the spring of 1984. If the EUR document represents the high point of trade union unity after 1972, it nevertheless failed to resolve many of the fundamental issues which separate Italian trade unions and which have re-emerged to shatter that hard-won unity. The main issue over which the unions have been divided is precisely how they should participate in the management of the economy and at what level. The catalysing element has continued to be the debate over the reform of the wage indexation system.

How then do the Italian unions propose to insert themselves into the management of the economy?

The CGIL was the first union to develop a view, publishing its Factory Plan ('Piano d'impresa') in October 1979 (31). The CGIL's view is that the enterprise should develop a plan which it should then submit both to public agencies and to the union. The enterprise would then discuss the plan with the union and the result of the discussions would be transmitted to the public agencies. Thus the enterprises would be required to coordinate their decisions and to take into account all their consequences and the union would need to decide on its own strategy and priorities so as to be able properly to evaluate the enterprise's decisions (32). The CGIL's position is a rejection of corporatist alliances between state, unions and employers' associations; it is different from systems of worker participation via membership of an advisory board; it is different from workers' control via an investment fund (33). (As we shall see, these two latter positions are those eventually adopted by the UIL and the CISL respectively.) These CGIL rejects these worker participation models in so far as they unquestioningly accept the capitalist system as an immutable economic and social reality and, more importantly, because they restrict the activity of the union to factory horizons and prevent it from looking beyond to the relationship between the economy and the state (34).

The CISL was equally firm at its IX Congress in rejecting worker participation, arguing that this would lead to a confusion over the role of unions and managers, subordination of workers' interests and unacceptable limitations to the bargaining functions of unions (35). The CISL rejects worker participation ('cogestione') but is in favour of self-management ('autogestione') in the cooperative sector of the economy (36), but for the rest it puts forward its plan for a solidarity fund.

The solidarity fund ('Fondo di solidarietà') proposes a levy of 0.5 per cent on the wage packet to form a fund which would be used, under worker direction, for new industrial investment, particularly in the South (37). The CISL's proposals, which can be traced back to 1956 and the discussions on the Vanoni Plan (38), aim to increase the area of influence of the union and of the workers within the economic system through the acquisition of a limited but significant quota of resources and their allocation to social objectives. The union thereby hopes to achieve social control of the economy, starting at the level of the enterprise but aiming at the reorientation of the entire development of the social and productive system through more participative forms (39).

The UIL's proposals on this matter are less clear, but a careful reading of the concluding document to the VIII Congress (40) leads to the view that the UIL favours worker participation ('cogestione') in state run industries and hopes to be able to incorporate the new proposals being formulated at the European level (presumably the Commission's Draft Fifth Directive on worker participation [41]).

On the issue of how and at what level the union inserts itself into the management of the economy, each of the unions produced a response in tune with its own tradition. The CGIL, with the Factory Plan, emphasises the political, and sees itself as participant in and controller of the planning process. The CISL, with the Solidarity Fund, stresses the social, and sees itself as a protagonist, if only partial, in the process of accumulation. The UIL, with its tendency towards worker participation, stresses the institutional, and sees the union more closely confined within the enterprise structure (42). The unions were deeply divided on this issue and their divisions could no longer be masked by unitary or internationalist rhetoric.

If the autumn of 1969 marked the beginning of trade union unity, the autumn of 1980 marked the beginning of its demise. On 10 September 1980, FIAT announced the dismissal of 14,000 workers in an attempt to re-establish the profitability of its automobile division. The FIAT management clearly believed the unions to be weak, and that the time had come to shift the balance of power in the factories back towards the management. They were basically correct. The strike showed up the unions' lack of policy alternatives in times of economic recession and showed how little influence the unions had really managed to exert over investment and production decisions (43). The union (the FLM, the unified metal workers' union, the principal promoters of trade union unity) called an all out strike which lasted thirty five days, but which was ended by a mass demonstration on 14 October in Turin of 40,000 workers who rejected the leadership of the FLM and demanded the right to return to work. The terms negotiated for the return to work - 23,000 workers were to be laid off with 93 per cent of their wages paid by the CIG, but with no guarantee of re-employment - were drastic and the reaction of the work force was violent, since the call for the return to work was far from unanimous.

The political importance of the strike is clear when one notes that the government fell during the course of the dispute and the President of the Republic refused to approve a new cabinet until after the strike was over. Its effect on the morale of the unions was also clear. Union membership had risen steadily from 1968 to 1980, but between 1981 and 1983 membership of the CGIL fell by 7.5 per cent, of the CISL by 5 per cent and of the UIL by 3 per cent (44) and clear ideological divisions appeared in the industrial working class. By 1983, 60 per cent of unionists in the industrial sector expressed dissatisfaction with their union leadership, and of these, some 40 per cent (the highest proportion) named too much political activity as their major cause for complaint (45). But if the unions were failing to represent the interests of the working class, it was at least in part because that class had become progressively less homogeneous. Twenty three per cent of unionists claimed to belong to their union for ideological reasons ("class unionism"), 32 per cent wanted the unions to concentrate on defending the interests of the workers in the work place ("old style reformist unionism"), the same number (32 per cent) expected their unions to participate with government and employers in economic and social decision making ("new style reformist unionism") and a maverick 10 per cent had joined the union for the advancement of personal interests (46). Furthermore, 40 per cent of those interviewed believed that they could improve their lot without the unions (47), and 80 per cent of unionists believed that disputes should be resolved by collaboration between employers and employees in committees of which both groups were members. These figures are difficult to interpret. Some sociologists of labour might attribute these attitudes to a tactical and transitory "confusion" in the mind of the worker which is limited to the present socio-economic conjuncture, the result of which has been increasingly to unite both employees and employers in the fear of bankruptcy and in the need to fight together to obtain the state guarantees of survival (CIG, restructuring aid, early retirements, and so on). Others would argue that it is not the worker who is confused, but the sociologist of labour, hidebound by a class view of industrial production and unable to see the factory as the locus not only of division and conflict, but also of cooperation and collaboration.

Whatever the explanation for this apparent or real lack of homogeneity in the Italian working class, the subsequent conflicts among union leaders, between the leadership and the grass roots and between the unions and the employers federations over the reform of the wage index-ation system were both protracted and bitter. From the unions' point of view, wage indexation had been effective in defending (and even in-creasing) the purchasing power of workers - but at a cost. Firstly, since the mechanism was automatic, the unions lost much of their nego-tiating role over salaries. Secondly, they lost what little influence they had gained over economic policy. Thirdly, whilst the system pro-tected lower paid workers very well, it penalised workers on higher than average wages. Fourthly, wage indexation was increasingly perceived as the major cause of inflation, and consequently unemployment. From April 1981, it was clear that the wage indexation system was no longer non-negotiable.

From 1981 to 1983, various reform proposals were put forward, only to founder in the quagmire of union-party relationships. The PCI was far from keen to see any solution which might lead to the extension of tripartism, since such arrangements tend to bypass opposition parties, and the PCI has been in opposition since 1947. Between 1976 and 1979 the PCI had sought to develop an "historic compromise" with the DC and the PSI, and in return for consultation over government programmes had called for austerity and working class restraint. In 1979, the elec-torate firmly rejected this strategy and the following year, Party Secretary Berlinguer abruptly changed tack and began to support workers' struggles in order to rebuild the party's credibility within the working class, denouncing structural problems rather than the cost of labour as the cause of inflation (48). By calling Luciano Lama (General Secretary of the CGIL) into line, the PCI forced a split in the union between the Communists and the Socialists (about 25 per cent of CGIL members are also members of the PSI, as opposed to about 56 per cent who are members of the PCI). The Christian Democrats, who had also lost support as a result of their flirtation with the PCI, were quite happy to use this occasion to snipe at the new government (June 1981) under Republican, Giovanni Spadolini (the first non-DC prime minister since 1945). In fact six governments fell between 1979 and 1983, and three of these crises were precipitated by the PSI. Confindustria also mounted a sustained attack on the government's economic policy and on wage index-ation, threatening to break the agreement on indexation if reform could not be achieved.

As far as the unions were concerned, the CISL was divided between the leadership and the grass roots, as it had been earlier over the proposal of the Cossiga government to set up a Solidarity Fund. The split bet-ween leadership and grass roots was not confined to the CISL, however: in March 1982, 250,000 metal workers demonstrated in Rome and shouted down the UIL leader Giorgio Benvenuto for opposing the call for a gen-eral strike. An eight-hour general strike eventually took place in June 1982, forced by the grass roots on their reluctant leaders. The same month, both Confindustria and Intersind (the employers' federation for the state run industries) broke the 1975 agreement. Six months later, in January 1983, after heated bargaining, the employers, the unions and the government were able to sign a "major agreement" ('Grande accordo'). This in fact turned out to be little more than minor tinkering and it soon proved to be unsatisfactory to all parties. The resolution of the problem had to await the firm intervention of Bettino Craxi (leader of the Socialist Party and prime minister since August 1983), who unilaterally decreed the revision of the wage indexation system in February 1984.

The CGIL could not accept the revision of the wage indexation system without some tangible reward such as the reform of the taxation system and new employment policies (49). The UIL was prepared to accept, since many of its (generally better paid) members had lost out due to the erosion of differentials caused by wage indexation and flat rate increases. The CISL - more surprisingly - also accepted the reform, largely for political reasons. By breaking with the CGIL and appearing moderate and realistic, the CISL sought to gain a new legitimacy from its intimate association with the government. It was the CGIL which most closely represented the views of the rank and file and the factory council militants who organised strikes and pressured the PCI into calling for a referendum on the issue. When the referendum was finally held, in June 1985, the proposal to restore the four points cut from the indexation scale (worth about £11 a month) was defeated by 54.3 per cent to 45.7 per cent. Campaigning and voting in the referendum took place along party political lines - the DC and the PSI both urging a "no" vote, and Craxi threatening to resign in the event of a "yes".

The referendum result was certainly a setback for the CGIL, and it represents the final act in the dissolution of the unity pact so unevenly maintained over the previous thirteen years. The CISL had been severe in its criticism of the CGIL, especially of its alleged subordination to the will of the PCI, and the referendum result helped to create a more favourable climate for the establishment of a PSI/CISL axis (50). Perhaps rather perversely, however, the referendum also cleared the air, and the following months saw a tentative reconvergence of views on at least some of these issues. By the beginning of the 1985-1986 wage round (a significant moment since contracts for ten million workers are renewed on a three yearly basis) the CGIL had accepted that a reform of the wage indexation system was necessary and it abandoned its demand for flat rate increases, recognising that percentage increases would have to be reinstated. This is a return to the pre-1969 situation. In return for its shift on wage indexation the CGIL demanded that employers stop the practice of giving incentive payments to foremen (their way of subverting flat rate increases) and start paying workers for increases in productivity. They also demanded a return to greater shop floor bargaining.

In this, the CGIL is to some extent recognising that there has been a substantial shift in workers' attitudes over the last few years. Inflation and flat rate increases have eroded differentials and the purchasing power of some workers, but advertising and consumerism have encouraged workers to give priority to alienated needs - power, possessions, money. The erosion of differentials and the lack of job satisfaction have led to the re-establishment of meritocratic principles in the place of the class solidarity based on equal treatment which was defended to the death up to a few years ago. Sixty five per cent of industrial workers now believe that their union should fight for differential increments based on job classification, productivity, danger and physical strenuousness of work, compared with 50 per cent in 1971 (51).

There has also been a convergence of views between the unions on the issue of the 'Cassa integrazione guadagni' (CIG). The CGIL accepted in

September 1985 that it was necessary to accept fewer institutional guarantees for workers in exchange for new labour policies from the government and the extension of factory bargaining. The CISL and the UIL had for some time held the view that the CIG relieves both the unions and the employers of the responsibility of finding long term solutions to the problems of industrial employment - the number of workers receiving CIG benefits had grown to 436,000 by September 1985. The CGIL accepted that workers who were laid off and who could be shown by their employers to be redundant, should lose their jobs and be 'employed' by public agencies on retraining schemes and paid at the same rate as under the CIG. The CIG system has, in any case, been much criticised for its abuses. Some workers, for example, have been laid off for ten years or more and have found second jobs but continue to claim CIG benefit. Nevertheless, opposition from the factory councils and from the unemployed was strong - the factory councils stood to lose all guarantees of re-employment for CIG workers, and the unemployed demanded to know why CIG workers should receive better treatment than the 'genuine' unemployed. Not surprisingly, perhaps, it is the employers who are least keen on the dismantling of the CIG. The system has proved very convenient to them in the past since the costs and the responsibility for lay-offs has been shifted to the state: it was relatively easy for FIAT in 1980 to lay off 23,000 workers and transfer them to the CIG; to have sacked them would have led to insurrection. Rather than see the complete abandonment of the CIG system, FIAT, for example, would prefer a more flexible system which would permit large scale early retirement (52).

CONCLUSION

Since 1968-1970 the Italian labour movement has tried to bring about a radical transformation of its role in society, with consequent modifications in its organisation and in its relations with its members and with other workers. Briefly stated, the unions have attempted to shift the focus of their action from the bargaining area to the more widely political. Some commentators have even gone so far as to talk about the "unionisation of society" or even a "social revolution" (53).

The experience of the 1980s does not confirm this view. The political parties have recovered their role and re-established their influence over the unions, albeit in a rather different way than previously (54). This in turn has adversely affected the autonomy of the unions and undermined the unification process begun in 1972. The 'reform strategy' of the unions brought few results in the long term, and the strategy itself entered a crisis as a result. The union strategy, based firmly on egalitarianism and job security, created considerable pressure and generated a rupture between the union leaderships and the better qualified and more highly paid workers who were anxious to restore differentials. The rigid defence of employment levels to some extent prevented the work force from adapting to the changes in the economy brought about by the crisis. The great leap forward towards the democratisation of the economy has not happened (not least because of falling union membership).

The economic crisis is clearly a major factor in this retrenchment. In particular, the rapidly changing modes of production have forced the unions to react, often negatively and with an eye to the past, but the sporadic nature of change has broken·down the homogeneity of the working class and thrown its representatives into some confusion. The existence of trade unions in Italy is not challenged, but the threats to their policies (both formation and implementation) and the modes of representation of the interests of their members is clear.

So what of the future? Will the CISL's new found legitimacy bear fruit in terms of real advantages for workers and social reforms or does its incorporation indicate its basic irrelevance both to the rank and file and to the government? Will the CGIL's apparent isolation result in a weakening of its position in the factories or will its identification with the defence of workers' interests result in its strengthening, and if so will it be able to manage a readjustment between its market and political objectives? Will the UIL become irrelevant in this 'battle of the giants' or will it, like its Socialist Party ally, lay claim to the middle ground and the representation of Italy's growing middle classes?

However matters develop in the future, the Italian trade unions have at least begun to recognise their previous limitations and an effort is being made, especially by the CGIL, to reshape their traditional activities and functions. The active role played by some of the trade unions in the peace movement, for example, may be seen as an indication of their desire to break out of the strait jacket of representing only the workers in the work place (55). Even when representing the working class, they have begun to accept that they must also represent the non-working class (being unemployed) and the non-working class (having a different sociological base or working in sectors not previously unionised) because all these groups have interests which overlap.

The unions in Italy are facing a profound crisis, but the crisis in union membership and activity are not such as to allow facile predictions of a qualitative shift in industrial relations towards a non-mediated relationship between the employer and the worker, to the exclusion of the union. The unions are still deeply rooted in the social fabric of the country and will continue to be able to play a central role in the process of change and evolution towards new power relations. If the crisis has revealed the weaknesses of the union movement, the most recent developments have indicated a new suppleness and a readiness to meet the challenges of the late 1980s.

NOTES

(1) Benjamin C Roberts, Towards Industrial Democracy: Europe, Japan and the United States, London, Croom Helm, 1979, p. 11.
(2) We use the term neocorporatism to distinguish from the corporatist experiments of the 1930s in fascist Italy and Germany. For fuller discussion of this issue, see L. Panitch, 'Recent theorisations on corporatism: reflections on a growth industry' in British Journal of Sociology, vol. 31, 1980; R. Jessop, 'Corporatism, parliamentarianism and social democracy' in P. Schmitter and G. Lehmbruch (eds.), Trends towards Corporatist Intermediation, London, Sage, 1979; Marino Regini, 'Sindacati e stato nell'Europa occidentale', Democrazia e Diritto, vol. 21, no. 5, 1981, pp. 69-80.
(3) Mario Telò, 'Sindacato europeo e parti sociali nella crisi di rappresentanza', in Paolo Perulli and Bruno Trentin, Il sindacato

nella recessione. Modelli e tendenze delle politiche contrattuali in occidente, Bari, De Donato, 1983, p. 181.

(4) Marino Regini, 'I dilemmi del sindacato di fronte alla crisi', in Perulli and Trentin, op. cit., p. 212.

(5) Bruno Trentin, 'La crisi della forma-sindacato e le possibili evoluzioni del sistema di relazioni industriali' in Perulli and Trentin, op. cit., pp. 35-36.

(6) Regini, art. cit., (1981) p. 213.

(7) This discussion of stable and unstable neocorporatism and incorporation is taken from Regini, art. cit., (1981).

(8) Trentin, art. cit., p. 40.

(9) Telò, art. cit., p. 184.

(10) Regini, art. cit., (1983) p. 216.

(11) Gino Giugni, 'Per una riforma della contrattazione collettiva', in Perulli and Trentin, op. cit., p. 217.

(12) For further details of this period, see Bruno Salvati, 'The birth of Italian trade unionism 1943-54' in Stuart J. Woolf (ed.), The Rebirth of Italy, 1943-50, New York, Humanities Press, 1972.

(13) Peter Lange and Maurizio Vannicelli, 'Strategy under stress: the Italian union movement and the Italian crisis in developmental perspective', in Peter Lange, George Ross and Maurizio Vannicelli, Unions, Change and Crisis: the French and Italian Trade Union Strategy and the Political Economy, 1945-1980, London, George Allen and Unwin, 1983, pp. 114-115.

(14) Tiziano Treu, 'Italy' in Benjamin C Roberts (ed.), Towards Industrial Democracy: Europe, Japan and the United States, London, Croom Helm, 1979, p. 82.

(15) Lange and Vannicelli, op.cit., pp. 128-129.

(16) Ibid., pp. 136-137.

(17) Ibid., p. 153.

(18) Ibid., pp. 156-157.

(19) Treu, art. cit., p. 90.

(20) For a detailed discussion of the background to the 'Statuto dei lavoratori' and the legal framework of industrial relations in Italy, see Giovanni Contini, 'Politics, law and shop floor bargaining in postwar Italy', in Steven Tolliday and Jonathan Zeitlin (eds.), Shop Floor Bargaining and the State, Cambridge University Press, 1985.

(21) Sergio Turone, Il paradosso sindacale, Bari, Laterza, 1979, pp. 187-188.

(22) Lange and Vannicelli, op. cit., pp. 164-165.

(23) CISL, 'Tesi programmatiche approvate dal IX Congresso Confederale' (Roma, 7-12/10/81) in Conquiste del Lavoro, supplemento no. 92, ottobre 1981, p. 67.

(24) CGIL, 'Tesi programmatiche approvate dal X Congresso', Rassegna Sindacale, vol. 27, no. 43, 26/11/81, p. 142.

(25) Ibid., p. 143.

(26) Lange and Vannicelli, op.cit., p. 97.

(27) Ibid., p. 98.

(28) On the issues raised by the 'hot autumn' of 1969 and on the development of trade union unity, see inter alia Lange and Vannicelli, op. cit., Georges Couffignal, I sindacati in Italia, Roma, Editori Riuniti, 1979, and Dominique Grisoni and Hugues Portelli, Le lotte operaie in Italia dal 1960 al 1976, Milano, Rizzoli, 1977.

(29) CGIL/CISL/UIL - Comitato direttivo unitario, 'Proposte per una svolta di politica economica e di sviluppo civile e democratico'

43

(EUR Roma, 13-14/1/78), in Rassegna Sindacale (inserto speciale), vol. 24, no. 2, 19/1/78.

(30) Ibid., p. vi, my emphasis.

(31) CGIL, 'Democrazia industriale', Documento approvato dal Consiglio della CGIL, tenutosi ad Ariccia dal 10 al 12 attobre 1979, in AA. VV., Il piano d'impresa e il ruolo del sindacato in Italia, Bari, De Donato, 1980, pp. 89-115.

(32) Giuliano Amato, 'Premessa' in ibid., pp. 5-6.

(33) Bruno Trentin, 'La frontiera della programmazione e i compiti del sindacato', in ibid., p. 20.

(34) Michele Magno, 'Il ruolo del sindacato nel caso italiano', in ibid. p. 69.

(35) CISL, 'Mozione politica generale del IX Congresso CISL', Conquiste del Lavoro, supplemento no. 92, ottobre 1981, p. 61.

(36) Ibid., p. 69.

(37) For a description of and comments on the 'Fondo', see Conquiste del Lavoro, supplemento no. 9, 30/5/83.

(38) An historical survey of the background to the proposal can be found in Franco Archibugi, 'Fondo di solidarietà: gioco agli equivoci' in Conquiste del Lavoro, 16/2/81, p. 5.

(39) Tiziano Treu, 'Fondo di solidarietà: un'idea da far funzionare', Il Progetto, vol. 1, no. 1, gennaio-febbraio 1981, p. 66.

(40) UIL, 'Documento conclusivo approvato dal VIII Congresso', Lavoro Italiano, vol. 7, no. 23-24, 16-23/6/81, pp. 40-42.

(41) For the text of the Draft Fifth Directive with subsequent amendments see EEC, 'Council Directives on procedures for informing and consulting employees', in Official Journal, no. C217/3, 12/8/83.

(42) For amplification of this point and further discussion of the issues involved, see Franco Carinci and Marcello Pedrazzoli, 'Una legge per la democrazia industriale', Mondoperaio, no. 1-2, gennaio-febbraio 1983, pp. 34-45, and the debate which followed in Mondoperaio over the next six months.

(43) Joanne Barkan, Visions of Emancipation: the Italian Workers' Movement since 1945, New York, Praeger, 1984, pp. 166-170.

(44) European Trade Union Institute, The Trade Union Movement in Italy (Info 11), Brussels, ETUI, 1985, pp. 9-10. Despite this fall in numbers, Italy still has very high rates of unionisation. In 1983, 45.5 per cent of Italy's 14.8 million wage earners were members of unions. The working members of the three confederations totalled 6.75 million, divided as follows: CGIL 46.8 per cent, CISL 34.9 per cent, UIL 18.3 per cent.

(45) AA.VV., Il lavoratore post-industriale: la condizione e l'azione dei lavoratori nell'industria italiana, Milano, Angeli, 1985, p. 453.

(46) Ibid., p. 448.

(47) Ibid., p. 464.

(48) Barkan, op. cit., pp. 162-163.

(49) Donald Sassoon, 'Italian unions' in Marxism Today, April 1984, pp. 5-6.

(50) This view is expressed by Pierre Carniti, former General Secretary of the CISL, in an interview in Panorama, 29/9/85, p. 243. Carniti's term of office came to an end in July 1985. In early 1986, Craxi offered Carniti the prestigious job of chairman of the RAI, the Italian state broadcasting corporation.

(51) Il lavoratore post-industriale, p. 428 et seq.

(52) This is the view of Cesare Annibaldi, FIAT's external relations director, interviewed in L'Espresso, 29/9/85, p. 189.

(53) Il lavoratore post-industriale, p. 428.
(54) On the trade unions and the political system, see: Mimmo Carrieri
     and Carlo Donolo, 'The political system as a problem for the trade
     unions in Italy: 1975-1983', in Otto Jacobi et al., (eds.) Economic
     Crisis, Trade Unions and the State, London, Croom Helm, 1986.
(55) For an account of the involvement of the Italian trade unions in
     the peace movement, see William Brierley, 'Italian politics and
     the peace movement' in Journal of Area Studies, no. 9, Spring 1984,
     pp. 18-23.

3 Labour confederations and Socialist governments in France, 1981-1986

JEFF BRIDGEFORD AND PETER MORRIS

The years 1981 to 1986 placed French labour confederations in a situation without precedent in their long history; central government was firmly in the hands of a political force theoretically sympathetic to their aspirations. Earlier periods in which the left had held office (the Popular Front, the immediate post-war years, even the Republican Front of 1956-57) were all marked by 'unstable coalition' rather than by 'stable majority' government and all succumbed within a couple of years to outside pressures from the right. This is not to say that the first two periods did not have long lasting consequences for the French trade union movement. The Popular Front marked the coming of age of French unionism as a mass structured force with the formal negotiating and representational rights it had hitherto lacked. The post-war years saw individual unions and confederations acquiring durable influence and status within a number of key sectors of the French economy (e.g. transport, energy manufacture and supply) and the establishment of workplace committees ('comités d'entreprise') on which labour was represented. This second period, however, also witnessed the consolidation into a seemingly ineradicable split within the French union movement into Communist and non-Communist segments. What was new about the period 1981-86 was that for the first time the Socialist Party had unfettered control over all the institutions of central government; that its parliamentary majority was absolutely secure; and that for the first three years the Communist Party provided some members of the ministerial team.

Thus it might be imagined that 1981 provided the best possible environment that the French labour confederations have ever experienced to consolidate and develop their interests and powers. Yet it is abundantly clear that this has not proved to be the case. By 1986 the overall image of the French trade union movement was of an already weak institution becoming a dangerously enfeebled one. The indicators of this decline are obvious. As is well known, the French labour confederations have always been weak in overall levels of unionisation, which have rarely gone above 25 per cent of the labour force. In the last five years, that figure has fallen still further and under 20 per cent are now (1986) described as unionised. Two of the three major labour groupings - the Confédération Générale du Travail (CGT), and the Confédération Française Démocratique du Travail (CFDT) - have suffered particularly severe losses, whereas the other, Force Ouvrière (CGT-FO), has managed to improve its position slightly. Between 1974 and 1983, the CGT lost 830,000 members and it is significant, given that labour confederations like all mass organisations always exaggerate their size, that in 1983 it was claiming no more than 1.6 million members; in the late 1970s the figure claimed was 2.5 million (1). In the same period, CFDT membership fell from over one million to under three quarters of a million. According to Frank Wilson, these figures are even worse than they appear in that an increasing proportion of union membership is made up of retired workers (2). The CGT-FO has always been coy about its membership figures but recently the figure of 600,000 has been put forward (3). The two confederations have also performed poorly in nation-wide elections for industrial tribunals ('conseils de prud'hommes'), workplace committees and social security boards where the whole labour force - not just affiliated trade unionists - votes. In the 1983 elections for workplace committees, the CGT for the first time in its history obtained under 30 per cent of the votes (in 1967 it had 45 per cent) and the CFDT vote, at 21.9 per cent, also showed a slight fall. The CGT-FO increased its share to 11.1 per cent. The percentage of votes going to non-unionised delegates (22.8 per cent) made that category the second largest group on the committees. Along side this decline in membership had gone, not surprisingly a fall off in levels of income leading, particularly in the case of the CFDT, to some acute financial difficulties. Less causally linked (for reasons that will be explained below) to the decline in confederation strength but nevertheless a real feature of trade unionism in the 1980s has been a sharp fall in the number of days lost through strikes: in the year from June 1984 to June 1985, or example, they fell by one third.

On the one hand, therefore, the French labour confederations in the 1980s have experienced an extended period of strong left wing government; on the other the CGT and the CFDT at least have endured a decline in their membership levels, resources and in what might be described as their representative legitimacy. (It is perhaps a measure of the latter that the French press in the run-up to the 1986 legislative elections was able to devote so little space to their interventions, or non-interventions, in the campaign.) This juxtaposition of left government but declining unionism forms the background to the present chapter. The chapter does not intend either to condemn the Socialist governments for having, by their actions and inactions, caused the present weakness of French organised unionism; nor does it seek to argue, as some social theorists (such as Alain Touraine) that traditional trade unionism is doomed to disappear, irrespective of what governments do, by the changing economic, political and indeed cultural structures of post-industrial societies like France. Our aims are much more modest. We seek to show firstly how the changed economic circumstances of France in the late 1970s combined with the particular structures of left wing politics, of which the labour confederations are a part, to produce the presidential and parliamentary victories of 1981. Then we examine the legislative performance of the Socialist governments in so far as they affected and were affected by the interests of the labour confederations. Finally we offer a number of tentative suggestions as to why, when the Socialists lost control of the government - though not of course of the presidency - in March 1936, the overall relations between the confederations and the government seemed as weak as they are customarily portrayed as being.

THE LABOUR CONFEDERATIONS AND THE VICTORY OF 1981

The base line definition of independent trade unionism is of a group of workers formed into an association which exists to promote and defend their collective interests in the institution from which they derive their wages and which is not controlled by the owners or managers of that institution. (Those that are so controlled, company unions, are known in French as 'syndicats jaunes' and are loosely organised into the Confédération des Syndicats Libres.) In most countries where independent trade unionism exists, individual trade unions are organised into one or more national confederations which purport to speak for all the affiliated groups and thus give an impression of labour solidarity that will strengthen their bargaining power. The extent to which such national confederations are able to control the actions of affiliates varies widely from country to country; moreover the fact that there exist in a country like France more than one national confederation shows the extreme difficulty in obtaining the 'worker unity' which ideologies of the labour movement have always proclaimed.

French trade unionism is characterised by two related features which have severely impaired its effectiveness as an economic pressure group. The first is the fragmentation of its organisational structure. For all that the separation of union and party is a fundamental part of the belief system of French trade unionism, the CGT, the CFDT and the CGT-FO hold profoundly antagonistic political sensibilities and values that cannot be reconciled and that make coordinated worker action impossible to achieve except in particular circumstances. Thus the labour confederations reflect the rivalries and competitiveness that are a feature of left wing politics in France. Indeed, affiliation to a particular confederation is, in the case of the CFDT and the CGT-FO, a good indicator of overall political attitude, while - paradoxically - the most overtly politicised union, the CGT, is the one most likely to attract the ordinary, 'non-political' worker. The second feature of trade unionism is the underdeveloped nature of industrial relations in France and the generally poor ability of labour organisations to impose solutions to industrial conflicts or even to control strategy in such conflicts. There are many reasons for this: intense employer hostility to bargaining at plant level over wages and conditions of service; the legal framework for worker representation committees which insists on the pluralism of unions and thus entrenches inter-union competitiveness and the aforementioned inter-union political hostility. The result is that French trade unions have very rarely been able to impose collective bargaining practices on companies or been able to impose closed shop arrangements over the head of the legal prohibitions on such arrangements. In a few areas - docks, printing, energy supply, transport, broadcasting, education - coverage has remained good, but in general what might be called the bread and butter attractiveness of union membership to ordinary members has been limited and as a consequence rates of unionisation have been low. This is not to say, of course, that industrial relations are 'good' or that strikes are infrequent, but it is to argue that the institutionalised capacity of unions and confederations is low.

An important consequence of this has been that in order to make themselves heard, the labour confederations have been, despite the contrived apoliticism of trade union discourse, active at least as much in the political as in the economic market place. Most strikes in France take place over ordinary labour-related issues: wages, conditions of service and so on. But two of the three major confederations are staffed by highly politicised personnel, at both national and local level; and even the resolutely apolitical CGT-FO comes from a 'labourist' tradition within the old Socialist Party and is marked by an ineradicable anti-communism that provided the impetus for its creation in 1947. (The initial funding for its creation came from the USA and it was revealed in 1985 that President Reagan's special funds to sponsor anti-communist political movements - the National Endowment for Democracy - had in the preceding twelve months given it $830,000.) In the case of the CGT, its political alignment is manifest. From 1947 to the present day, national and local leadership of the confederation and its most important affiliates has been dominated by the French Communist Party (PCF) (4). The CFDT refuses to accept that it is in any sense the 'labour spokesman' of the Socialist Party (PS). Sectors of its leadership, however, played a large part in the convening of the 1974 Assises du Socialisme which saw the consolidation of the PS after the presidential campaign of that year and even today the confederation elite is close to various factors within the PS. The result of this politicisation, enforced as it is by the relative weakness of shop floor unionism and perpetuated as it has been by political disagreement, is to give to each confederation a solid core of leaders and activists, whose motivation is intense just because it is ideological. Their enthusiasm cannot easily be dampened by failure at factory and bargaining level and they guarantee a visibility and credibility to the confederations as political actors which in terms of political muscle they probably do not merit. Moreover, in times of social crisis (e.g. 1968), governments have to talk to someone and the confederations' legitimacy benefits accordingly; while in times of left wing political harmony (the early and mid-1970s) the confederations were capable of mobilising large groups for short, one day mass protests which had propaganda value at least.

The role of the confederations in the run-up to the 1981 presidential election has been the subject of analysis by G. Ross and others (5). The general conclusion of this analysis seems to be that the victory of François Mitterrand, because it was initially won at the expense of the Communist Party, marks a defeat for the CGT (Ross talks of a "political disaster" [6]) and an embarrassment for the CFDT which, after 1978, had moved away from a position of commitment on behalf of the PS to one of deliberate political isolationism. This was the so-called policy of 'recentrage' or 're-syndicalisation'. While such a conclusion no doubt accurately reflects the strategic calculations of the confederation leaderships, it may be thought to do less than full just ;e to the longer term social and economic goals of the confederations, to their influence on the 1981 programme and to the result of the election.

The background to the Mitterrand victory was of course the recession that began in the mid-1970s and deepened after 1978. Economists conventionally define a recession as a situation in which the growth of over-all demand in a country's economy slows down to a point where its gross domestic product hardly changes over an extended period. An inevitable consequence of the overall slow down in the growth of demand is that demand for labour will also weaken. It does not necessarily follow from this that real wages will also fall in a recession since price levels are equally subject to the squeeze effect of falling demand; but recession conditions do mean that levels of unemployment are highly likely to rise. And risen they have in all the mature industrial economies of Western Europe including France in the last ten years. The rise, more-over, has been speeded up by the declining ability of many industrial sectors to cope with the intense challenge being presented by the high technology, low wage economies of the Far East. Thus even when domestic demand recovered in European countries, it has been met not by domestic production (which generates jobs) but by overseas imports (which do not). The old equation recession equals unemployment still holds true; the old equation recovery equals rising employment does not. In France by the end of 1981, the unemployment rate stood at 2 million; real disposable income started to fall in 1980; investment fell, as did the strike rate.

Mitterrand's victory was due in substantial measure to the belief that the economic policies of his predecessor had failed and that the neo-liberalism which had been a marked feature of the political discourse of both Giscard d'Estaing and Barre was responsible or the rapidly worsen-ing economic situation. Whether or not such a belief was valid is beside the point; what matters is that government economic policies were blamed. The major polls were unanimous in attributing Giscard's defeat to this factor above all others. Thus the politics of economic decline (to use James Alt's phrase about Great Britain) benefited the political left in France whereas elsewhere they worked to the advantage of the right. Worker militancy - defined in terms of strike levels, union ability to mobilise protest movements - had weakened. But since these are, for the reasons outlined above, rather poor indicators of confeder-ation capacity in France, the election of 1981 provided an opportunity for the realisation of their aims. As we have seen, whatever their immediate pre-election calculations, two of the three confederations were identified with the coalition of political forces which won in 1981. Even the CGT-FO had, in its leader André Bergeron, a member of the PS. And, of course, the formally autonomous Fédération de l'Éduca-tion Nationale represents a profession which has long had very strong links indeed with the local and central structures of the PS. To be elected in 1981, Mitterrand had to demonstrate two things: first that he was not the prisoner of the PCF, and second that he was still authentic-ally a candidate of the left. The PCF campaign and performance allowed him to do the former; his programme guaranteed the latter. Anti-Commun-ist trade unionists in the CFDT were reassured and voted Socialist in greater numbers than ever before (50 per cent in 1981 as opposed to 23 per cent in 1973 and 36 per cent in 1978). Communist-voting CGT members (57 per cent of the total confederation membership in 1981) were able without difficulty to transfer their votes in the second round of the election to a candidate who was, because of his programme, recognisably 'unitaire pour deux' (7).

The confederations moreover had brought a significant input to the policy package that Mitterrand was pledged to introduce. For all the watering down of the Common Programme of the left and of the 110 Propositions of the Socialist Party, Mitterrand's 1981 programme did offer a distinctive choice rather than a mere statement of good intentions. The stress was on nationalisation; greater state control over credit; an expansionary budgeting policy; interventionism in industrial policy; the revival of the planning mechanism. These were all welcome to the CGT and had been part of its economic thinking. As we have see, the majority of the CGT membership did vote for the Communist candidate (Marchais) in the first round of the presidential elections and fewer of its members voted Socialist than in 1978. Nevertheless, the programme was by no means unacceptable to the CGT membership nor (as pre-election tensions and disagreements about the PCF electoral tactics had demonstrated) to many permanent officials within the regional and industrial federations. As far as the CFDT is concerned, the very fact that the 110 Propositions were reminiscent in their economic orientation of the Common Programme was not an incentive to enthusiasm. Once again, however, the coalition building that had gone on in the 1970s meant that ideas advocated by the CFDT were represented - in particular proposals for improving plant level bargaining, decentralisation, self-management and employee involvement in decision taking. Even the nationalisation programme would have one advantage for the CFDT - since it would by definition extend the public sector which in France (as elsewhere) is always the sector in which union rights are most securely entrenched. This same consideration also applied to the CGT-FO given the importance within it of civil service federations.

SOCIALIST GOVERNMENTS AND THE TRADE UNIONS

In this section we shall discuss the ways in which successive Socialist governments of the Mitterrand presidency have affected, or been affected by, the position of French trade unions and confederations. For convenience the discussion will be structured along four dimensions:
    a) access to decision making within government itself,
    b) labour law,
    c) social policy,
    d) economic policy.

a) Access

The trade union confederations were in something of a dilemma. How could they succeed in influencing the decision making machinery of the Socialist government whilst still retaining their commitment to self-proclaimed independence? Given the importance to the syndicalist myth of the separation of spheres between union activity and political activity, it is perhaps not surprising that direct government linkages were fairly restricted. There was no direct equivalent of Ernest Bevin or Frank Cousins. Only one trade union leader actually became a government minister - André Henry of the Fédération de l'Éducation Nationale was head of the short-lived Ministry of Leisure. Nevertheless, a number of full-time trade union officials did take up senior appointments within the ministries and public sector institutions or as heads of specialist agencies. A few came from the CGT - René Bidouze and Jean-Louis Balland went as advisors to Anicet le Pors, the Minister responsible for the Civil Service, and Jacques Chauvineau became a member of Charles Fiterman's staff, as did a prominent railway workers' union official, André Laumin (8). One out-of-favour CGT secretary Christiane Gilles left to work at the Ministry of Women's Rights. Hubert Lesire-Ogrel went to the

Ministry of National Solidarity and Social Affairs, René Decaillon went to the Ministry of Labour, Henri Fauqué went to the Energy Ministry, Francine Collet went to the Ministry of Posts and Telecommunications and Jeanette Laot became an advisor at the Élysée Palace. Hubert Prevot became the head of the Commissariat for Economic Planning, Michel Rolant went to head the newly created National Agency for Energy Affairs (9). At a later date, after the announcement of the plans for restructuring the steel industry, the leader of the Metal Workers Union of the CFDT, Jacques Chérèque, went to become a Super-Préfet responsible for job creation in Lorraine (10). CFDT influence was reinforced by the relatively high proportion of members of ministerial staffs who were CFDT members (11). For instance, Pierre Mauroy had a 'Groupe Matignon' which met regularly to discuss government policy and which had a CFDT member and one also from CGT-FO (12).

Initially the Socialist government was quite anxious to be seen to involve the trade unions in the decision making process. Trade union and party officials boasted about the variety and intensity of links between the different bodies. The CGT explained that the trade union confederations had been consulted on economic planning, industrial policy, nationalisations, agricultural policy, the status of the civil service, immigration policy, health, transport policy, vocational training and education; they were not consulted on the decentralisation issue, however (13). According to René Mouriaux, contacts between officials and civil servants were incessant (14). Pfister has described the visits of trade union leaders to the Hotel Matignon (15). However, contacts were variable - relatively good with the traditionally sympathetic ministries such as Employment, but markedly less so with for instance the Ministry for Industry. As time went on and the period of 'mandate politics' gave way to the more familiar experience of governing under pressure, so the frequency of contacts declined. Once the Socialist government began to respond more and more to other forces, so it was less prepared to listen to the voice of the labour confederations, something bemoaned by the latter's leaders and officials alike. The trade unions were not consulted on the first set of austerity measures. The Prime Minister's office lost its team of advisors specialising in trade union affairs. Moreover, with the Cabinet reshuffle of March 1983, there was a Minister of Social Affairs, but no Minister of Employment (16). The trade unions were supposedly involved in negotiations prior to the second set of austerity measures, but this did not materialise (17). At a sectoral level, for instance, trade unionists complained that in spite of enormous problems in the ship-building industry, the newly appointed Minister for Industrial Redevelopment, Édith Cresson, was apparently not even prepared to meet trade union representatives (18).

Trade unions and the Socialist government had negotiated amicably during the first few months of the administration, but at the first sign of a change in government strategy the Socialists seemed to revert to a Jacobin imperiousness which encouraged the exclusion of the trade union confederations. They in turn lapsed into a sulkiness (justified once again by reference to their 'syndicalist' values) which reinforced this exclusion. The two groupings thus reverted to a stance which in any case they probably found the most comfortable and which certainly accords better with the traditional distanced relationship between government and labour confederations in France.

b) Labour law

Legislation has always been central to the pattern of industrial relations in France. Workplace representation for example, has been strictly codified. Personnel delegates were instituted in 1936 to represent
collective or individual grievances of a firm regardless of whether the
latter were members of a trade union or not. Workplace committees were
set up in 1945 to advise on the running of the firm and to oversee the
management of the work force's social benefits (canteens, libraries,
Christmas parties, holiday homes). The trade unions did not have the
automatic right to represent the interests of the work force although in
practice they did manage to ensure that their candidates were elected.
Indeed the hostility of employers to trade union 'interference in company management' meant that it was not until 1968 that trade union
sections were officially recognised within the workplace and trade union
delegates were permitted to represent the interests of their members
within the firm itself. Therefore, it is not surprising that labour law
should receive considerable attention (19). Indeed it could be argued
that the government made their greatest single contribution to the
fortunes of employees and trade unions with the introduction of the
Auroux Laws, named after the Minister of Labour at the time, the Socialist Mayor of Roanne, Jean Auroux.

The laws had complementary goals, but in essence they were to improve
the rights of employees and trade unions, above all within the workplace. The first law, on the institutions representing the work force
(28 October 1982) aimed to improve workplace representation in its
various forms and particularly in small firms. Trade union sections
could now be set up in firms with fewer than fifty employees. Union
dues could now be collected in the workplace during working time. Firms
were required to provide trade union premises. Trade union sections
could now invite other trade unionists on to the firm's premises. The
trade union delegate was entitled to an increase in paid time off for
trade union activities. Trade union delegates were to have improved
protection against being sacked. The workplace committee's rights were
increased - it should be informed of the impact of the introduction of
new technology; it should be informed if the firm invested in another
firm or received investment from any other firm; it could give its
opinion on increases in the prices of the firm's products; depending on
the size of the firm, it could solicit specialist information concerning
the running of the firm. Where firms were too small to have a workplace
committee, the personnel delegate could take on these responsibilities.
Finally, workplace committees could be set up not only at plant level
but also at company level - a particularly important initiative given
firms' increasingly complex structures.

The second law, on collective bargaining and the regulation of collective disputes (13 November 1982), aimed to improve collective bargaining, whilst also strengthening the position of trade unions. At industry level, the employers and the trade unions had an obligation to
negotiate each year on wages and every five years on job regradings. At
the level of the firm, annual negotiations were to be held on real wages
and work times. Moreover, if a plant level agreement contained provisions which contravened agreements which had already been negotiated at
a higher level, trade unions (with a majority in the workplace committee elections) could reject the agreement - thus helping to strengthen
the position of the trade unions with relatively large grass roots

membership and to de-legitimise the activities of the smaller unrepresentative unions. There was also the possibility of easier recourse to arbitration under the aegis of the Ministry of Labour - a procedure which hitherto had hardly ever been used.

The third law, on health and safety committees and working conditions (28 December 1982) aimed to allow employees and trade unions more influence regarding health and safety at work. If conditions were considered hazardous, employees were not entitled to stop work on a particular job, but the health and safety committees which normally have trade union representation had the right to demand the intervention of a works inspector.

There was a fourth law on workers' rights in the enterprise (4 August 1982). Hitherto disciplinary procedures had not featured as part of labour law, with the result that in practice employees could be disciplined and even sacked at the whim of their employer. As a result of this measure, the law established what may or may not be considered suitable for inclusion in disciplinary procedures. The other aspect of this law granted employees the right of expression as to the content and organisation of their work and the definition and the implementation of actions designed to improve working conditions in the firm (20).

Two further laws on the democratisation of the public sector (27 July 1983) and on trade union education (31 December 1985) aimed to improve the institutional position of the trade unions. With the former, trade unions were to represent the work force on the board of nationalised industries and with the latter, trade unions were to be granted certain facilities for the training of their members.

Two types of comment are worth making about these laws. Firstly, their introduction was not necessarily supported by all the trade union confederations. The CFDT was, on the whole, very much in favour, which is perhaps not surprising given its role in the initial process of formulation and the overall commitment to the more decentralised approach to power relationships that it has always favoured (21). Curiously it was particularly enthusiastic about the right of expression, a right which by-passed traditional workplace representation and thus weakened the potential for trade union control. The CGT was in favour, but not surprisingly claimed that the reforms did not go far enough - employees needed to be granted further means for solving the problems in the workplace (22). The CGT was caught between the desire to avoid a weakening of the authority of its central organisation and the desire to take advantage of its relatively better presence at grass roots level. The CGT-FO was particularly concerned about the potential reduction of the role of the trade union both at national and local level (23). Desjardins provides further evidence of trade union differences concerning the law on the right of expression (24), and yet, according to figures produced by the Ministry of Social Affairs, CFDT enthusiasm and CGT-FO reluctance have been somewhat tempered at shop floor level. In those firms where negotiations on the right of expression have taken place, 78 per cent of CFDT trade union sections signed agreements, thereby demonstrating less than total support, whereas as many as 62 per cent of CGT-FO trade union sections signed, thereby demonstrating a considerable interest in procedures which their leadership sometimes gave the impression of holding in disdain (25).

Secondly, it is not clear how well the laws have actually been implemented, in spite of the glowing appraisal of their value made by Jean Auroux's successor, Pierre Bérégovoy (26). By the beginning of 1985, 2,618 agreements on the right of expression had been signed, covering over two million employees (27). What does this mean in practice? At a training weekend organised by the metal workers union of the CGT, the opinion seemed to be that in a well organised firm this right of expression offered no particular advantages, in fact it was a diversion, but in firms with low unionisation every little bit helped (28). As for the law on collective bargaining, the Ministry of Social Affairs has shown that 66 per cent of those firms surveyed (a total of 10,225) had entered into negotiations in 1984 - a significant increase on 1983 when only 42 per cent had negotiated (29). Clearly a large percentage still had not, even though there was no compulsion to negotiate 'in good faith' nor of course to reach an agreement at the end of the bargaining process. Of the 62 per cent that did negotiate, approximately two thirds did in fact come to an agreement. Moreover, according to another part of this same 1984 review, the quality of the information provided by the employers as a basis for negotiation was distinctly variable. Further research is needed to provide a clearer picture of the implementation of these laws and indeed of the others. Have new employees actually been able to take advantage of the new health and safety regulations with impunity? Have the representatives to the enterprise committees had access to more detailed information and has this extended their influence? Equally, what sanctions are to be used against employers who refuse to countenance the introduction of these new laws in their firms?

In spite of these doubts regarding the application of the laws, a particularly vulnerable area after the 1986 legislative elections, it is clear that the Socialist governments have reinforced and extended the formal rights of employees and also of the trade unions in a number of different ways. Other ways in which the government helped the institutional state of unions and confederations were by increasing the financial grants that were available to them from the Ministry of Labour; and by including trade unionists in the new categories of those eligible for entry to France's famous administrative training college, the École Nationale d'Administration.

c) Social policy

On entering office, the Socialists immediately carried out a series of social welfare measures which increased the real value of the minimum wage, pensions, family allowances, housing and disability benefits (30). Subsequently benefits and the minimum wage were relatively well protected: from 1981 to 1985 the purchasing power of the minimum wage increased by 15.5 per cent, pensions by 25 per cent, family allowances for families with three children by 16 per cent and with two children by 46 per cent (31). In an interesting article, Jean-Pierre Jallade has shown that the universality and adequacy of welfare benefits were improved, even if proportionality and progressivity were not (32).

On another tack, in January 1982 the Socialist government issued a regulation introducing the fifth week of paid holidays and the thirty-nine hour week without loss of earnings (33). This measure further illustrated the considerable differences that existed in the trade unions over policy objectives: the CGT and CGT-FO were adamant that this reduction in the working week should not lead to a commensurate cut in wages, the CFDT an the other hand was prepared and almost seemed anxious to accept it as part of an overall strategy to create jobs (34). The final decision was taken by François Mitterrand against the advice of his Prime Minister (35). The commitment to a thirty-five hour week by 1985 was discreetly dropped, partly because of the problem of deciding corresponding wage levels (36). In its place, negotiations on the reduction of the working week were to have been held on an industry-wide basis: in the gas and electricity industries and in the Paris Métro, for instance, the working week for all employees was down to 38 hours by January 1983. Indeed by April 1983, 24.6 per cent of all employees were contracted to work less than 39 hours (37). (Of course, in other, particularly ailing, industries like steel and ship building, the work-ing week was often much shorter than this, but this was for quite different reasons [38].) The length of the working week was one of the major issues, along with the introduction of new technology, procedures for redundancies and the status of short-term contract workers, to be debated and incorporated into a national agreement on more flexible working arrangements (39), but the major trade union confederations finally decided not to sign it. The CGT had always been opposed to the idea of bartering hard-won rights for dubious gains: if the CNPF (the Conseil National du Patronat Français - the French employers' federa-tion) was so keen then something must be wrong. The CFDT and the CGT-FO had been initially quite favourable to the idea, but grass roots opposi-tion, the fear of playing into the hands of the employers and the fear of being isolated as the only major trade union confederation prepared to countenance such a move, particularly if it brought no clear advan-tages, continued to explain their ultimate reticence (40). By the end of the Socialist government's period of office, the number of hours actually worked per employee per week had stopped falling (41).

The government had in part at least responded to the trade union confederations' demands on social welfare policy. This legitimised the trade unions as appropriate interlocutors, but equally it could be argued that later, when the Socialist government was less attentive to the demands of the trade unions, that the latter became de-legitimised. Moreover, the confederations found themselves in the usual dilemmas that confront unions when their political allies are in power. Why should employees bother to join unions if major advances in social welfare provision could be achieved within the workplace but as a result of government policy? Should confederation leaders risk alienating their own grass roots supporters to facilitate the policies of a government with which they are broadly in sympathy?

d) Economic policy

In the sphere of economic policy, government/union disagreements have been much sharper and this is hardly surprising given the problems the labour market faced. Initially, the Socialist government spoke to the concerns of the labour movement by engineering a Keynesian expansion of the economy, with the emphasis on job creation, which was generally welcomed by the trade union confederations. This was an extremely difficult undertaking at a time when international orthodoxy was much less sympathetic to such policy than it had been twenty years earlier (the Wilson government of 1974 found this out too). After twelve months, with a growing budget deficit, relatively high inflation and a deteriorating balance of trade, the Socialist government introduced its first package of measures advocating economic restraint. Although the package included a four month wage freeze, an increase in social security contributions and a reduction in future public expenditure (42), the reaction of the unions was overall relatively muted (43).

However, although there were short term improvements in the inflation rate and the deficit in the trade balance, international speculation led to a further devaluation of the franc in March 1983. Accompanying this was a second package of austerity measures which entailed cuts in public expenditure, higher charges for public utilities and social security contributions and also an obligatory loan to the state (44). On this occasion the reaction of the unions was more critical (45) but their criticism led to little in the way of action (46).

The Socialist government had committed itself to reducing the rate of inflation and following a policy of economic modernisation. Initially this meant in industrial terms providing considerable support for the sunset as well as the sunrise industries. By the time Laurent Fabius became Minister for Industry in February 1983 the emphasis switched to support for the latter but at the expense of the former. In the coal industry this would lead immediately to 6,000 redundancies and to 25-30,000 redundancies in all by 1988 (47). The steel industry was set to lose 20-25,000 jobs by 1987, with the majority of the redundancies being made in the Nord-Pas de Calais area, a region which has consistently suffered from problems of de-industrialisation (48). It was particularly as a result of the government's decision not to support ailing nationalised industries that grass roots trade unions became more militant, at least in some sections (steel). There was however nothing in the coal industry to compare with the length and bitterness of the British miners' strike of 1984-85, in spite of the CGT's hopes that French miners would be inspired by the actions of their British counterparts.

Socialist economic policy had mixed results. It succeeded in reducing the rate of inflation from a high of 14 per cent in 1981 to 4.7 per cent in 1985, but industrial production stagnated and economic growth was also slow (1.1 per cent averaged out from 1980 to 1985) (49). Socialist government economic policy, along with other international factors, was responsible for the dramatic rise in unemployment which after peaking at the end of 1984 has still not descended below 10 per cent of the working population (50), in spite of a variety of employment policy initiatives. Solidarity contracts were introduced to encourage early retirement or a reduction in the length of the working week which in turn would be counter-balanced by the hiring of new employees; subsequently this scheme lost its impetus and was used more defensively, to avoid redundancies. In 1983, 167 solidarity contracts were concluded (347 in 1982) covering 90,581 employees on reduced hours; 6,800 jobs were preserved in this way but only 1,896 new employees were taken on (51). The Socialist government's major programme for reducing unemployment was a YTS-style scheme for young people which was set up towards the end of 1984 and which provided placements for 78,000 young people by March 1985 (52).

Another important feature of economic policy with which trade unions have been dissatisfied has been the government's policy on wages. Although, as has been shown above, benefits and the minimum legal wage have kept well ahead of inflation, the same cannot be said of wages in the rest of the economy. According to a survey carried out by the Centre des Revenus et des Coûts, purchasing power for a couple with one

salary and two children increased for all categories from 1981 to 1982
except for those where the wage earner was a middle manager ('cadre
moyen') or senior manager ('cadre supérieur'). By the following year it
declined for families where the bread winner was an office worker or a
skilled worker also. For the period 1983-84 all categories, including
unskilled workers and labourers (but not senior managers) experienced a
reduction in their purchasing power (53). It cannot, however, be argued
that the dissatisfaction of the confederations was linked exclusively to
insufficient wage levels. They disliked the way that after the initial
period public sector wage levels were once again imposed from the centre
rather than negotiated. Perhaps more intriguingly, Edmond Maire, leader
of the CFDT, spoke out against generalised wage increases whose effect
would be to increase unemployment.

After an initial period of economic expansion, the Socialist government switched to a policy which stressed the virtues of low inflation,
international competitiveness and economic modernisation. Trade union
confederations like the CFDT which stressed the importance of solving
the unemployment problem and those like the CGT and the CGT-FO which
stressed the importance of keeping wage increases ahead of inflation
were both ignored. Employees in general benefited from the Socialist
government's anti-inflation policy, but at the expense of jobs and
higher wages. In terms of economic policy formulation, the trade union
confederations were more or less excluded.

GOVERNMENT-UNION RELATIONS, 1981-86

From the evidence given above it is clear that the Socialist government
of the Mitterrand presidency did enact a large body of legislation that
was favourable to the interests of the labour confederations and for a
period at least, did facilitate the entry of some trade union officials
into the policy making communities. It is difficult to see, therefore,
how the charge that the governments were 'anti-union' can be made to
stick. Yet none of the confederations demonstrated in the 1986 elections any enthusiasm for mobilising their resources in support of the
out-going parliamentary majority. This is the more remarkable, given
that the programme of the right for those elections contained several
items that were quite hostile to the rights that trade unions now
possess. Not one of the trade union confederations in 1986 advised its
supporters to vote for the left (54); and while this omission can be
explained by reference once again to the 'apoliticism' of French trade
unionism, such an explanation is unconvincing given what we know about
the political linkages and attitudes that they have. This section will
attempt to consider the evolution of government-union relations during
the first five years of the Mitterrand presidency and the apparent
mutual indifference to each others' fate that was evident in 1986. But
we will also look at the implications of the fact that by 1986 the
resources of the confederations - both material and moral - were even
weaker than they had been in 1981. Not only had the advent to power of
the left failed to mobilise support around the trade unions, but the
subsequent five years saw a further reduction in their income and membership. The much trumpeted revival in the fortunes of the CGT-FO only
means a modest increase in the vote obtained by its candidates in the
so-called professional elections. Polls show that French people have in
general even less confidence in trade unions in 1985 than they did in
1982 and this applies as much to the 'reformist' confederations like the

CGT-FO as to the more ideologically radical ones like the CGT and the CFDT (55). Martin Schain has observed that younger workers are the least impressed with trade unionism and that they rate the CGT and CFDT lowest of all (56).

As regards the first set of issues - government-confederation relations - it is important to distinguish between what might be called policy making influence and political support. Initially, both in the union sphere and in the sphere of economic and industrial policy, the confederations were accorded access to their proposals and were taken seriously. This period coincided with the political honeymoon which Mitterrand saw himself as enjoying. More prosaically, this could be seen as a period when mandate politics prevailed in France. Like many such periods (though not all, as the case of Mrs Thatcher shows), it did not last long before being replaced by the more familiar experience of economic crisis (brought on by the currency crises, the yawning balance of payments gap and inflation). At this stage, economic decisions had to be taken quickly and there was no inclination, just because there was no immediate need, to take confederation views into account. For their part, the confederations would not want in any case to be identified with measures aimed at reducing demand, controlling wages etc. This would be bad for their self image. It is true that, as we have seen, the CFDT leader Edmond Maire did during the 1982 debate about the 39 hour week articulate sentiments about wages and hours that would seem to be heresy to a 'normal' trade unionist concerned with maximising the former and reducing the latter; but his position, though supported by Prime Minister Mauroy, was significantly overruled by Mitterrand himself. Subsequently, the relationship between government and confederations at policy making level was at worst non-existent and at best, to paraphrase Jack Hayward, a case of intermittent consultation rather than effective sharing of decisions (57).

Given that French labour confederations have always rejected the role that neocorporatist politics would assign them - a notional influence in policy formulation in return for the national policing of agreements - this distancing that took place after the initial stage of the Socialist government was probably not unwelcome, particularly since the benefits of closer cooperation were so nebulous. But there remains the issue of the 'non-bargained' support that existed between confederations and government. Here the politics of the left coalition and the profile of the Socialist Party itself are the principal factors. From 1981-84, the government was a coalition of the PS and the PCF - but a coalition in which the former exercised a clear predominance. At first the PCF could do little other than manifest loyalty to the new order which meant that the CGT leadership would too. Yet it was known that the most powerful influence within the CGT, Henri Krasucki, was a Communist hard liner, opposed to the political pact that had been made in 1981 with the victorious Socialists and that he had absolutely no desire to make the Socialist experiment succeed. His replacement of Seguy as CGT General Secretary in 1982 was a signal that the confederation was going to do nothing to help the new government, even though for the moment it could not break with it, still less break it. (Seguy's 'openness' in 1977 and 1978 after the breakdown of the Union of the Left made him the prime candidate for sacrifice as expiation of and explanation for the appalling Communist result in the 1981 election. Communist Party orthodoxy was that his willingness to allow a remarkably high level of discussion and even dissent at the 1978 CGT Congress explained why Marchais' 1981 message that there was no hope for workers outside the Communist Party was not sufficiently heard [58]). This charge was quite absurd in itself, the more so given that if there is such a thing as a 'CGT vote', it was more pro-Communist in 1981 than it had been in 1973 and 1978 (59). Once the Socialist-Communist Alliance started to disintegrate - which it did as soon as the popularity of the government began to decline - so the CGT became more willing to criticise particular measures (eg. the austerity programme of 1983). This willingness to criticise was tempered only by its need not to provoke the government into sacking its Communist ministers. The change of government of 1984 did, of course, lead to the end of the PCF-PS alliance. Hitherto the CGT had attempted to portray itself as a guarantor of social peace; now it rapidly reverted to its preferred image of intransigent guardian of the working class against the treacheries of social democracy. The self portrait was undoubtedly sincere - but it was wholly unreal. The re-structuring of French industry took place with little of the union resistance that accompanied similar exercises in the United Kingdom. A series of one-day protests and the 1985 'Tour de France de la Classe' produced little response. In the run-up to the 1986 election, the CGT campaigned against government proposals to make working hours more flexible and its press constantly denounced the failures of the out going (Socialist) administration.

There is no reason to be surprised by this absence of PS-CGT solidarity, given what we know about the CGT's relationship with the PCF. What is perhaps more worthy of comment is the coolness that existed in 1986 between the Socialists and the CGT-FO and also between the Socialists and the CFDT. The confederation leaderships had, of course, reasons to be dissatisfied with the government's record. Yet they knew that in 1986 they faced the prospect not simply of a return to right wing government but to a right which had embraced more free market, and hence anti-union, policies than had been the case in the 1970s when Gaullist and Giscardian ministers sought to incorporate trade unions into at least some aspects of decision taking. The answer to this indifference seems to reside in the growing distance that existed between the Social-ist Party and unionism particularly after the replacement in 1984 of the old-style 'labourist' Prime Minister Pierre Mauroy by the 'innovator' Laurent Fabius.

It is clear that a multitude of forces were weighing down on the Socialist administration but interestingly it was not specifically to-wards trade unions that the Socialist government looked for allies. The lack of institutional links between the Socialist Party, in or out of government, and the trade unions has hampered the mutual understanding of each other's objectives and preoccupations. The Socialist foothold in the CGT was enhanced slightly at the 40th Conference in 1978. It was very soon down graded again and now counts for naught given the overall presence of the PCF at every significant level of the confederation's organisational structure. More generally such links that have developed between the PS and the confederations have been fostered by individuals and factions within the Socialist Party and officials from the trade union confederations, in a semi-occult fashion. For example, Jacques Delors, Finance Minister from 1981 to 1984, has always been close to the CFDT but is not a Socialist leader. These unofficial links have been destined to produce rivalry as much as common identity. Mitterrand for example has still not forgotten that in his first presidential campaign (1965) the CFDT declined to express a preference between him and

Lecanuet, his centrist rival (60). His lack of empathy with the present CFDT leader Maire is well known and is made more total by the latter's political connections with Michel Rocard, the leader of the 'social democrat' wing of the PS and Mitterrand's most enthusiastic intra-party rival.

CONCLUSION

Party-confederation politics cause hostility and misunderstanding and have tended to reinforce potential fragmentation within the Socialist Party - clearly, from the party's point of view, a process to be discouraged. Within the CFDT there has been a similar potential for internal strife between Rocardians and supporters of CERES, the left wing and self-styled 'socialist conscience' of the PS. The potential for misunderstanding is further enhanced by the sociology of the Socialist Party. Although it is relatively well supported at election times by industrial workers - arguably the backbone of the trade union movement - the Socialist Party institutions are relatively resistant to them. Indeed its debating society atmosphere has discouraged trade unionists from remaining members. This exclusivity is at its most noticeable in the upper echelons of the party: only one per cent of post-1981 Socialist deputies are industrial workers and none of the June 1981 Council of Ministers, with the result that very few Socialist leaders have direct knowledge of the central features of trade union activity. Socialist Party leaders have also not been socialised into an unquantifiable feeling of what might be called 'labour sentimentalism', so prevalent a feeling on the other side of the Channel.

Once the initial policy of the Socialist government changed, therefore, the non-Communist confederations were not involved in the pre-decision consultations. When the ideology of market oriented growth was proclaimed in 1984, they had no part in it. And when the 'social democratisation' of French socialism was introduced in 1985 at the Toulouse congress they were absent from the celebrations. That absence, however, is a testimony to the continuing 'apartness' of the French political experience. In the countries of Europe where social democracy is the dominant style in labour politics, union-party connections have always been very close. In France, just at the moment when the Socialist left prepared to adopt social democracy, its links with organised trade unionism seemed weaker than ever.

NOTES

(1) Le Monde, 20.3.86
(2) F. Wilson 'Trade unions and economic policy' in H. Machin and V. Wright (eds.), Economic Policy in Mitterrand's France, London, Frances Pinter, 1984, pp. 257 and 261. See also Libération, 26.7.84.
(3) See a not disinterested source, Union des Industries Metallurgiques et Minières, L'Audience des Organisations Syndicales, 1985, p. 8.
(4) The best study of the relationship between the CGT and the Communist Party is provided by G. Ross, Workers and Communists, See also his chapter in M. Kesselman (ed.), The French Workers' Movement, London, Allen and Unwin, 1984.
(5) See Ross in Kesselman, op. cit., esp. pp. 62-67; F. Wilson,

op. cit.; P. Morris, 'The left and the trade unions in France' in Journal of Area Studies, no. 7, 1983.

(6) See Kesselman (ed.), op. cit., p. 67.
(7) Morris, art. cit., p. 17. The expression means that one partner in a couple claims that the relationship works even when there is ample evidence to the contrary.
(8) R. Mouriaux, La CGT, Paris, Seuil, 1982, p. 191.
(9) H. Hamon and R. Potman, La Deuxième Gauche, Paris, Ramsay, 1982, pp. 341-342.
(10) Libération, 4/5/84.
(11) D. Dagnaud and D. Mehl, L'Élite Rose, Paris, Ramsay, 1982.
(12) T. Pfister, La Vie Quotidienne à Matignon au Temps de l'Union de la Gauche, Paris, Hachette, 1985, p. 259.
(13) Institut Syndical Études Recherche Economiques Sociales, Rapport Annuel sur la Situation Économique et Sociale de la France (10 Mai 1981 - Décembre 1982), 1984, p. 76.
(14) R. Mouriaux, Les Syndicats dans la Société Française, Paris, Fondation Nationale des Sciences Politiques, 1983, p. 172.
(15) Pfister, op. cit., pp. 109-111.
(16) S. July, Les Années Mitterrand, Paris, Grasset, 1986, p. 87.
(17) Ibid., pp. 153-154.
(18) Interview CGT-FTM, 26/2/85.
(19) For the best overview of French labour law, see Y. Delamotte, Le Droit du Travail en Pratique, Paris, Éditions d'Organisation, 1983.
(20) Les Nouveaux Droits des Travailleurs, Paris, La Découverte-Maspero/ Le Monde, 1983.
(21) Ibid., pp. 135-142.
(22) Ibid., pp. 142-144.
(23) Ibid., pp. 144-146.
(24) B. Desjardins, 'Réflexions à partir d'une loi expérimentale' in Travail et Emploi, June 1985, pp. 25-30.
(25) Bilan Annuel de la Négociation Collective 1984, Ministère du Travail et de l'Emploi et de la Formation Professionnelle, June 1985.
(26) European Industrial Relations Review, July 1984, pp. 29-31.
(27) S. Volkoff, 'Expression des salariés bilan statistique de 3000 accords' in Travail et Emploi, March 1985, pp. 79-86.
(28) D. Linhart, 'Le droit d'expression des salariés' in Revue Française des Affaires Sociales, 2/1985, pp. 87-103.
(29) Bilan Annuel de la Négociation Collective 1984, op. cit.
(30) Le Monde, 4/6/81.
(31) Les Notes Bleues, Ministère de l'Économie, des Finances et du Budget, 15-21/7/85.
(32) J-P. Jallade, 'Redistribution and the welfare state: an assessment of the French Socialists' performance' in Government and Opposition, Summer 1985, pp. 343-355.
(33) Libération, 2/2/82.
(34) Le Monde, 6/2/82, 12/2/82. 13/2/82.
(35) Pfister, op. cit., pp. 128-130.
(36) ADA, Bilan de la France, Paris, Table Ronde, 1986, p. 284.
(37) Travail Informations, Ministère des Affaires Sociales et de la Solidarité Nationale, Jan/Feb/March 1984.
(38) For details concerning the shipbuilding industry, see J. Stirling and J. Bridgford, 'The industrial relations of decline: British and French merchant shipbuilding' in Industrial Relations Journal, Winter 1985, pp. 7-16.
(39) Le Monde, 18/12/84.

(40) Le Monde, 22/12/84, 23-24/12/84.
(41) Bulletin Mensuel des Statistiques du Travail, February 1986, p. 9.
(42) Le Matin, 14-15/6/82.
(43) For the CGT statement, see G. Alézard, Le Peuple, no. 1138. For the CFDT statement, see CFDT Syndicalisme, 8/7/82.
(44) Le Matin, 26/3/85.
(45) For the CGT, see L. Viannet, Le Monde, 6/4/83. For the CFDT, see E. Maire, Le Monde, 29/3/84. For the CGT-FO, see A. Bergeron, Le Monde, 29/3/84.
(46) Le Monde, 9/4/83.
(47) Libération, 3-4/3/84.
(48) Libération, 30/3/84.
(49) Le Point, 17/2/86.
(50) Les Notes Bleues, 7-13/4/86.
(51) European Industrial Relations Review, October 1984, pp. 12-13.
(52) M. Elbaum, 'Politiques de l'emploi en 1984' in Dossiers Statistiques du Travail de de l'Emploi, September 1985, pp. 24-29.
(53) Libération, 29-30/4/85.
(54) Le Monde, 14/3/86.
(55) Le Nouvel Observateur, 20-26/12/85.
(56) Kesselman, op. cit., p. 273.
(57) J. Hayward, The State and the Market Economy, Brighton, Harvester, 1986, p. 66.
(58) Ross in Kesselman, op. cit., p. 67 and note p. 73f.
(59) Morris, art. cit., p. 17.
(60) Kesselman, op. cit., p. 77.

4 Trade unions and industrial relations in Spain: the response to the economic crisis

RICHARD HAWKESWORTH AND LLUIS FINA

From the early 1970s onwards, most of the Western world has been faced by the so-called 'economic crisis'. The causes of it are varied as have been the economic policies to mitigate it. Measuring the crisis in terms of indicators such as unemployment, inflation and the balance of payments, Spain has been no exception to the experience of crisis. Indeed, as will be seen below, Spain's economic problems can be said to have been worse than many other Western European countries. Furthermore, they have occurred within the context of radical and major political and social change. This situation sets Spain apart from other West European countries in the analysis of the response to the economic crisis. Since the trade unions and the other actors on the stage of industrial relations - the employers and government - have been an intrinsic part of this political and social change, their response to the crisis cannot be fully assessed without taking full account of such change.

THE HISTORICAL LEGACY IN INDUSTRIAL RELATIONS

The turning point in industrial relations came in 1975 with the death of General Franco. This effectively ended forty years of a political, social and economic order in which an authoritarian, fascist dictatorship held control via a variety of state intervention measures. Under Franco, freedom of political parties was removed and the economy was strictly controlled, at least until the early 1960s, by the state both internally and with respect to external interdependence, the basic ideology being nationalism, Catholic corporatism and economic autarky (1). Although some modification did occur in the years after about 1960, high tariffs and also the imposition of quotas shielded firms from external competition in order to foster industrialisation and growth via import substitution. In industry, importance was attached to the state holding company, INI. However, the system penalised exports - the very sector which was able to finance this type of industrialisation - and the cost of autarky was high, in the form of, inter alia, low effi- ciency, inflation and severe problems of external deficit and foreign currency shortages. Only after 1960 did the orientation of this policy shift, to greater liberalisation and export substitution.

In the area of labour and labour relations, Franco's brand of corpor- atism meant that all free trade unions were banned and free collective bargaining was not permitted (2). Strikes or any individual or collec- tive action which in any way disrupted the norm of production were seen as seditious acts and a crime against the state. In an attempt to achieve unity and reduce the class struggle all participants in produc- tion were considered part of the national-syndicalist community which, in turn, meant that all employees and employers, according to branch of activity or service, had to become members of 'vertical' trade unions ('sindicatos'), that is, single corporative organisations of workers and employers under the direction of the state. Of the outlawed trade unions, the UGT (the General Union of Workers) re-organised its leader- ship abroad and attempted to influence events from outside. In the Basque region the ELA-STV (a regional trade union) succeeded in retain- ing some contact with its rank and file. The CNT (National Confeder- ation of Labour) attempted to re-establish itself in Spain but was generally unsuccessful.

After 1958 some change was permitted within industrial relations. The Law of Collective Agreements added to the existing system a new and more flexible mechanism for the fixing of wages. However, it was basically controlled liberalisation, seeking to contain changes which were already in evidence, particularly the tendency amongst the larger firms for earnings drift above the rates laid down by the Ministry of Labour. Such a tendency was the result of increasing economic liberalisation, notably the opening-up of the economy, greater foreign investment and the em- ployers' attempts to increase productivity.

One of the main and unintended consequences of the introduction of this controlled form of collective bargaining was in the area of worker organisation. The new negotiating role given to the unions and, at the level of the plant, to the works councils ('jurados de empresas') which had been introduced in 1953 - as an instrument of participation and consultation within the vertical framework - created a dual level of bargaining. Also it increased the development of worker organisation in the plants, noticeably as elections for the workers' representatives in the works councils were progressively democratised during the early 1960s and because, after 1964, some separation was established in the vertical unions between workers and employers. The net result was what is known as 'entryism' ('entrismo'), that is groups of workers - known subsequently as Workers' Commissions (Comisiones Obreras [CC.00]) - who presented grievances or claims to management and who increasingly put forward candidates at official works councils elections. Such groups became increasingly politicised and were promoted by the (illegal) Communist Party (PCE). The UGT, which was in effect the labour arm of the Socialist Party (PSOE), rejected entryism and refused to participate within the vertical system.

At first the authorities tolerated this new movement of workers and it was even thought that the CC.00 could assist the Franco regime by giving some credibility to the vertical system. However, the CC.00 was too successful and after the 1966 elections the unions were purged of CC.00 candidates. This, coupled with recession and rising inflation in the late 1960s and early 1970s led to attempts by the regime to control the situation by reimposing state regulation of wages under the guise of 'incomes policies'.

The implications of the above for industrial relations were that, despite the fact that on paper the vertical structure appeared much the same in 1975, when Franco died, as it had fifteen years earlier, the position and strength of the workers had changed significantly even in the face of repeated suppression by the government. Entryism had indelibly left its mark on the labour scene. Workers had increasingly gained more strength, divesting power from the higher levels of the unions to the level of the shop floor, even though the unions still exercised control over the collective bargaining framework. When Franco died and the early attempts by the government of Arias Navarro to establish 'Francoism without Franco' failed, it was the existence of a workers' power base at plant level which enabled the labour movement to mobilise its strength on a broad front to promote political change and also changes within industrial relations, notably the freedom of association, the right to strike and free collective bargaining.

THE ECONOMIC CRISIS IN SPAIN

In the 1960s, Spain's economy had experienced a high rate of growth (one of the highest in Western Europe) resulting from foreign investment, tourism and the increasing shift towards exporting (by the late 1960s nearly half of Spain's exports were going to the EEC). However, in 1973 the oil crisis hit Spain very hard - more so than many other Western countries - both on account of its high dependence on imported energy, particularly oil, and as a result of the lower growth in those very economies which had assisted Spain's 'economic miracle' in the 1960s (via tourism, remittances from migrant workers, foreign investment and the purchasing of Spain's export goods). The net result was a significant reduction in the growth potential of the economy, thereby affecting real GNP and unemployment and also introducing severe inflationary pressures from 1974 onwards. (See Table 4.1) Even prior to the oil shock, inflation had become an issue as workers, seeking to exceed the Francoist pay norms (for political as well as economic reasons) fuelled inflation. With the massive rise in oil prices starting in 1973/74 (and again in 1979) inflation became the leading economic issue for the rest of the decade and into the 1980s. There was also increasing concern about unemployment which rose significantly after 1979 to become the highest (as a percentage of the labour force) in the OECD (3). (See Table 4.2)

In terms of the structure of unemployment, Table 4.2 shows that from 1977 to 1985 (years for which comparable data is available) unemployment has been a significantly greater occurrence amongst the young (16-24) particularly in 1985 and especially for teenagers who are now more likely to be unemployed than employed. Taking the whole 16-24 age group, unemployment rates reached 48.7 per cent in 1985 which contrasted with 14.6 per cent for the post-24 groups as a whole. More than in any other OECD country, the problem of unemployment is concentrated amongst teenagers and young people.

Table 4.1

Rates of increase in GNP, inflation, productivity
and unemployment in Spain, 1970-85 (%)

	GNP (in real terms)	GNP deflator	Real GDP per employee	Unemployment rate (%)
1970	4.1	-	4.1	1.2
1971	4.9	7.1	4.7	1.7
1972	8.1	8.2	6.7	2.2
1973	7.8	11.4	6.2	2.8
1974	5.7	16.6	4.6	3.0
1975	1.1	16.7	3.0	3.8
1976	3.0	16.7	5.2	4.8
1977	3.3	22.8	3.1	5.3
1978	1.8	20.2	4.3	7.1
1979	0.2	16.7	2.4	8.7
1980	1.5	13.9	4.8	11.5
1981	0.4	13.6	2.8	14.4
1982	0.9	13.7	2.5	16.3
1933	2.5	11.9	3.1	17.8
1984	2.0	11.3	3.2	20.6
1985	2.1	8.8	3.2	21.9

Sources: (1) GDP at market prices: Instituto Nacional de Estadística, Contabilidad Nacional de España (Base 1970).
(2) Unemployment rate: 1970-76: Grupo de trabajo de Empleo (1979), p. 40. 1977-85: Instituto Nacional de Estadística, Encuesta de Población Activa.

-oOo-

Table 4.2
Unemployment rates (%) by age and sex

	Male		Female		Total	
Age groups	1977	1985	1977	1985	1977	1985
16 - 19	14.5	54.3	16.3	52.2	15.3	56.3
16 - 24	10.5	42.2	9.8	47.8	10.2	44.6
25 - 54	3.8	15.6	2.5	16.2	3.5	15.8
55 and over	3.0	11.4	0.6	4.8	2.4	9.8
Total	5.1	20.4	5.6	25.5	5.3	21.9

Source: Ministerio de Trabajo y Seguridad Social, Boletín de Estadísticas Laborales.

The only counterbalancing features have been the stability in the participation rates of young female adults (20-24)) - though these are low by European standards - and an increase (29 to 35 per cent) in the rates for females of 25-54 years, due in the main to changing social factors and job patterns. (See Table 4.3) Also the rate for young male adults (20-24 years) has increased slightly despite a four fold increase in unemployment. The main problems have occurred in the two extreme age groups, both for males and females, where there has been a consequential rise in post-compulsory education and in the number of pensioners.

Table 4.3
Participation rates (%) by age and sex

Age groups	Male		Female		Total	
	1977	1985	1977	1985	1977	1985
16 - 19	60.0	42.5	46.8	32.2	53.5	37.5
20 - 24	62.1	66.8	54.4	54.8	58.5	61.1
25 - 54	95.8	94.1	29.0	35.0	61.8	64.2
55 and over	47.9	37.1	13.1	9.8	28.1	21.8
Total	75.2	68.7	27.5	27.8	50.3	47.5

Source: Ministerio de Trabajo y Seguridad Social, Boletín de Estadísticas Laborales.

Apart from its direct effect on inflation, the wage explosion of the early 1970s appears to have had a real and negative effect on employment though other factors are also implicated in this decline, as will be indicated below. After reaching a peak in 1974, employment thereafter declined in a continuous and dramatic fashion until 1985. In the context of, for example, the EEC such a trend in employment has been unusual. Taking the period 1977-1985 (for which comparable data is available) this fall in employment in Spain accounted for 84.6 per cent of the rise in its unemployment which itself rose by 2,227,000 over the same period, accounting for 21.9 per cent of the labour force in 1985. (See Table 4.1) In contrast with the experience of other countries within the OECD, the labour force barely rose during this period (an increase of only 343,000, from 12,922,200 to 13,265,800) mainly as a result of 'discouragement', that is, the detrimental impact of economic recession on the supply of labour services (implying a negative relationship between participation and economic activity).

As indicated above, inflationary pressures arising from increased energy costs and the wage explosion - notably before the pay policies negotiated after 1979 (discussed in a later section) - both contributed to the fall in employment and the rise in unemployment though, in a closed and highly protected economic system (hallmarks of the Franco period) most firms were able to pass on wage increases into higher prices with the help of a loose and accommodating monetary policy. However, two other factors also contributed to the reduction in employment. These were, first, the fiscal system and, second, certain changes in the labour and industrial situation.

The introduction of a more modern and efficient fiscal system and its extension to medium and small-sized firms (as well as large) reduced the fiscal isolation of these firms and brought them into the arena of real market forces. Also, the re-establishment of freedom of association for workers and the legitimisation of trade unions and their activities have posed, for some firms, too large a threat to their continued survival after many decades during which they have been accustomed to the old paternalistic and authoritarian mode of conducting industrial relations using the repressive powers of the state as a recourse, when the employers deemed it necessary. Lastly, the opening-up of the economy, particularly with membership of the EEC in prospect, forced the rationalisation of many firms. This process is still continuing. The net result of all the above factors has been a good record on productivity (see Table 4.1) especially when compared with other OECD countries (4) despite the fact that output growth after the boom of the 1960s was generally slower.

The main questions which arise from the above analysis of the extent and nature of economic problems in Spain are: first, how have such problems been tackled and, second, how and to what extent have the trade unions been involved in the policy processes which have sought to mitigate the economic problems? In answering these questions the main complicating factor, as indicated in the introduction, is that the economic crisis in Spain has occurred at a time of radical political and social change. Given that the trade unions played a key logistical role in bringing about such change, it is important to the analysis to assess the major institutional and policy developments in the area of labour and industrial relations and their interplay with economic problems.

THE TRANSITION TO DEMOCRACY, 1975-77

When Franco died in 1975 the exiled and clandestine political parties made moves to re-establish themselves within Spain. Their overriding aim was to return parliamentary democracy and freedom of association to the country. In the event, this took just over eighteen months to achieve, the first free elections since 1936 being held in June 1977. The role played by the mass mobilisation of labour was crucial to this development, especially in the early stages, for it overwhelmed and thwarted the attempt by the government of Arias Navarro to perpetuate 'Francoism without Franco'. Labour unrest soared in 1976, the explosive outcome of years of suppression by the state and reflecting the mixing of political and economic demands. In addition the unions frequently competed over strike calls and often had little control over local activity.

The reaction of the government to the labour unrest was to seek stability by issuing a decree (in December 1975) which enforced, for 1976, the pay norm of the previous April's incomes policy (maximum rise equivalent to the inflation rate during the previous twelve months). In reality, however, the government's situation was extremely tenuous as it was faced with overwhelming labour and political unrest and opposition. The appointment, by Franco's planned successor King Juan Carlos, of Suarez as Prime Minister was a significant move; contrary to expectations he effected a move towards the evolution of democracy by seeking a dialogue with all the involved parties for a 'negotiated break' with Francoism. On the political front the freedom to form political parties was established and this was complemented in industrial relations when the trade unions were made legal just two months later, in April 1977.

However, despite the legality of trade unions it was not clear in mid-1977 how industrial relations would develop. Basically, the old Franco-ist system was still very much intact and the workers' representatives in the plants were those who had been elected in 1975, prior to Franco's death. Also, whilst there was a degree of experience of a form of collective bargaining in some of the larger plants and in some industries, for the main part both sides of industry were, after nearly forty years of state control, essentially unfamiliar with and inexperienced in negotiations on wages, employment and other workplace issues. This situation was compounded, as a result of the emergence of new trade unions, by their mutual unfamiliarity and also a suspicion over the aims and ambitions of their respective rival union organisations, particularly between the two largest unions, the UGT and the CC.OO. Compared with the CC.OO, the UGT was not initially in a strong position having rejected entryism in the 1960s. However, until the Socialist Party (PSOE) emerged as a serious political contender, the moderate UCD government viewed the strengthening of the UGT favourably - to counter the Communist-influenced CC.OO - and it even allowed the UGT to hold a conference in April 1976 when it was still illegal (three months later the CC.OO had to hold its own congress in secret).

On collective bargaining and strikes the government had made some moves though they represented a compromise at a time when democracy was still in its infancy and economic problems were pressing. Decrees in March and December provided a temporary legal framework for strikes and workers' representation. In plants of less than 250 workers (this was later reduced to 50) there were to be open lists of workers in the elections to the works councils. This was the preferred position of the CC.OO which favoured a (single) workers' movement (as in Portugal) and not separate union lists which was the stance preferred by the UGT and which were to be allowed in the larger plants. In the event and not surprisingly in view of the CC.OO's entryist policy within the plants, the first post-Franco elections to the works councils were easily won by the CC.OO. (See Table 4.4)

Table 4.4
Results of works council elections 1978-1982 (%)

	1978	1980	1982
CC.OO	34.45	30.86	33.40
UGT	21.70	29.27	36.71
USO	3.87	8.68	4.64
ELA/STV	1.00	2.44	3.30
INTG*	0.32	1.01	1.17
Other and non-affiliated	38.66	27.74	20.78

*INTG = Intersindical de Trabajadores Gallegos

Source: Ministerio de Trabajo

At the end of 1977 there were three major issues to be resolved. First, there was the question of establishing a permanent legal framework for industrial relations which would effectively replace the existing legislation, the major bulk of which had been inherited from the Franco regime. Second, there was the need to develop and establish a political constitution; and third, there was the major issue - largely

neglected until now because of the political transition - of the economic crisis, especially of inflation. As will be seen in the next section, the analysis of the trade unions' response to such economic problems must necessarily take cognizance of the political and social changes which impinged on the situation throughout the period. This is a
major distinguishing characteristic of this case study of Spain in the
1970s and 1980s.

THE RESPONSE TO ECONOMIC PROBLEMS: THE MONCLOA PACT, 1977

One of the most significant instruments implemented in response to the
economic crisis has been the series of pacts (accords) which have been
agreed between various of the social partners though there have been
interruptions to the succession of pacts and the participation of the
CC.OO has been erratic. The focus of their content has been wide-
ranging, incorporating economic, social and labour issues as well as the
common theme of a centrally determined pay norm for the year ahead.
Such width in the pacts has been a way of attempting to resolve problems
of inflation and of directly tackling unemployment, productivity and the
development of the industrial relations framework which was largely left
to evolve via a concertation process between the main social partners.
To some extent the inclusion of non-wage issues has facilitated the wage
element within the pacts themselves though actual progress on some of
the many non-wage issues has often been slow.

The Moncloa Pact (October 1977) was negotiated between the centrist
government (UCD) and the political parties, but it did not include
either the trade unions or the employers' confederation CEOE (formed in
September 1977). The content of the Moncloa Pact was very wide and
covered economic, social and political issues and problems. The impact
of some of its content has continued to be felt throughout the 1930s.
However, the CEOE was not favourably disposed to it because of its
inclusion of new corporate and wealth taxes, a tougher monetary policy
and the dismantling of some financial privileges. On the trade union
side, the socialist UGT was uncertain about its own position and about
the future of industrial relations and therefore did not sign. The
CC.OO was more favourably disposed but did not wish to compromise its
position in view of the pending elections to the works councils. The
government, however, pressed for an accord with the political parties to
provide a more immediate avenue for tackling the economic crisis. The
trade unions at this time were relatively weak in terms of membership
and even though their influence was greater than density figures suggest
(particularly later as collective bargaining developed and coverage by
agreements increased to a high level) there was no guarantee that the
unions could 'deliver the goods' with respect to the principles and
policies negotiated in the pact. The main economic problem was inflation which was running at nearly 30 per cent (August 1976 to August
1977) and there was a large deficit on the current account. Thus a pay
norm of 20-22 per cent for 1978 was agreed, based on expected rather
than past inflation as had been the case with Franco's pay policies and
in 1976. Also, the norm was backed by a tighter monetary policy with
money supply growth restricted to 17 per cent for 1978.

The pact was significant in reducing inflation, in fact more than
planned so that real wages actually rose. The current account also moved
into the black in 1978. However, there was a high cost for such

success, notably in terms of unemployment. The 1978 rate of increase in unemployment - which was much higher than expected - was the highest for the period from 1977 to 1985. Also, conflict remained at a high level (see Table 4.5) which surprised many commentators at the time who thought that the CC.OO would not only put the norm into practice (the PCE having signed Moncloa) but would be able to influence adherence to it. Retrospective analysis suggests that autonomous factors were active, such as the trade unions manoeuvring for position and also exercising a degree of strength, both of these being reactions to years of repression by Franco within the firms. At the time there was little progress on most of the non-wage aspects of Moncloa but some - such as fiscal and monetary reform and the increase in the state-financing of the social security system - have since been implemented. Overall, the Moncloa Pact had the virtue of distilling the main issues and focusing attention on them, particularly in view of the severity of the economic situation.

Table 4.5
Labour disputes in Spain
1975-85*

	Number of disputes	Workers involved (000's)	Working days lost (000's)
1975	3,155	647.1	1,815.2
1976	3,662	2,555.9	12,592.7
1977	1,194	2,955.0	16,641.7
1978	1,128	3,836.9	11,550.9
1979	2,166	4,706.9	16,311.3
1980	1,365	1,170.1	6,177.5
1981	1,307	1,126.3	5,153.8
1982	1,225	875.1	2,787.6
1983	1,451	1,483.6	4,416.7
1984	1,498	2,242.2	6,357.8
1985	1,092	1,511.2	3,223.8

* Since 1979, not including Cataluña

Source: Ministerio de Trabajo y Seguridad Social

1979: APPROACHES TO POLICY

In 1979 the government sought to build on the wage pact principle established with Moncloa though this time it opened up discussions with the trade unions in an attempt to provide a firmer foundation for and acceptance of any pay norm that could be agreed, thereby hopefully reducing conflict and improving the macroeconomic stability it was seeking. However, it was aware that such agreement with the unions and the employers might be difficult in view of certain fundamental problems.

The first problem concerned the CC.OO which, backed by the PCE, had emerged as the strongest union in the 1978 elections to the works councils and, to some extent, was seen as the real voice of the labour movement at this time. The CC.OO made it clear to the UCD government that all major policy issues had to be open for negotiation which, in turn, should be between all the parties. This meant agreement on political as well as economic, social and labour issues between the unions, employers, government and the political parties. Furthermore, the CC.OO wanted a three-year pact, enabling it to reinforce its then relatively advantageous position within the labour market. The CC.OO's views on the government's proposals for discussions on a pact coincided with those of the PCE both in terms of the desire for a wide-ranging accord and of its duration, the latter point potentially assisting the PCE politically in the light of the possibility of a forthcoming parliamentary election.

In contrast to the CC.OO, the UGT wanted a much narrower focus in any agreement with the UCD government. Basically, it desired to confine the issues to pay and to labour and economic questions and, furthermore, to develop this within a tripartite framework, that is, without the political parties per se. The PSOE was also of the same view, having been opposed to the Moncloa Pact (even though it signed, for reasons of establishing some stability at a delicate time, politically and economically). Thus the gap between the UCD government and the UGT - in terms of an accord - was not a wide one in principle. What was wrong was the timing. With the Constitution approved by Congress in October 1978, it was likely that Suarez, then (1979) in mid-term of office (1977-81) might call an election - which he in fact did, for March 1979. The PSOE did not wish to see the UCD's hand strengthened by an agreement with the socialist UGT which would, in effect, last throughout 1979.

In the event, a tripartite agreement was not reached and the government unilaterally declared, in December 1978, a pay norm of 13 per cent (11-14 per cent band with provision for renegotiation if inflation was higher than expected). Immediately the UGT and the CC.OO opposed the declaration, displaying a degree of common understanding over an issue which would have had implications for pay bargaining throughout 1979. The outcome of the government's measures was not entirely successful. Whilst wage rates were close to the norm, earnings drift was much higher than with Moncloa and industrial conflict reached a record level (for the post-1977 period), affecting many firms. Also, unemployment rose from 7.1 per cent to 8.7 per cent of the labour force though the rate of increase did decline compared with 1978.

THE POLICY FOR 1980: THE ACUERDO MARCO INTERCONFEDERAL (AMI)

The approach to a pay policy for 1980 was influenced by four main factors. First, a shift in policy by the government; second, the high levels of conflict seen in 1979; third, a change in strategy by the UGT and fourth, the moves towards a more permanent institutional framework for industrial relations. Since the policies would be the outcome of a concertation process, the government felt that it would increase the chances of success in terms of their actual implementation and adherence to them, and also reduce industrial conflict. For the UGT, it was precisely on the labour and economic issues that it altered its position, developing separate initiatives to its rival union, the CC.OO. The Constitution (1978) had included a section - as a result of pressure from the PCE and CC.OO - that "the law shall establish a workers' statute" which was to be built on the basic principles of the Constitution - freedom of association, collective autonomy and the right to strike. After the 1979 parliamentary elections, the UCD government had offered the unions and the employers, in accordance with its new strategy, the opportunity to negotiate, between themselves, the basic principles for a workers' statute. The UGT used this offer to improve its standing and its appeal to the vast majority of the workers in the labour market who were not members of a union. (Trade union density figures are not accurately known but have been, and are, around 20 per cent - membership amongst women being particularly low. The reasons for low density include the absence of a well developed check-off system, the tendency for collective agreements to be extended to nearly all workers in a bargaining area - this 'free-rider' issue is currently being discussed, with proposals to introduce a levy on workers covered by the collective agreement - and to a certain extent the politicisation of trade unions.) The UGT was aware of its weak position compared with the CC.OO at this time, as shown in the 1978 works council elections and as reflected by its influence at plant level. Thus it now decided on a policy of co-operation. In July 1979 it signed the Acuerdo Basico Interconfederal (ABI) with the CEOE (which also made concessions to reach an agreement) to discuss the future basis for the industrial relations framework. The CC.OO refused to sign unless the government was also a signatory, acting as guarantor for the implementation of the agreed principles, discussions on which showed a wide gulf between the UGT and the CC.OO over the role of unions (the UGT's position) in the plants and in the works council elections.

On pay the UGT also cooperated with the CEOE and for similar reasons as above. For its part, the CEOE felt a pact could contribute to reducing inflation further and also reduce conflict which had risen steeply in 1979. The outcome of discussions was a bipartite pact, the Acuerdo Marco Interconfederal (AMI), a two-year accord which, for 1980, had a pay norm of 13-16 per cent based on an expected inflation rate of 14 per cent and, for 1981, had a (revised) norm of 11-15 per cent based on an expected rate of 13 per cent. The AMI also incorporated a number of economic and labour issues. One of these was the criterion - later adopted in the Workers' Statute (1980) - that the representative character of trade unions would be determined by the election of staff representatives and members of the works councils (see footnote 5).

The CC.OO did not sign the AMI. It was still pressing the principle that any pact should include agreements on a wide range of issues including political ones (it held this position until early 1981). Second, it opposed the UGT's policy of promoting union sections within the plant (the union sections principle was, however, incorporated into the Workers' Statute, as the UGT had pressed for and for which it had developed a separate position from that of the CC.OO with regard to co-operation with the CEOE). Third, the CC.OO wanted pay norms to be based on past inflation and not expected because it felt the latter would lead to a fall in real incomes. Finally, the CC.OO objected to the measures on productivity and absenteeism.

The decision by the UGT to cooperate paid off in the 1979/80 works council elections as, in terms of seats gained, it caught up with the CC.OO. Interestingly the 1980 AMI pay norm was very close to that originally asked for by the CC.OO and this tended to further marginalise the CC.OO. The norm, in both years, was fairly closely adhered to (Table 4.6) despite the opposition of the CC.OO (and even in plants where CC.OO was dominant) and inflation in 1980 fell quite significantly. Conflict declined from the high levels of 1979 further evidence

Table 4.6

Social pacts in Spain, 1980-85

Pay and outcomes

Date	Title	Main signatories	Expected inflation %	Pay norm %	Outcomes increases (%) in			
					Cost of living	Wage rates	Earnings per worker	Hourly earnings
Jan 1980	Acuerdo Marco (AMI)	CEOE, UGT	14	13-16	15.6	15.3	16.1	13.5
Feb 1981	AMI (Revision)	CEOE, UGT	13	11-15	14.6	13.1	15.4	19.1
Jun 1981 (for 1982)	Acuerdo Nacional de Empleo (ANE)	CEOE, UGT, CC.OO, government	12	9-11 (private) 8-9 (public)	14.4	12.0	14.0	15.4
Feb 1983	Acuerdo Inter- confederal (AI)	CEOE, UGT, CC.OO	12	9.5 - 12.5	12.2	11.4	13.7	15.3
1984	no pact	-	8	-	11.3	7.7	10.0	12.4
Oct 1984 (for 1985 and 1986)	Acuerdo Económico y Social (AES)	Part 1: CEOE, UGT and government Part 2: CEOE and UGT	7 (1985) 8 (1986)	5.5 - 7.5 7.2 - 8.6	8.8	7.4	8.7	9.3

Sources: Various

that the CC.OO was perhaps not as powerful as previously in manipulating workers in the plants. For the UGT the AMI reflected an awareness of inflation as a major problem and that cooperation with the CEOE could assist its own position. Furthermore, the AMI started discussion on other areas such as productivity and absenteeism, areas which would be important policy issues in the future.

THE ACUERDO NACIONAL DE EMPLEO (ANE), 1982

As a result of the UGT's (successful) strategy described above, the CC.OO changed its tactics when discussions on a pact for 1982 were opened, in early 1981. Whilst it still preferred a pact involving all major issues, it was now prepared to compromise, even to accept the principle of pay norms based on expected inflation. The move towards an agreement was reinforced by the attempted military coup (February 1981). In June 1981 the first tripartite pact involving the unions was signed. This was the Acuerdo Nacional de Empleo (ANE), covering a pay norm of 9 to 11 per cent (which was based on an expected inflation rate of 12 per cent, implying a fall in real wages; this fall did in fact occur, for the first time in the period since 1970 and also including a variety of important non-wage issues. (See Table 4.7)

The CC.OO had pushed for a solidarity pact on employment, partly to improve its own standing and also because of the high and increasing rate of unemployment. Thus an ambitious programme to create 350,000 jobs by the end of 1982 was included. Arising from the Workers' Statute there was also to be reinforcement of the unions' involvement in these state institutions pertaining to labour matters (6). The ANE's comprehensive incorporation of wider non-pay issues was also reflected in its agreements on the coverage of unemployment benefit, on the negotiation of check-off facilities for union dues and on state aid for the unions #13 millions to be paid over 3 years as compensation for the confiscation of union assets by Franco). On the employment creation side, the focus was on reducing overtime as standard practice, early retirement at 64 (instead of 65 which was the age for both men and women) with the jobs it was claimed would be created being filled by unemployed youths (important in the light of high unemployment amongst young people), the end of moonlighting (especially in public administration), re-training schemes and a reduction in firms' social security payments.

The pay norm of the ANE was closely followed during 1982 even though it was realised that such adherence would lower real wages and conflict fell dramatically in terms of working days lost. Also, for the unemployed, the trend towards lower coverage of benefits - produced by reforms in 1980 - was reversed. However, the unemployment rate itself continued to rise and placements (as shown by employment contracts) fell from a high of 1.96 million in 1981 to 1.6 million in 1982 (7).

The ANE covered 1982, the year the new socialist government of Gonzalez was elected (October) with a substantial majority. The economic situation it inherited was a serious one in may respects. The second oil shock of 1979 had produced external current account deficits that reached -2.4 per cent of GDP in 1981-82 compared with an average of -0.6 per cent for the OECD (8). Unemployment, after showing some deceleration in 1979, began to rise again reaching, in 1982, another peak (with a 32 per cent rate of increase in the number of unemployed), the

Table 4.7
Social pacts in Spain, 1980-86
Main non-pay issues

Accord   Issues

AMI   Guidelines for reducing annual hours worked and absenteeism.
1980-81   Recognition of union sections in plants.
          Focus on bargaining at factory level.
          Inclusion of productivity clauses.

ANE   Job creation (350,000 new jobs by end of 1982).
1982   Check-off system to be negotiable in firms with over 250
          employees.
          Government aid to unions (£13 million to be paid over three
          years for compensation of assets confiscated under the Franco
          regime).
          Institutional reinforcement of unions in the labour market.
          Moves towards ending moonlighting ('pluriempleo').
          Reduction in overtime (to create jobs).
          Recommendations for early retirement at 64 (men and women
          - the current retirement age is 65 for both) to create
          jobs for young people.
          Retraining schemes, negotiation of absenteeism and reduction
          in firms' social security payments.

AI   Reiteration of reduction of overtime, moonlighting and
1983   retirement age.
          Standard hours to be reduced from 42/43 hours per week to 40,
          plus holidays to rise from 23 to 30 days per year.
          Tripartite body to alter structure of collective bargaining
          (to sector level).

AES   Employment: government funds of £240 million for new
1985-86   investment.
          Also solidarity fund of £240 million financed equally by
          government and a levy on employees.
          Employment legislation to increase flexibility in the labour
          market.
          Compensation for the unions' confiscated assets.
          Extended coverage of unemployment benefit to at least 43 per
          cent of the unemployed by the end of 1985 and 48 per cent by
          the end of 1986.
          Reiteration of overtime (as in ANE and AI) by negotiation.
          Negotiation of changes to structure of collective bargaining
          (as in AI).

previous peak being in 1978 which had been a consequence of the Moncloa
Pact's tight monetary policy.   Also, the public sector deficit had been
rising rapidly (-2.0 per cent of GDP in 1980, -3.3 per cent of GDP in
1981 and -5.9 per cent of GDP in 1982).   This was due to the growth in
public sector employment (policies to improve the provision of public
services such as health and education, and the rise in public administration [autonomous government, etc.]), the incorporation of loss-making
firms into the public sector (to preserve jobs), and most importantly
the increase in expenditure on the social security system, particularly

on pensions (rise in both coverage and average payment) at a time when the system was constrained by unemployment and also reductions - under the pacts - in employers' social security contributions. In terms of inflation, despite the adherence to the pay norms other cost factors (notably oil) tended to militate against an improvement. Table 4.1 shows a fairly constant GNP deflator from 1980 to 1982.

The above factors shaped the government's economic policy response, as did the recognition of the failure of the expansionist, neo-keynesian policies in France, from 1981 to 1982, by the new, socialist government under Mitterrand. The macroeconomic policies finally adopted were generally tight, similar in philosophy to those of Mitterrand's 'politique de rigueur', that is, reducing the PSBR, containing public sector wage increases and devaluing the currency (to attack the external deficit). Unemployment was to be tackled directly by attempting to create conditions favourable to employment promotion, particularly measures to give labour contracts greater flexibility to reflect, much more, the market conditions in industrial sectors. Such a view was then gaining more prominence amongst the OECD countries.

In industrial policy the main focus was on restoring profitability to the sectors in crisis, particularly via the reduction in over-manning which, as described earlier, has been a consequence of job security within the Francoist system. The restructuring policy really got under way with the Decree of November 1983 and led to opposition from the CC.OO because the policy aimed to increase productivity and profitability by reducing employment in the crisis industries (reductions of 5.6 per cent in footwear, 14.2 per cent in electronics components, 18.7 per cent for textiles, 27 per cent for naval shipyards and 29 per cent for iron and steel). Firms were not obliged to participate in the plans but the tax advantages and financial subsidies and credits which accrued to them if restructuring did take place made it attractive to do so. Furthermore, with entry to the EEC then an increasing likelihood, firms' competitiveness would be a crucial factor as Spain's domestic markets were opened up.

In the light of the above problems the government's response was to throw responsibility on to the two sides of industry and not, as the previous government had done with the ANE, be a signatory to any agreement. This would free the government from having to offer too many quid pro quos to the other participants particularly ones which, given the increasing budget deficit, would be likely to add further to state spending. Furthermore, the introduction of an industrial policy which sought rationalisation might prove difficult and thus a strategy which encouraged concertation between the two sides of industry but which did not directly involve the government, might not be as compromising nor as constraining to it. This strategy has since continued though, as will be seen, accord between all the main social partners has progressively been difficult. For the first year of the new, socialist government, however, agreement was reached after lengthy discussions between the CEOE, the UGT and the CC.OO. This was the Acuerdo Interconfederal.

THE ACUERDO INTERCONFEDERAL (AI), 1983

As with previous pacts, the AI incorporated both pay and non-pay issues. For the former a norm of 9.5 to 12.5 per cent was agreed, the expected rate of inflation being 12 per cent which implied a fall in, or at best, a constancy of real wages. The outcome was a slight rise, the result of both adherence to the norm and a slight dip of actual inflation below expected. Industrial conflict, however, increased especially in the public sector as a result of a tight policy. On the non-pay side the majority of issues included in the pact were a reiteration of the ones raised in the AMI and for which legislation still had to be passed. New areas included the claim for a 40 hour standard week, the replacement of the old Francoist pay ordinances by negotiated agreements (giving some flexibility in pay differentials), and the move to establish a tri-partite body to discuss the structure of collective bargaining.

The AI was a positive response by both main unions and the CEOE to the new government's strategy of a bipartite accord. For the UGT its participation in an accord was a continuation of a deliberate strategy of cooperation which had begun with the ABI and AMI. For the CC.OO its signatory status had started nearly two years later than the UGT, with the ANE, and had now extended to a second successive year in the AI because, given the large parliamentary majority of the new socialist government, it would not have been strategic for the CC.OO to have distanced itself too much from policy-making at that time. However, it became apparent towards the end of 1983 that a further pact was going to be difficult to achieve. In the event no central agreement was reached. The government did not press hard for an agreement, believing that the economic situation and market forces would constrain wage increases and inflation.

Whilst the CC.OO had signed the AI it was now increasingly critical of the government's economic and labour policies, notably the threat to the security of employment, the legal process required to reduce hours worked (as set out in the AI), the extension of union sections to plants under 50 workers (this it felt would serve to benefit the UGT more), and the government's decision to extend the mandate of the works councillors elected in 1982 to 1986 with future elections to be held every four years not two (9). This last measure was aimed at reducing the pre-occupation of unions with fighting elections and to extend the UGT's 1982 majority to the end of the government's limit of office. This would further marginalise the CC.OO and dampen opposition to policies.

The CC.OO's criticism also extended to pay. The expected rate of inflation for 1985 was 8 per cent, a figure which the UGT and eventually the CEOE used as a basis for their initial position. The CC.OO, how-ever, wanted a slightly higher norm of 8.75 per cent, arguing that the cost of living had risen faster than expected in recent years. This was certainly true of the ANE. Also, it was reluctant to enter an agreement without the government though, as stated above, the latter preferred not to be a participant relying, if necessary, on the market situation to influence events.

In relation to the previous years where pacts had been agreed, the 'no-pact' situation was not as successful. Industrial conflict in-creased significantly though much of the increase was due to union opposition over industrial restructuring, that is, its impact on employ-ment. The unemployment rate increased by three percentage points to over 20 per cent and though productivity rose, it was losses in employ-ment which contributed to its rise rather than increases in output. On the pay side, real wages fell - though less than the authorities actually envisaged - as inflation exceeded the expected rate (9 per cent as opposed to 8 per cent, December to December).

THE ACUERDO ECONOMICO Y SOCIAL (AES), 1985 and 1986

In the light of the above results both the UGT and the CEOE felt that an accord for 1985 could be to their mutual advantage. For the former it could serve to prevent further falls in real wages and for the CEOE a means of reducing industrial conflict. The government also saw benefits from an accord for the remaining two years of its office and pledged itself to a wide range of non-pay issues that would please both sides of industry and thereby effect an agreement. However, as with the AI, the CC.OO was opposed to any agreement which reduced the security of employment, a feature which had begun in 1977 and had recently (August 1984) been included in 'Modifications to the Workers' Statute' ("...to adapt the institutional framework governing the labour market to circumstances governed by the recession..."). For the AES, discussions took place for a modification (loosening) of Article 51 of the Workers' Statute - whereby an employer must follow detailed procedures on dismissals, involving authorisation from the local labour office and this point, pressed for by the CEOE, caused the CC.OO to withdraw from the negotiations. It also felt that insufficient funds were being made available for employment creation and it wanted to see a more progressive tax system and a reduction of the working week to 38 hours, as well as action on retirement at 64 (referred to in the ANE).

The wide-ranging pact which was finally agreed by the other parties for 1985 and 1986 was called the Acuerdo Económico y Social (AES) and contained two parts, the first being a tripartite (government, CEOE and UGT) accord covering, inter alia, taxation, public spending and employment legislation. Part 2 was a bipartite pact (CEOE and UGT) on pay, productivity, absenteeism and the structure of collective bargaining. On pay the CC.OO had felt that the norms for 1985 and 1986 were underestimates of inflation. The outcome was that, for 1985, the norm was closely adhered to and real wages fell only fractionally. The pay norm of 5.5 to 7.5 per cent for 1985 contributed to bring about single figure inflation for the first time since 1972. However, the unemployment rate continued to rise - as a result of both a tighter macroeconomic policy and the impact of industrial restructuring - though the rate of increase was not as great as 1983-84.

Whilst Part 2 re-addressed issues raised in previous pacts (overtime, moonlighting, etc.), Part 1 - the tripartite element - focused on employment creation (state spending and also the solidarity fund financed by both employees - via a levy - and the state to promote jobs and reduce regional imbalances) on extending unemployment coverage and increasing social security. Increased employment flexibility - favoured by the CEOE but which has persistently been opposed by the CC.OO - has not been easy to bring about. However, it is an issue which is likely to be pressed in the future and though the CEOE has recently asked for an easing of dismissals in small firms (without having to approach the labour inspectorate for approval) this represents a more reasonable claim by the employers than previous ones which sought virtually the overall disappearance of employment protection norms.

The progress of the AES has not been smooth since mid-1985. Significant problems have arisen over the State Pensions Reform Bill (effectively reducing most initial pensions) which has been opposed by the UGT as well as the CC.OO which has had the effect of making the UGT appear more independent of the government. Likewise the government has been under attack from the CEOE for its lack of (agreed) consultation over reducing firms' contributions to social security, and the UGT has also criticised the government for its slow implementation of the (agreed) increases in coverage of unemployment benefit. Thus the non-pay issues have been somewhat problematical but the divisions and disagreements between the unions and the government have not resulted in any unanimity between the two main unions themselves.

CONCLUSION

One of the main conclusions from the foregoing analysis is that the trade unions' response to the economic crisis in Spain has largely taken the form of active participation in a concertation process which has proceeded almost continuously since 1979 and has resulted in a series of pacts covering both pay and a wide variety of non-pay issues. The emphasis has been on collective responsibility by the social partners from both sides of industry for the negotiation and implementation of the policies covering such areas, in order to strengthen the commitment and adherence to the agreed principles and instruments at a time of economic instability and political change and consolidation.

On the union side, however, there have been considerable differences between the two main unions, the Communist-influenced CC.OO refusing to sign four of the six pacts since the end of 1979, mainly on account of its opposition to pay norms, its criticism of the inadequacy of employment creation and, as a corollary, its defence of employment security. However, the UGT has adopted, since mid-1979, a policy of cooperation with the CEOE, seeing this as a means of gaining support from workers - many of whom are not unionised - and promoting itself as the 'responsible' union at a time of crisis. Although a major union prior to the Franco regime, the UGT, like the CEOE on the employers' side, was essentially a relatively new organisation after 1975 because it had not been party to the entryist strategy pursued by the CC.OO. Thus the UGT (and CEOE), being better organised at the top than at the enterprise level (compared with the CC.OO) saw it as in their interests to conclude central framework agreements because these enabled them to bargain at a level where their organisational strength was greatest. As a quid pro quo for their cooperation, the UGT and the CEOE were able to influence the development and evolution of the institutional framework for the union organisations and for collective bargaining.

In all the pacts a wide variety of issues and areas for further discussion have been negotiated. On the non-pay side, in addition to negotiations on the future framework for industrial relations, the main focus has been on unemployment and on employment creation measures, either by affecting the supply side (reductions in hours, moonlighting and the retirement age), by direct job creation (government or tripartite funding measures) by increasing the flexibility of labour markets and by concentrating on the structural side of labour and product markets (retraining and the adoption of new technologies). Job creation was initially the quid pro quo for the CC.OO's participation in the pacts (as with ANE).   After the AI, however, the CC.OO became marginalised as it repeatedly criticised the (as it saw it) inadequacy and failure of the policies to lower unemployment, thus leading to its refusals to sign the pacts.

It can be argued that the pacts have incorporated too many issues in the negotiations.   Some of them belong more directly to a parliamentary process (social security reform for example).   Their inclusion in bipartite or even tripartite pacts resulted in a lengthy process of gradualism and may have delayed adjustment and prevented urgently needed reforms. Alternatively, such 'gradualism', together with a strong focus on consensus and concertation between the social partners, can also be seen as the only legitimate and effective way forward and solution to economic problems in a nascent democracy.   In this respect, as Perez Diaz (10) has noted, one of the positive effects of the pacts (or the experience of "societal corporatism" as he calls it) has been the legitimisation of the capitalist system in Spain which, for complex historical reasons, was a process which had yet to be completed.   Union leaders, trained in the school of political opposition to Francoism, involving attempts to break the wage norms imposed during the regime (and being successful) have, since 1979, increasingly moderated their demands, a feature which has been the consequence of a more pragmatic approach by the unions and the rank-and-file workers at a time of economic difficulties and the consolidation of democracy.

In economic terms, the pacts have been associated with a reduction of inflation.   Pay norms based on expected inflation have normally been adhered to which has contributed to lower inflation and progressively lower pay norms.   However, when the AMI was signed in 1979 it was not clear if the norms would be accepted at levels below the central framework.   The practical effectiveness of the AMI (and later pacts) as a means of supervising wage negotiations at lower levels was not clear since Spanish legislation did not confer on these parties the authority to set standards.   Neither was it clear to what extent the sector/provincial organisations within the CEOE and the UGT were legally bound to respect the central guidelines.   However, as noted, adherence to the norms has been good.   One effect of this has been that real wages have been significantly lower than in the early and mid-1970s (11).   Such reductions in real wages have been important for unit labour costs especially in the export sector.   However, the lowering of real wages has not been translated into a reduction in rates of unemployment and, whilst the pacts have contained measures to combat the problem, industrial policy has, in recent years, sought to increase efficiency by reducing work forces in the crisis industries.

It might be argued that given the economic situation in Spain in the late 1970s, inflation would have been contained without the need to impose pacts, as was the understanding in 1984.   However, without the pacts and their progressively rather than dramatically reduced norms, the price paid in terms of conflict and economic and political instability might well have been too high.   Thus, at a time when social pacts have lost ground in Western Europe, they have played a significant role in Spain with regard to attempting a solution to economic and labour questions and have served as a vehicle for union participation within the context of an on-going concertation between both sides of industry.

NOTES

(1) S. Lieberman, The Contemporary Spanish Economy, London, George Allen and Unwin, 1982, chapter 3.

(2) L. Fina and R. I. Hawkesworth, 'Trade unions and collective bargaining in post-Franco Spain' in Labour and Society, vol. 9, no. 1, January 1984.

(3) OECD, Economic Outlook, Paris, various dates.

(4) Ibid.

(5) The principle established in the AMI was that trade union sections could be set up in undertakings employing more than 250 workers. In the case of collective agreements at provincial or national level, bargaining rights are enjoyed by trade unions, their federations or confederations covering at least 10 per cent of the works committees or staff representatives within the geographical area or field of activity to which the agreement relates (for the 'autonomous communities' the figure is 15 per cent). The figure of 250 was later reduced to 50.

(6) J. M. Zufiaur, 'El sindicalismo español en la transición y la crisis' in Papeles de Economía Española, no. 22, 1985, pp. 202-231.

(7) Ministerio de Trabajo y Seguridad Social, Boletín de Estadísticas Laborales, no. 15, March 1985.

(8) OECD, Economic Report on Spain, Paris, various dates.

(9) Boletín Oficial del Estado, 8 August 1985.

(10) V. Perez Diaz, 'Políticas económicas y pautas sociales en la España de la transición: la doble cara del neocorporatismo', in J. Linz (ed.), España: un presente para un futuro, vol. 1, La sociedad, Madrid, Instituto de Estudios Económicos Collección Tablero, 1984.

(11) A. Espina, 'Política de rentes en España, 1977-86' in Papeles de Economía Española, 22, 1985.

See also International Labour Office, The Trade Union Situation and Industrial Relations in Spain, Geneva, 1985.

PART II
EASTERN EUROPE

5 Trade unions and economic crisis in Poland

FRANCES MILLARD

INTRODUCTION

Since 1956 Poland has experienced periodic upheaval generated by a coincidence of economic difficulties and political unrest. Yet up until 1980 the trade union movement was neither the object of government concern nor a focal point of workers' strategy. Since 1980, however, trade unionism has been a central issue in Polish politics. In 1980 independent trade unionism developed, symbolised by the ten million strong union Solidarity. The 'old' official state-sponsored unions continued to exist, but they suffered a massive haemorrhage of their membership to Solidarity and some of the smaller new unions. In December, 1981 the Polish leader General Jaruzelski instituted a nineteen-month period of martial law. All existing trade unions, including Solidarity, were at first suspended, then banned. The new military regime then set out to recreate trade union structures to provide some channels of workers expression but without sacrificing its own political control. This chapter will look at the background to these developments in order to provide an interim examination of the achievements of and constraints faced by the Polish government in the attempt to develop 'new' Polish trade unions in the context of continuing economic crisis.

One reason why trade unions traditionally failed to function as vehicles of popular protest in Poland lies in the concept of the role and nature of trade unions under socialism. Trade unions in the social-ist states of Eastern Europe, including Poland before 1980, have seldom been regarded as vigorous, effective organisations for the represent-ation of working class interests. With the partial exception of Hun-gary, the official concept of socialist trade unions emphasises their production functions, including the fulfilment of the economic plan and the maintenance of labour discipline: since the plan itself allegedly embodies the needs of society and not the pursuit of profit as under a capitalist system, it follows that striving to implement the plan serves the interests of the working class. Similarly, disruptive actions such as strikes are deemed as particularistic and egoistic manifestations harmful to the public interest. Further, trade unionism is avowedly subordinate to the 'leading role' of the Communist Party (1).

This model of official trade unionism partly explains why working class protest in Poland for so long by-passed the trades unions. Economic grievances were significant, but the unions served to articulate only minor issues, and spontaneous protest actions took the place of regularised institutional channels of interest articulation. This in turn meant that working class protest in Poland, while emphasising immediate economic demands, has gone beyond the economic sphere to make political claims for new institutions to represent working class interests. The years of major working class turbulence - 1956, 1970, 1976 and 1980-81 - all saw the vigorous expression of economic grievances resulting from shortages of consumer goods, lack of housing, inadequate access to the health service, price rises, and pressure to keep wages down. In 1956 the political expression of workers' interests was through spontaneous workers' councils, which the party-government authorities gradually subordinated and emasculated. The developments of 1980 were the culmination of a lengthy experience of protest, concession and disillusion, leading Polish workers to the conclusion that gains could be permanently achieved only through legally guaranteed structures of independent trade unions devoted to the defence of their members' interests.

In 1980 the impact of economic crisis was increasingly making itself felt as the most severe of the post-war period, with an unprecedented negative economic growth rate (2) having been registered in 1979. The manifestations of crisis included profound dislocation of the planning process, chronic shortages of both producer and consumer goods and of energy, massive foreign debt, high inflation, shortages of basic foodstuffs, lengthening housing queues and inadequate funding of social services. The impact of these economic difficulties on the population was heightened because they followed a period of expansion and increased prosperity which led to rising expectations; because of the collective memory and experience of previous upheaval; and because for the first time both the working class and the intelligentsia came together in a united effort to exact permanent concessions from the regime.

These concessions, temporary though they were to prove, were embodied in the famous Gdansk Agreement of August 1981 (3) which gave official confirmation of the birth of Solidarity. The Agreement and others like it embraced a wide range of economic, social and political issues: legal recognition of 'independent, self-managing' trade unions and a commitment to their participation in economic decision-making; wage rises to compensate for price increases, a commitment to greater investment in housing and social services, the right to strike, a new law on censorship, the release of political prisoners, and many others. The provisions were not only designed to provide some redress for economic hardship but also to ensure institutions for the articulation of occupational interests as well as the conditions necessary to safeguard the gains and the new institutions. In particular, Solidarity recognised that trade union independence required the mechanism necessary to preserve and protect it, namely the right to strike. Similarly, the demand for a strictly delineated and legally limited system of censorship stressed the new union's need for a system of open communication and dissemination of information as essential conditions for independent unionism. The union accepted the legitimacy of censorship in areas such as national security but wished to safeguard its own existence.

For the Polish regime 1980-81 was a period of economic crisis compounded and reinforced by political crisis. Both aspects had international dimensions embracing the problem of Poland's enormous hard currency debt and the pro-Solidarity sentiments of western governments alongside the anti-Solidarity sentiments of the Soviet Union and other Warsaw Pact countries. At the same time the Party itself, especially its rank and file, was spawning moves for genuine internal democratisation, while Solidarity not only proved immune to the Party penetration and domination previously used to subordinate autonomous movements but also increased the scale of its political demands. The government mounted a sustained propaganda offensive against Solidarity. It emphasised Solidarity's role in exacerbating economic crisis because (inter alia) of its widespread use of strike action, its commitment to the five-day working week, its pursuit of higher wages and greater social expenditure. With the introduction of martial law the Government attack centred on the alleged imminence of civil war, fomented by extremist 'anti-socialist' elements within Solidarity. This view served as the justification for the suspension of civil liberties, mass internments, and numerous political trials of the martial law period.

The 'vision' proffered by General Jaruzelski in the period since martial law claims to be based on the lessons of pre-1980 injustices as well as the 'distortions' of the Solidarity period. Jaruzelski propounds the prospects of a society based on a 'social contract' between rulers and ruled, major instruments of which are seen as economic decentralisation and a reconstituted trade union movement. Party, government, and populace are to forge a new partnership to overcome the economic crisis, re-establish the momentum of social progress and ensure political stability.

This is a daunting task for the Polish authorities, given the depth of economic crisis, the traditional assertiveness of the Polish working class, and the lack of regime legitimacy, reduced if not engendered by the suppression of Solidarity and the heightened coercion of the post-1981 period. At the same time they must contend with the continued existence of Solidarity, now operating as a clandestine underground movement.

The brief experience of autonomous trade unionism was profound in its impact. The government's new trade union proposals thus could not ignore this experience, despite its determination to prevent the development of genuinely independent structures able to mount an effective challenge to its own policies and methods. At the same time it needed - for purposes of establishing some minimum degree of legitimacy - to avoid the political embarrassment of unchannelled popular protest, since the 'leading role of the party' rested on the claim that the Party represented the interests of working people with policies designed to embody the public good. Certain concessions have been granted to the new trade union structures in order to attract members and to give the unions some credibility. Yet these concessions entail some risk that the unions may provide the future focus for renewed protest if genuine economic improvement is not forthcoming. The position has been further complicated by the inability of the Jaruzelski regime to try to buy popular support by offering economic concessions. Despite some degree of stabilisation (4), the economic crisis has remained such that bribing the population with increased access to consumer goods, shorter housing queues and the like is not an option. Indeed, restrictive austerity measures, including massive price rises, are seen as necessary to restore some form of equilibrium to the economy. Similarly, the economic situation poses a dilemma for the new trade unions. They need to behave 'responsibly' within the confines of the established order. Yet if they cannot achieve tangible results for their members, they will be rendered as irrelevant as their predecessors, the old state-sponsored unions. Although they can assume a monopoly in the organisational sphere and the support of the official press, they have on their flank underground Solidarity, also determined to maintain its strong hold on the loyalty of the population (5). This, then, is the context of trade union developments since the introduction of martial law.

THE NEW TRADE UNIONS

In October 1982 in an atmosphere of some controversy the Sejm (the Polish Parliament) passed the new law (6) regulating trade unions, thereby also rendering illegal all existing union organisations, which had previously been suspended but not formally banned. New unions were to be permitted to register from 1 January 1983, while in the meantime 'initiating groups' were to lay the foundations for subsequent developments. Initially trade unions were to be permitted only at enterprise level, with regional and national structures scheduled to emerge gradually over the next three years.

The new trade union law and a 'model statute' issued to provide guidance for setting up a new trade union generally followed the previous pattern of trade union regulation, but the influence of the Solidarity experience was not absent. Clearly a simple return to the old system of state-dominated, production-oriented unions would have served no useful purpose. At the same time, however, we should stress that what appear to be departures from pre-1980 practice are couched in vague legal formulations which are relatively easy to circumvent in practice; indeed, considerable scholarly controversy continues in respect to certain phrases in the new legislation (7).

Trade unionism is open to all, save soldiers, police, prison officers and state employees of certain ministries, including Justice and Foreign Affairs. Unions may be formed either on the basis of the sector of employment (this was the old system, with trade union structures paralleling ministerial structures and embracing all employees in a given branch of the economy) or on the basis of type of occupation. To facilitate the establishment of the new unions, in the first year the initiative of at least ten (but from 31 December 1983 at least thirty) individuals at their place of work was sufficient to inaugurate the process of setting up a trade union in the enterprise. If more than one union should request registration at a single workplace, the provincial court may defer registration until agreement is reached on a single union.

The trade union statute places great emphasis on the 'voluntary' and 'autonomous' nature of the new trade unions. No external body has the right to interfere in the internal affairs of a union so long as it acts within the law, in which case recourse is only to the courts. Clearly the stress on the independent and 'self-managing' character of the unions and the prohibition of external intervention by administrative or economic organs of the state is a legacy of Solidarity's own emphasis on the need for independent trade unions. Similarly, the description of the functions of the new trade unions stresses their role in defending their members' interests, rather than - as was previously the case - their role in stimulating production and labour discipline. Articles 5-7 list the functions of trade unions as: representative and defensive functions, participatory functions and educational functions in that order. As well as the defence of the rights and interests of members in regard to the occupational, economic and social conditions of their work, the unions are also charged with defending social, cultural and living conditions of members outside the workplace. Article 6 specifies trade union jurisdiction (not of course exclusive) in the fields of leisure, sport and physical recreation, housing, environmental protection, pricing policy and the cost of living. Article 21 provides for trade union participation in the process of preparing laws and other decisions by state authorities affecting the rights and interests of working people and their families. Deputy Premier Rakowski, also a parliamentary deputy, argued in the Sejm that this provision stressed the role of trade unions as integral elements of the socialist system and reaffirmed the necessity of the independent, autonomous social control provided by trade unions to protect workers against bureaucratic distortions by state authorities (8). However, Article 3 prohibits trade union activity directed against the basic principles of the socialist system as defined by the Constitution, and specifically against the principle of the social ownership of the means of production and the leading role of the Communist Party (PZPR).

Union rights in support of their functions are in theory wide ranging. Trade unions have the right to complete information concerning the socio-economic conditions of the country, province and place of work, buttressed by the right to conduct their own independent research, to publish their findings and to have access to the mass media. All these provisions testify to the continuing impact of the Solidarity period. Most innovative of all, however, are the provisions regulating the conduct of collective disputes with the organs of the state. In the period before the emergence of Solidarity, Polish law simply ignored the possibility of collective disputes, which were seen as "a phenomenon exclusively confined to the conflicts of interest between capital and labour under capitalism" (9). Now the trade unions have the right to organise strikes and other protest actions in pursuit of the economic and social interests of their members, but only when other means, including arbitration, have failed; the strike is a weapon of last resort. This is certainly a restricted right. The formulation appears to exclude the possibility of sympathy strikes, while 'political strikes', though not defined, are explicitly prohibited. Strike action may also be temporarily banned in an area declared a natural disaster zone. In addition, the right to strike is not universal: it is prohibited among others to those working in the gas and petroleum industries, communications and transport, the fire and health services, and those engaged in the production, storage and distribution of foodstuffs. Despite these limitations (many of which also characterise liberal democratic states), the acknowledgement of the right to strike clearly has significant potential implications.

Many provisions of the new Trade Union Law have not yet been seriously tested. Both government and the new unions have been treading a cautious and flexible path. If the government wishes to reduce its emphasis on coercion, which after all is an expensive and rather limited way of ensuring cooperation, then it must provide the conditions in which trade unionism can serve as some sort of genuine channel for the expression of workers' interests and grievances. At the same time the government is also clearly determined to prevent a resurgence of the genuine working class autonomy which existed in 1980-81. Yet official perceptions of the economic situation establish limits to what can realistically be conceded.

The leaders of the new trade unions, on the other hand, need to win the confidence of the working class, still bitter at the suppression of Solidarity and suspicious of government manipulation. The process of legal regulation has been dynamic, with pragmatic adaptation to changing circumstances. Indeed, amendments to the Law have already been considerable, including changes made in July 1985 giving the unions greater power over factory-level wages and in areas such as the distribution of factory-owned housing, as well as greater powers to defend the rights of individual employees.

Yet what must have been the worst fears of government and the new unions, namely a total lack of response by the potential membership, have not materialised. The structure of the new trade unions has developed rapidly. In the first year only local enterprise-level unions were permitted for most industries with inter-plant organisation to follow in 1984 and national organisation to develop in 1985. In practice, the development of new structures proceeded somewhat faster than was at first envisaged, with the government arguing that fragmentation and lack of coordination were hampering the development of a strong trade union movement. By October 1983, a large number of 'federations' had been registered with the courts, including the Federation of Trade Unions in Light Industry, the Federation of Mining Trade Unions, the Federation of Thermal Power Workers' Trade Unions and the Federation of Trade Unions of Health Service Workers. In September 1984, delegates from these new national bodies met and decided to arrange a national coordinating conference on the further integration of the trade union movement. This meeting took place in Bytom in late November; it voted by 534 to 430 to establish a National Trade Union Accord (OPZZ) and elected a 210-member Council (10). The Council of State gave its consent to the OPZZ and the new body was legally registered in April 1985. By June the impounded assets of Solidarity had been transferred to the new national trade union organisation.

These developments undoubtedly owed much to the need to demonstrate that the new trade unions would indeed prove effective bodies in defending the rights of the working class. There could be no pretence of this so long as the trade union movement was fragmented into thousands of separate unions based on the factory or workplace and characterised by low membership figures. In addition, it seemed clear that government worries about a massive 'Trojan horse' strategy by Solidarity were unfounded. Rather than encourage their supporters to join the new unions and change them from within, the Solidarity Temporary National

Coordinating Commission in these early stages of the formation of the new unions urged a policy of non-cooperation and attempted to discredit the unions.

At first workers and employees did prove rather reluctant to join the new enterprise-level unions. Indeed, Communist Party members were instructed not to join en masse in order to give credence to the 'independence' and self-governing nature of the unions; in other words to try to prevent condemnation of the unions as instruments or appendages of the Party. Yet it was obviously insufficient, and the numbers joining the unions remained very low. In February 1983 - almost two months after the new statute came into effect - the Trade Union Minister Stanislaw Ciosek reported the registration of 5,600 new unions with a total of one million members. A few days later, Deputy Premier Rakowski announced that it was time to lift the restrictions on union membership by full party members (11), probably in an attempt to boost membership figures.

Membership clearly did rise steadily throughout the ensuing months. By October 1983, official statements claimed 18,000 registered trade unions with 3.5 million members. However, the attractions of union membership were clearly greatest in smaller enterprises and outside the great industrial complexes where Solidarity had been so strong. The major provincial newspaper of the Baltic coast region Glos Wybrzeza, noted that Gdansk, the birthplace of Solidarity, occupied last place in regard to unionisation, with only 16 per cent of workers having joined the new unions. The newspaper openly admitted that there remained "an atmosphere of mistrust ... and conditions of continuing bitter struggle against the political opposition ..." (12). Similarly in the large Warsaw plants where Solidarity had been a major force, membership in the new unions remained low: at Huta Warszawa, the Warsaw steelworks, membership in October 1983 was put at less than 10 per cent of the work force, with "almost no members" in the iron foundry (13); a similar situation prevailed at the major agricultural machine plant at Ursus.

In 1984 membership continued to rise. By the time of OPZZ's founding conference in November, the total claimed was over 5 million, roughly half the total Solidarity membership. This, however, included some 600,000 retired workers, and the authorities conceded that the new unions remained weak in major industrial complexes (14). The slow but steady increase in membership continued in 1985, by which time the new unions appeared to have attracted nearly 6 million members. This compares unfavourably with previous rates of near 100 per cent unionisation, but given the circumstances it is not a derisory achievement. Nonetheless, the old Solidarity strongholds such as the Lenin Shipyard in Gdansk and Huta Warszawa and Ursus in Warsaw were still proving resistant to the new union structures.

The reasons for this success are certainly manifold and one cannot at this stage gauge the significance of each individual factor; however we can comment generally on some of the attractions of trade union membership. Firstly, membership of traditional Eastern European state-sponsored trade unions has always conveyed substantial material benefits, and the new Polish unions are no exception. At the level of the enterprise, trade unions are given a significant role in the allocation of subsidised holidays, factory-controlled housing and enhanced sickness and welfare benefits. The distribution of such benefits and other material advantages of union membership, including subsidies on commuter tickets, summer camps for children, the provision of refrigerators, vouchers for car purchase and the like, have received considerable publicity in the local press. Although in many instances benefits are intended for distribution without regard to union membership, there are indications that the unions have accorded preferential treatment to their own members (15). In this sphere, the enterprise-level unions initially benefited from the transfer to their coffers of local funds raised by Solidarity, thus enhancing their capacity to make special payments to needy cases; one plant in the Bialystok area distributed 160,000 zloties derived from this source, as well as donating 40,000 zloties collected by Solidarity for a maternity clinic to that same end.

In addition, the factory-based unions began from the outset to press provincial authorities to take on projects of widespread appeal: the Wloclawek provincial authorities promised, for example, to allocate housing for health personnel and to consider the building of a new hospital in the town of Michelin, to try to increase the number of garden allotments and to provide help with workers' transport. The press continue to lay great stress on the importance of meetings between trade unions and provincial government and party authorities and the concrete achievements and potential of the unions.

Secondly, the new trade unions have already been extremely anxious to be seen as acting on behalf of their members. They have been cautious, but they have not remained silent or passive on issues of obvious general concern; indeed, they have been quite responsive on many issues which have provoked outbursts of discontent in the past. Clashes have occurred particularly in the sensitive areas of wages and prices. Government legislation has attempted to curb wage increases. At their second national meeting with Party and government leaders in May 1984, union leaders placed particular emphasis on growing income differentials between social groups as a consequence of the fact that more 'profitable' enterprises would be able to grant higher wage increases than the 'less profitable'. Again, in early 1985, when the government announced consultation with the unions over proposed variants for price increases, the unions, both individually and through the OPZZ, rejected all variants as inflationary and leading to a reduction in workers' living standards. The Federation of Metal Workers issued a statement condemning the new arrangements for price increases in language reportedly so strong that government censors banned its appearance in the press (16). The unions have also raised demands for increased government spending on health and social welfare programmes, which, they have argued, are notably higher in the other East European socialist countries. Conflict with individual unions has also been apparent. For example, in September 1984 the print union, with a claimed unionisation rate of 40 per cent, unilaterally terminated its collective wage agreement, negotiated in 1970, and demanded immediate discussions about a new settlement. The union also demanded substantial new funding for the industry, whose investment programme had been squeezed by the restrictions on Western imports, its major source of equipment. Similarly in 1986, the Miners' Union vigorously opposed the government's order extending the principle of Saturday working in the extracting industries. Backed by the national OPZZ, the union threatened to initiate dispute procedures to re-establish voluntary Saturday working, which had been rescinded in the early days of martial law.

The government has clearly made a number of concessions to the new trade unions, and press reports continue to emphasise their credibility as representatives of their members' interests. The weekly journal Polityka claimed considerable optimism in assessing the new unions' ability to steer a path between the old Central Council of Trade Unions, "which was at the beck and call of the government, and Solidarity, which carried out the role of opposition"; it hailed the large number of local union achievements throughout 1983 and 1984: of 556 conflicts investigated, 462 were concluded amicably without recourse to judicial arbitration, and 90 per cent of these ended in accordance with union views (17). When the Ministry of Justice contested an arbitration agreement reached between the Executive of the Opole Automobile Repair Service Trade Union and the plant management, the Supreme Court upheld the agreement (18). On wider issues, too, the government has attributed influence to the unions: when the government withdrew its proposed price increases in favour of a more gradual pricing reform, it announced that it had listened carefully to and taken account of union protests.

Similarly, the amendments introduced to the Trade Union Law in July 1985 were defended as necessary to increase trade union powers. Although the government refused to alter its position regarding the decentralisation of wage agreements, the amendments did give the unions a greater role in these local negotiations, as well as more power in the division of the enterprise social fund. In the specific case of the printers mentioned above, the government did grant important pay and investment concessions, while remaining adamant that a new collective agreement could not yet be negotiated. Yet when after almost twenty months of frustration, the printers' union declared an overtime ban and called a token half-hour stoppage for 21 May 1986, the government hurriedly offered assurances that an interim wage agreement would be urgently forthcoming. The union called off the proposed industrial action but served notice that it was prepared to utilise the disputes procedure to the full.

There are thus substantial reasons why individuals would be prepared to join the new trade unions, if not necessarily to play an active role within them. They are an officially acknowledged structure representing workers' interests, even though what they can achieve will obviously be limited to marginal gains within the existing system; and they offer material benefits to their members. This of itself might be sufficient to generate a 50 per cent membership rate, especially when coupled with traditional high rates of unionisation. It must also be remembered that not all Poles joined Solidarity or felt a burning sense of betrayal at its suspension and prohibition; the 'old unions' continued to exist up until the declaration of martial law, albeit in shrunken form, and there were also a number of small unions which set themselves up as 'independent, self-governing unions' in the spirit of Solidarity but without formal allegiance to Solidarity's national or regional structures. These people would perhaps see little obstacle to membership.

Yet another reason why membership of the new unions has risen steadily is perhaps even more speculative. The Solidarity underground leadership has been somewhat divided in its views of how to respond to the new officially sanctioned unions. Many have urged a total boycott and have sought to discredit the new organisations. Others, however, like Zbigniew Bujak, the leader of underground Solidarity, and the historian Bronislaw Geremek, gradually abandoned the policy of non-cooperation and began to speak out in favour of Solidarity members' joining the new trade unions. This constituted a strategy of transforming the new unions from within. It is impossible to estimate the significance of this development, although it is clear that former members of Solidarity have joined the new unions; nor is this necessarily incompatible with continuing support for Solidarity itself.

The relative success of the new trade unions in attracting members does not imply, however, that the unions can look forward to continuing steady gains in acceptance and legitimacy. The economic situation still presents major obstacles to more than very marginal achievements, and questions of wages, prices and working conditions will continue to be major areas of potential conflict with government policy. The current 'economic reform' is difficult to assess, but if it is successful in creating a genuinely decentralised economy with individual plants being judged on their efficiency and 'profitability', then trade unions are unlikely to succeed in their aim of negotiating wages at branch level rather than at enterprise level. If wages in turn become in practice dependent upon the 'profitability' of individual enterprises so that successful plants are able to offer higher wages and better working conditions, this is an obvious recipe for resentment at the resulting inequalities. Thus far the impact of the reform has been limited by a number of factors, including central allocation of scarce inputs, ministerial interference in the running of the 'autonomous' enterprises in their sectors, and a pricing system which is inadequate to the task of 'measuring' profitability. The government has also been unwilling or unable to curb wage increases to the extent that it deems desirable.

However, although there has been something of a cushion to soften part of the impact of change, tensions are already evident. When the print workers demanded further investment, this was because new investment was seen as facilitating the efficiency and thus the profitability of their industry. This argument would apply to most of the industrial sector; in other words, central government policy and priorities will strongly influence conditions enhancing or retarding the ability to improve productivity, on which wage rises are to depend. There is evidence to suggest that conflict over inequalities between workers has already surfaced over the issue of the social and housing fund. The determination of this fund is complex (and currently under review), but there is greater potential for the fund in the industrial sector than in the service sector, where 'profitability' indicators are problematical. The Federation of Health Service Workers is one union which has already protested against the proposals endorsed by the OPZZ in November 1985 (19).

The 1986 Party Programme reiterates official determination to proceed with the decentralisation of the economy, despite the relative lack of success so far in reducing the economic power of the central government bureaucracy. Indeed, it is difficult to see how the authorities could do otherwise than to continue on the course they have laid down for themselves. However, it also seems very likely that the unions will become a major source of institutional resistance. This is certainly the Hungarian experience; in Hungary issues of profitability and wage differentials have generated trade union resistance to the extension of the market-oriented reforms of the New Economic Mechanism. Interestingly, the Catholic Church has emerged as a proponent of reform and has - if somewhat obliquely - offered its support in calming any discontent which may arise from growing income differentials (20).

Another obstacle to the development of mass popular trade unionism within the confines of the existing framework lies in the existence of conflict between the trade unions and the so-called workers' self-management councils. Self-management councils have a chequered history in Poland (21) and it is not altogether clear why the Jaruselski regime determined to reactivate them in February 1982. In most plants they appear to be virtually impotent as instruments for asserting workers' control over enterprise management, and one reason offered for this is the existence of conflicts of jurisdiction and status with the trade union in the enterprise (22). In other firms, they have provided a substitute for trade union membership, giving workers an alternative forum for their grievances. Thus the council at Huta Warszawa, where trade union membership is estimated at some 20 per cent of the work force, has a reputation for particular vigour; it also enjoys the support of underground broadsheets distributed at the steel mill. Indeed, some councils have been openly criticised for functioning as centres of "political opposition", i.e. agents of underground Solidarity. The Elana fibre plant in Torun is the most dramatic example (23), not only because its membership includes former Solidarity internees, but because of its running battles with management. It has achieved considerable publicity for its persistent determination to bring together representatives from other self-management councils in large firms for the type of horizontal coordination and linkage reminiscent of similar efforts in Torun to link democratised local party structures during 1981. In the spring of 1986, the Supreme Court found in favour of the self-management council: the director's attempt to prevent a local meeting to discuss economic reform with other enterprises and ministerial representatives was an infringement of the self-management statute (24). Elana shows the anxiety of the institutions of the state to be seen to be acting legitimately. It also illustrates the continuing importance of the largely unseen actor, Solidarity.

SOLIDARITY

The workers' councils are but one dimension of the activities of underground Solidarity, whose continuing clandestine existence provides an added dimension to the government-trade union relationship. Both the structure and membership of illegal organisations are difficult to assess, but a number of aspects seem fairly clear. Officially Solidarity has a four or five person (depending on who is in gaol) Provisional National Coordinating Commission. Zbigniew Bujak headed the Commission until the authorities finally caught up with him in May 1986. In theory the Commission coordinates the activities of twelve networks around the country, which in turn direct cells in all major factories, universities, hospitals and the like. The model is that of the 'secret state' of the wartime resistance, which set up a parallel underground administration to organise Polish society and provide the national education and culture threatened by the Nazis. In practice, the analogy is almost certainly more ideal than a reality, if not entirely fanciful. Yet the main aim, that of providing visible reminders of the continuation of Solidarity, with its vision of plural, independent trade unionism, has certainly been maintained, largely through clandestine publications and periodic demonstrations.

Solidarity has been able to maintain its underground press, with the regular appearance of journals such as Tygodnik Mazowsze with a claimed print run of some 30,000. Periodically the official press reports arrests for illegal dissemination of information, possession of illegal printing equipment or theft of paper and printing materials. Nonetheless, leaflets, bulletins and books of poetry, literature and history appear in vast quantities. Underground Solidarity has also called for protest demonstrations on anniversaries of national significance as well as to register its condemnation of specific government policies. May Day, the workers' day, has always been an occasion for official celebration by Communist Party regimes as a reaffirmation of the Party's ideological and political commitment to the working class. By providing alternative, and illegal, demonstrations underground Solidarity has been equally determined to demonstrate both the hollowness of the Party's commitment and the strength of its own position in Polish society. The May Day Solidarity demonstrations have continued to be impressive, given the government's willingness to utilise repressive means: pre-May Day arrests and harassment of known Solidarity sympathisers and activists; the use of riot squads armed with water cannon and tear gas; and the threat of severe reprisals for participants. Although official censorship makes accurate assessment of the extent and numbers of those attending difficult, Western journalists have consistently reported "tens of thousands" of Solidarity supporters on the streets of major Polish cities for alternative May Day protests since 1982. In Warsaw in 1985 more than 10,000 marched after paying homage at the grave of Father Jerzy Popieluszko, the pro-Solidarity priest murdered by Polish secret policemen (25). Similarly, thousands demonstrated in Krakow and Gdansk in protest against the arrest of Bujak. Protests at specific government policies have been less consistent. Despite confident calls by the Temporary Coordinating Commission, the response has usually been limited and scattered, with the largest demonstrations in Gdansk, Warsaw and Krakow to accompany the local election boycott in June 1984. Similarly, calls for work stoppages have met with limited response, which is not surprising given the risk of dismissal and heavy fines. The boycott of local and national elections also yielded disappointing results, with a turn out of 78 per cent claimed for the parliamentary elections in the autumn of 1985. The use of demonstrations as a means to bring mass political pressure on the government has clearly failed. The government can deal effectively with street protest without much difficulty. The underground leadership recognises this, although it is not itself without internal division and conflict (26); hence the greater sympathy for taking part in the new union structures and/or works' councils.

Nonetheless, the periodic manifestations of support must be of continuing concern to the government, which may have engendered passivity but which cannot claim positive commitment and support. Continuing harassment and vilification of the former Solidarity leader Lech Walesa belie the official contention that Walesa is merely an ordinary citizen with no political or social role. The estimated total number of political prisoners is not high (about 250), but political trials continue and penalties can be quite harsh: Bujak faces a charge of planning to overthrow the system of government which carries a maximum sentence of ten years in prison. However, the churches remain full and many congregations, like those at Ursus and Huta Warszawa, use religious services as a means of political expression, with visible Solidarity symbols and banners. The grave of Father Popieluszko has become a pilgrims' shrine. Many local priests continue openly to foster the spirit of Solidarity and to provide their premises and other means of physical support, despite the more cautious stance of the official Church hierarchy. Solidarity survives, if only to await the next Polish upheaval (27).

PROSPECTS

The regime has achieved some degree of economic and political stabilisation, yet there are few outside official Polish government circles who maintain much optimism either for a sustained economic revival or for the bridging of the moral and political gulf between the regime and the populace. Failure to pursue economic reform measures will mean the perpetuation of the structural imbalances and ad hoc central administrative intervention which generated and perpetuated the economic crisis. Cumulative economic hardship carries the risk of renewed outbreaks of popular discontent, fuelled by memories of Solidarity, if not channelled or directed by it. Economic reform does not guarantee an end to economic difficulties, as the Hungarian experience shows. Short-term setbacks and crises such as the impact of the Chernobyl disaster in the Ukraine are also impossible to predict but potentially very serious in their consequences. Even if the reform programme is pursued and some form of authentic decentralisation serves to revive the Polish economy, the benefits will not be immediate. The need to redirect resources from consumption to exports in order to service the foreign debt will place enormous strain on the relationship between rulers and ruled. In neither instance can General Jaruselski assume that the new trade union movement will absorb or divert popular resentment. If it remains passive, it will be discarded as the stooge of party and government; if it functions as a genuine representative and participatory structure, the regime will be back where it started. Jaruselski has achieved short term stability but for the longer term he needs the social contract of his own rhetoric. He needs a political solution, not merely an economic one, to what are inextricably entangled political and economic problems.

NOTES

(1) See for example Joseph Godson, 'The role of the trade unions' in L. Schapiro and J. Godson (eds.), The Soviet Worker. Illusions and Realities, London, Macmillan, 1981; J. L. Porket, 'Industrial relations and participation in management in the Soviet-type communist sytem' in British Journal of Industrial Relations, vol. XVI, no. 1, March 1978, pp. 70-85. Alan Ball and Frances Millard, Pressure Politics in Industrial Society, London, Macmillan, 1986 has a comparative chapter on trade unions in socialist states and liberal democracies.

(2) In Eastern Europe, only Czechoslovakia in 1962 had previously experienced a negative growth rate.

(3) The Gadnsk Agreement is reproduced inter alia in Kevin Ruane, The Polish Challenge, London, British Broadcasting Corporation, 1982, Appendix A.

(4) The extent of the stabilisation is controversial; see for example Zbigniew Fallenbuchl, 'The Polish economy under martial law' in Soviet Studies, vol. XXXVI, no. 4, October 1984, and George Blazyca, 'The Polish economy under martial law - a dissenting view' in Soviet Studies, vol. XXXVII, no. 3, July 1985; also Waldemar Kucynski, 'Bilans gospodarczej reanimacji (1982-1984)' in Aneks,

no. 38, 1985.

(5) For an assessment of public support for Solidarity, see David Mason, 'Solidarity, the regime and the public' in Soviet Studies, vol. XXV, no. 4, October 1983, pp. 533-545.

(6) Dziennik ustaw, no. 32, 11 October 1982, position 216; this is the source for all subsequent references to the Law on Trade Unions.

(7) See for example W. Goralski (ed.), Spor o Zwiazki Zawodowe, Warsaw, Instytut Wydawniczy Zwiazkow Zawodowych, 1982, 2 vols.; and A. Swiatkowski (ed.), Kompetencje Zwiazkow Zawodowych, Warsaw, Panstwowe Wydawnictwo Naukowe, 1984.

(8) Rakowski's speech is reproduced in the introduction to Goralski, op. cit., p. 7.

(9) Swiatkowski, op. cit., p. 331.

(10) 'Wlasna droga', Polityka, no. 48 (1439) 1 December 1984, p. 3.

(11) Financial Times, 22 February 1983.

(12) Glos Wybrzeza, 29-30 October 1983.

(13) Express Wieczorny, 20 October 1983.

(14) The Guardian, 26 November 1984.

(15) See for example J. Hausner and J Indraszkiewicz, 'Przepychanka' in Polityka, no. 45 (1488) 9 November 1985, p. 5; Express Wieczorny, op. cit.

(16) Financial Times, 5 March 1985.

(17) 'Wlasna droga', art. cit.

(18) S. Podemski, '2:0 dla zalogi' in Polityka, no. 50 (1493), 14 December 1985, p. 7.

(19) 'Z zycia Federacji ZZPOZ' in Sluzba Zdrowia, no. 47 (1976), 24 November 1985, p. 7.

(20) See Tygodnik Powszechny, 18 May 1986.

(21) See George Kolankiewicz, 'Employee self-management and socialist trade unionism' in J. Woodall (ed.), Policy and Politics in Contemporary Poland, London, Frances Pinter, 1982, pp. 129-147.

(22) Hausner and Indraszkiewicz, art. cit., p. 5.

(23) See for example Zygmunt Szeliga, 'W dwa ognie' in Polityka, no. 46 (1489), 16 November 1985, p. 5; see also Financial Times, 28 February 1984, 18 July 1984, 17 September 1985 and 24 September 1985.

(24) S. Podemski, 'Sad najwyzszy o konflikcie w "Elanie"' in Polityka, no. 19 (1514), 10 May 1986, p. 10.

(25) The Guardian, 3 May 1985; Financial Times, 2 May 1985.

(26) See for example Adam Michnik, 'List z Kurkowej' in Aneks, no. 38, 1985.

(27) This is Lech Walesa's view; see Financial Times, 17 September 1983.

6 Reality versus theory in the Yugoslav self-management system

MICA JOVANOVIC

Self-management was introduced into Yugoslav society in 1950, just five years after the end of World War Two. The kingdom of Yugoslavia emerged from the war in 1945 as a socialist country but with a completely destroyed economy. Was it justifiable to introduce self-management only five years after the war into a system which was totally disorganised both economically and socially? We will try to answer this question in the following pages.

DEVELOPING WORK INCENTIVES IN THE SELF-MANAGING ECONOMY

From the very beginning, the practice of self-management in Yugoslavia belied theoretical assumptions to a large extent. The reason for this can be found in the fact that three basic conditions for establishing such a system were not fulfilled either then or later. First, a developed economic foundation did not exist. Second, the working class's revolutionary consciousness was at a very low level. Despite the fact that a good part of the working class carried on its shoulders the weight of armed revolution which was a war of liberation from fascism, this proletariat was very poorly educated ideologically speaking and many of them did not know what they were fighting for. Third, in Yugoslavia there is no traditional work ethic. Great Britain has its Protestant work ethic according to which the basic assumptions are that the need for autonomy and personal success are satisfied through work; Hinduism teaches that work is the individual's obligation towards others

----

* The author would like to thank Prof. V. C. Fisera for his editorial assistance.

(family, friends, relatives, etc.), and Confuscianism recommends a rigid society with a fixed hierarchy in which the individual is absolutely subordinated and loyal to the group. In this regard, Yugoslavia does not have any culturally prompted positive relationship towards work. Of these three preconditions, the last two were never fulfilled, so a system of work motivation was never clearly developed in Yugoslavia either theoretically or practically speaking.

Furthermore, economic planning as such cannot help here as it does not solve organisational problems such as those of the labour process. Of course, the work of organisations in different economic branches must be coordinated. Planning must be founded on some assumptions about productivity, and for this to be accomplished, employees must be motivated to work. However, the lack of motivational mechanisms, as mentioned above, results in economic planning becoming little more than an expression of official government aspirations.

In recent times, there has been an attempt in Yugoslavia to create a so-called 'socialist work morale' which is to be constructed largely through the conferral of awards, medals and public praise on the best workers. Moral motivation has a certain significance for both the workers and for society as a whole. However, real work motivation must be founded on monetary (material) rewards for the worker (or punishment for not completing work obligations). In the worker's consciousness, moral motives are often reflected as material ones. We were convinced of this by a conversation we had with P. Pavlovic, foreman in the Bor Flotation Mining and Smelting Corporation (1). The conversation, which in some respects resembles the famous conversation between F. W. Taylor and Schmidt (pig-iron handler) (2), went like this:

We have been informed that you were decorated with the 'Decoration of Labour with Golden Wreath'. How did this recognition affect you regarding devotion to your job?

Yes, I received the Decoration. I feel that I deserved it because I was a very industrious worker. After receiving the Decoration I felt that I should work even harder in order to confirm and justify it.

Is that the only reason you worked better and harder?

Well, not only because of that. After receiving the Decoration I felt that my superiors monitored my work with greater care and word went around the shop floor that preparations were being made to promote the best workers.

So, you saw your moral recognition together with greater devotion to your job as a possibility of getting promotion?

Yes. When I received the Decoration I was just a normal worker on the flotation mills.

And then what happened?

Well, as you can see for yourself, I was promoted and now I'm a foreman. I don't do the hard work on the mills any more. Now I just supervise and coordinate the work of other workers in the group.

What about your salary?

I got a rise of about 30 per cent.

When you heard you had received the Decoration, did you think that it might lead to a better job or to a better salary?

P. Pavlovic thought about this question. At first he tried to explain that the Decoration only had a moral motivational effect, i.e. that he was proud to have received it from the President of the Republic. However, he finally admitted that the first thing that came to mind was a better job and better pay.

It is clear that moral motives are transformed into material motives. On the other hand, material incentives are reflected in the worker's consciousness as status symbols. A higher salary means a better social status as well. So it is no wonder that in enterprises a merciless battle is fought among the workers themselves for every three dinars (3).

The workers' standard of living in Yugoslavia is in constant decline. This is due to extremely high inflation (over 100 per cent in 1985) and very low labour productivity. Production is stagnating and the workers, through self-management decisions, try to keep up with inflation through enormous salary increases (even as much as 70 per cent a year). This results in a vicious circle where workers do not cover salary increases with increased productivity but with enormous increases in the price of their products. This, in turn, leads to even higher inflation. This makes the prediction of some Eastern critics of self-management, that "the workers will eat up the enterprises in Yugoslavia", an increasing reality. The problem of intensifying labour in Yugoslavia has its origins, as we have seen, in the actual production base of Yugoslav society, that is in the bad organisation of the entire Yugoslav economy.

Intensifying labour and increasing productivity, as we have already seen, are the basic problems of the Yugoslav economy and society as a whole. We have seen that the essence of the problem lies in the fact that Yugoslavia does not have a work ethic, or, according to some statistics, Yugoslavs do not like to work. Still, Yugoslavs are not lazy. This is confirmed by the extraordinary success of Yugoslav workers on work sites throughout the world, particularly in Western Europe. Does this mean that workers in Yugoslavia are not given the chance to show their work-oriented qualities?

Very frequently poor labour organisation or production capacities which have been built without a corresponding raw material base result in very low labour productivity, or in none at all. An example of this (and there are quite a few) can be found in the Obrovac Aluminium Plant near Zadar (4). This enormous industrial complex was built to extract aluminium ore, enormous amounts of money were invested, many workers were hired. Unfortunately, these workers had nothing to do - their productivity was zero. The reason: an incorrect estimate of the aluminium ore deposits, i.e. quantities were negligible and the aluminium plant stopped working before it even started.

In the end, it is the economic system which is the essential factor in labour productivity, both for individual and for total social reproduction. The worth of an economic system can best be tested by how much it stimulates the employable members of society to work and creativity. So what is the worth of the Yugoslav economic system according to these criteria? Labour productivity, as the most important qualitative factor in the economy, has declined considerably during the past decade compared to previous years (5). At the same time, inflation and unemployment have reached record levels and Yugoslavia's foreign debt has become enormous. The causes behind such unfavourable trends can be found primarily in an unstimulating economic system which did not succeed in 'coercing' employees to maximum work and creativity.

One explanation for the very low efficiency of the Yugoslav economic system is that it is an 'economy without coercion', an economy which displays an absence of objective criteria in the decision making process. There has been an erroneous assumption that workers, based on their own consciousness and without operationally established, rational criteria will make correct decisions and choose the best possibilities. This general assumption has resulted in numerous mistakes in specific sectors of socio-economic life (6). To mention the most evident: splitting the unified Yugoslav economy into six republican economies (7); atomising the economy into its lowest units called basic organisations of associated labour (8) (which is contrary to the modern economic law of concentrating and centralising the means of production and production itself); curbing rational market operations and abandoning the concept of a 'market-plan' economy, while introducing the concept of an 'agreement economy' in which the mechanism of agreement and understanding gives the integral system its characteristics along with a low level of responsibility, work and technological discipline.

What would be rational market operations? The market determines the structure of production and makes an efficient allocation of production factors and production processes. It offers objective criteria for determining the value of labour. By making a sharp distinction between work and idleness, it strongly encourages healthy competition between manufacturers and a constant rise in labour productivity. In this manner, it stimulates work and creativity as the real values of every society, regardless of the nature of social relations. Setting up homogeneous products at a uniform price, the market informs manufacturers that greater productivity and efficiency along with a better market orientation is the only way to be better than the others and to achieve better business results. Based on its objective standards, the market dispenses economic justice and makes a progressive differentiation between manufacturers. This is done without any administration and external control. For this reason, in the words of Z. Pjanic, it is the "cheapest and most suitable mechanism" (9). Yugoslavia, unfortunately, does not really have such a mechanism.

THE EXPLOITATION OF LABOUR IN THE SELF-MANAGEMENT SYSTEM

The exploitation of labour is a phenomenon which, according to Marx, is typical of capitalistic systems. Classical Marxist theory recognises exploitation in relations between the bourgeoisie which is the owner of the means of production (but does not work with them) and the proletariat which does not own the means of production (but works with them).

The proletariat works for wages which are determined by the owner of the means of production. However, these wages are far below the value of the real labour the worker expends in production. In this manner, the worker does not possess either his labour or the results of his labour, i.e. the worker is exploited by the capitalist. However, the proletariat's consciousness changes, the forces of production develop and come into sharper and sharper conflict with backward, conservative production relations which encircle them like a hoop. When the hoop of conservative production relations becomes too tight for the developed, progressive forces of production, the hoop bursts and a social revolution occurs.

This is how Marx, in his time, saw the relationship between the bourgeoisie and the proletariat, the exploitation of hired labour and the victory of the socialist revolution. Accepting these views of his in today's world would be too fundamentalistic. However, in countries with so-called 'real socialism', and in Yugoslavia, the relationship between the proletariat and bourgeoisie today is still understood in this manner. Marxism in its original form is fostered from high school textbooks to the university. It is not understood that the relationship between the bourgeoisie and proletariat is increasingly losing the characteristics of a direct conflict and taking on much more complicated dimensions (which we will speak of later). In their blind loyalty to Marx's original principles, some Yugoslav theorists and politicians do not notice some of the weak points in their own socialism which are very similar to relations in systems with an expressed exploitation of labour. The situation is similar in the countries of Eastern Europe.

Let us take them in order. In the Soviet Union with its socialist system of a planned economy, a state-owned monopoly governs the means of production. The workers do not work with means of production which are owned by them (and Marx says that labour will only be liberated when the means of production pass into the hands of the proletariat). This means that workers in the Soviet Union do not own the means of production. Therefore, they cannot decide on the fate of their products, since the owners of the means of production, i.e. the state, decides that. So in the Soviet Union the state's relationship to the workers is the same as that of the bourgeoisie to the proletariat in countries with bourgeois democracies: it exploits them and their work.

In Yugoslavia, the means of production have been in the workers' hands since 1950 when self-management was introduced. Therefore, the workers have been self-managing (with variable success) for 36 years already. What went on during all that time, though? The workers, in general, make decisions concerning local questions, and the country's global economic policies are governed by politicians (not economists)! So for many years the monopoly of politics over economics has been created, developed and consolidated. And politics relates to Yugoslav workers just as the bourgeoisie in bourgeois democracies, and the state in countries with 'real socialism'.

Here is a more specific example of worker exploitation in Yugoslavia. We recently spent some time in the Automobile Factory in Kragujevac which is an example of the successful self-management organisation of the work process. This factory, as is well known, aroused international interest by winning over the American market with its Yugo GV model. At $3,990, the car was the least expensive model on the American market, and this prompted American journalists to write about "the Yugoslav worker's slave labour". We were particularly interested in labour on the assembly line as well as work and productivity motivation. After speaking to the workers, we talked with the union president, the president of the workers' council and one of the factory directors. When asked why the assembly line in this factory runs 10-12 per cent slower than the same assembly line in the Fiat factory in Turin, they explained that in the name of socialist humanism and the humanisation of labour, they did not want to exhaust the maximum bio-psychological and physical potentials of the workers. So while worker potential in Fiat is utilised at about 90 per cent, it is below 80 per cent in the Kragujevac factory. However, research has shown that the Turin worker is paid 87.3 per cent of his labour, while in the Yugoslav factory, this is only 45-50 per cent, in the words of those employed on the assembly line. So, is the worker exploited more if he uses 90 per cent of his potential and is paid approximately that much, or if he uses around 80 per cent and is paid for less than half? Of course, other elements concerning the worker's position in the two systems, such as job security, have been disregarded, but this does not undermine the validity of the basic point.

Certainly this assumption about the assembly line in the above factory is the fruit of local politicians' political demagoguery and not the idea of a rational economist. At the same time, this example indicates the dangerous effect that the monopoly of politics over economics has on the Yugoslav working class. And not only the working class, but on Yugoslav society and self-management as a whole.

THE CAUSES OF INDUSTRIAL CONFLICTS IN YUGOSLAVIA

At first glance, it appears that in Yugoslavia industrial relations conflicts do not arise for the same reasons as they do in Great Britain. It is assumed that conflicts (especially strikes) cannot appear in a society where the workers themselves are the owners. However, this theoretical assumption is very often disproved in practice.

The well-known Yugoslav theoretician E. Kardelj has talked about "conflicts in self-management interests" (10). He has divided these different interests, which continuously appear and clash, into three groups: partial (or personal), collective (or joint) and general (or social). Today, these interests are in total chaos in Yugoslavia. Interests within the same group come into conflict and those from different groups also clash.

In this sense, Kardelj's theoretical division has lost its direct relevance. According to him, partial interests are those shown by an individual worker in his basic organisation of associated labour. This would primarily be a battle for a better salary or for an apartment (11). Collective interests appear between different work groups in a basic organisation of associated labour. In the same vein, these interests are very apparent and very strained between basic organisations of associated labour which are a component part of a broader association of labour - the work organisation. Basic organisations of associated labour which make up a work organisation are usually technically-technologically united, i.e. they work together on prescribed production. Conflicts, however, do appear, when the joint product captures a market and it is necessary to divide up joint income in accordance with the basic organisations' share of manufacturing the product. Then workers in every basic organisation think that their contribution in manufacturing the joint product was greater than the contribution of other basic organisations of associated labour. Then conflicts arise along the lines of 'all against one, one against all' or 'every man for himself'.

General interests, or those that concern all of society, are a special case. These are interests which emerge from the republics and provinces that make up the Yugoslav federation, but instead of these different interests dialectically giving birth to one joint interest, the opposite has occurred - these different interests estrange republic from republic, republic from province, province from province. The root of the problem lies in unequal cultural, social or economic development. Yugoslavia is a small country (around 250,000 km²) of stark contrasts. For example, the highly developed republic of Slovenia, located in the north western part of Yugoslavia, has enjoyed an economic and social development similar to that of the modern nations of Western Europe, but only 200 miles south east we encounter at times almost a kind of medieval Islamic despotism (the republic of Bosnia and Herzegovina). Such differences in economic potential create permanent strains in relations between republics and make it impossible to coordinate interests. For these reasons it is very hard to reconcile the opinions of the representatives of the republics in the Yugoslav Parliament. Consequently, laws promulgated at the federal level are often not adopted or must wait several months before being adopted. This happened with the law which was supposed to regulate the use of foreign currency earned through exports.

Even though at first glance it might seem that these conflicts are general and occur in many systems, not just in the self-management system, the situation is rather more complicated. If we start from the top, i.e. with the interests of republics and province, we see that solving problems at this level through mutual agreements and reconciliation is practically impossible. Theoretically, self-management enables the equal and democratic solving of problems through agreements in the Yugoslav Parliament. However, in practice things are quite different. When months pass with a conflict between republics going unresolved, the government enters the picture. The conflict is resolved, not in a self-management way, but administratively through government involvement. This is happening more and more frequently in modern Yugoslav practice, and "neglect of self-management" is increasingly being spoken of. When self-management is incapacitated at the very top, the effects are soon felt at the base, in the basic organisation of associated labour, and by the shop floor worker. This results in a basic industrial conflict in Yugoslavia in which it is impossible for the worker to implement self-management. While in theory Yugoslav workers were given the right to self-management by the Constitution (1974), denying workers the right to self-management means making it impossible for them to make decisions regarding production and particularly regarding income.

A special restriction to self-management appears in the form of "party state socialism" (12). The Communist Party (League of Communists) is the only party in Yugoslavia. According to its programme, it is the vanguard of the working class, or the vehicle of the 'dictatorship of the proletariat'. Its purpose is to protect the interests of its working class. After all, a large part of the party's membership comes from the working class. However, party leaders are often singled out and set up as a force above society and above self-management. Consequently, these party leaders have neglected self-management and have started to make decisions regarding questions of production and the economy in general. Party interference in the economy is increasingly apparent, and the result of this is poor earnings. Poor earnings are negatively reflected on the worker's income, i.e. lower employees' standard of living. A conflict then arises between the worker and his own party. The party makes fewer and fewer concessions to the proletariat, and the conflict is most often solved by workers abandoning their party, disillusioned with it and with self-management. Since the League of Communists is the only party, workers who withdraw their membership have no other political organisation to turn to and therefore disperse, every man for himself, into unorganised opposition.

As far as direct industrial conflicts are concerned, things sometimes do not differ much from similar situations in industrial relations in Great Britain. In Great Britain, these conflicts are shifted from the field of direct clashes between employees and stockholders to clashes between unions (as champions of the worker) and management (as champions of the stockholders). Conflicts most often arise during collective bargaining, and the two sides lock horns over the size of wages, the introduction of new technology and the resulting job losses, etc. In Yugoslavia, management functions are in the hands of administrative bodies chosen by self-management. The manager's power is limited by the workers' council which is, formally, the highest self-management body. The attitude in industrial relations is analogous to that mentioned above in Great Britain: in the place of the British stockholders, the Yugoslav government (or the party, as already mentioned) increasingly appears. Management organs are champions of government-party interests. The workers are located on the opposite side. Their interests, if the analogy with British industrial relations were complete, should be protected by unions. However, according to the Yugoslav Constitution, unions are socio-political organisations and they often protect the party's interests rather than the workers' interests. So workers remain isolated while the government, party and management functions are often united - on the other side. Weakened by this factionalism of power, workers in the battle for self-management turn to the only weapon left to them - strikes.

THE (DECLINING) IDEOLOGICAL HOMOGENEITY OF THE WORKING CLASS

The question of the ideological homogeneity of the working class is central not only to Yugoslav society but to the entire international workers' movement (if it still exists at all). Modern world trends indicate that not all of Marx's 'prophecies' have been fulfilled. If we start from the first socialist revolution, we see that it was not achieved in a highly developed capitalist country, as Marx predicted, but in feudalistic czarist Russia which at that time (1917) did not even have much of an authentic proletariat. Its landless peasants escaped from the feudal estates and went to the city where they became an industrial proletariat with a still undeveloped class consciousness. Furthermore, Marx expected capitalism to collapse quickly. Today capitalism is still strong and dynamic and there is no sight of a world revolution. In addition, even though there are still no solutions to some of its historical questions, the proletariat holds a very good position in modern capitalist systems, with well-organised and specific political economic powers and a better standard of living.

Late capitalism, or neocapitalism, places new questions about the modern proletariat at the centre of the problem. The key question is: what is the workers' social movement and does it exist at all in an 'affluent society' such as the highly developed western societies? Who makes up the substratum class of that movement? Is it just industrial workers in the traditional, i.e. Marxist sense, or some other social layers structured by class in the era of the scientific-technical revolution? Who is the subject of the revolution, if it is at all possible to speak of revolution in the West? (13)

It is interesting to note the concepts of some neo-Marxist theoreticians and leftist theoreticians in the West concerning the question of the modern workers' movement. For example, H. Marcuse (14) developed the well-known and frequently disputed theory about the integration of the working class into the capitalist system and about revolutionary radicalism shifting to marginal, 'non-integrated' layers and groups. The working class, according to Marcuse, continues to be the main subject of the revolution, but it is not revolutionary. P. Sweezy holds a similar opinion. For him the belief in the revolutionary character of the working class is called "traditional orthodoxy" as the centre of the world revolution is being transferred to national-liberation movements in colonies (15).

It is interesting that views on the disappearance of the proletariat as a revolutionary subject gained particular strength at the beginning of the 1980s. André Gorz expounds the thesis that the working class in the modern world is in a deep crisis, that it has been left behind by history and is losing its centrality. According to Gorz, the workers' movement has fulfilled its historical role and is therefore leaving the historical scene. With this departure, Gorz (very Shakespeare-like) bids the proletariat "Adieu!" (16). The well-known French sociologist Alain Touraine holds an opinion similar to that of Gorz. He feels that the workers' movement is outdated. In its place appear new social movements such as the anti-nuclear movement, ecology movement, etc. (17).

The homogeneity of the proletariat in countries with 'real socialism' is provided by way of coercion. The proletariat in Eastern European countries did not achieve its historical aspirations to take over the means of production (although recently the new Soviet leadership has tried to make some changes in this regard). On the other hand, this proletariat has the assurance of a very high degree of social security (job security, assurance of an apartment, assurance of basic foodstuffs). However, this sort of 'equality in poverty' had a very bad effect on working class consciousness in these countries, especially in the Soviet Union. The working class there is not vanishing from the historical scene because it has fulfilled its historical role, but because its role is being taken over by the state through coercion. Aware of the fact that it has lost its place in society, the proletariat in these countries (with 'real socialism') is fragmenting, frequently escaping into apathy, alcoholism and other social deviations.

Changes in the structure and physiognomy of the Yugoslav working class have come about in a different way. It differs from both the Western working class and the Eastern working class.   The Yugoslav Constitution assures the right to work with socially-owned means of production and the right to self-management. This should make the Yugoslav proletariat ehe most revolutionary in the world. However, a permanent deterioration in the standard of living has provoked changes in the workers' consc- iousness and egoism, envy and distrust have replaced collectivism, solidarity and the work ethic. Workers have less and less confidence in their own party (the League and Communists) and in its leading, vanguard role.   Fewer and fewer join the Communist Party, and workers very often resign from the party, dissatisfied with their social and work status. So the League of Communists is losing its cohesive force in gathering together and organising workers. On the other hand, workers, weighed down by worsening living conditions, are "escaping" to non-productive professions, motivated by easier work, the possibility of avoiding work obligations and - the greatest paradox of all - greater earnings.   The working class is thereby evolving into a bureaucracy, vanishing from the scene as a revolutionary subject, and is starting to swallow up the income of its former comrades.

THE ROLE OF THE TRADE UNION IN YUGOSLAV SOCIETY

The trade union system in Yugoslavia is not organised as it is in Great Britain, where each 'craft' has its own union (transport workers' union, miners' union, textile workers' union, etc.). These British unions are associated into the Trade Union Congress (TUC).   Unions in Yugoslavia are divided according to geographical-political positions.   Thus, each work organisation has its own union which, according to the Consti- tution, is a socio-political organisation.   All unions (which, as we indicated, are not organised by industry) are associated into the muni- cipal trade union council of the territory in which they are located. At the same time, all trade unions within each socialist republic are associated into the trade union confederation of that republic.   The republic trade union confederations are associated into the Trade Union Confederation of Yugoslavia.

It is clear that Yugoslav trade unions have not been successful in freeing themselves from the crucial influence of politics on the econ- omy.   In Yugoslavia, when the basic interests of the working class are in question, the trade union does not appear as the champion of worker interests.   Unions often show a hypocritical dualism, formally (by Statutes) setting themselves up as the main champions the working class at the point of production in the battle to achieve its direct goals. However, de facto, they often protect the interests of local political groups, whether these be personal interests or the interests of the local administration and Party.

Article 46 of the Statutes of the Trade Union Confederation of Yugo- slavia, which determines the role and tasks of the trade union to pro- tect the workers' interests, has the effect of empty political slogans (18).   Above all, we feel that the tasks of the trade union are given too generally and formalistically.   In the same vein, we feel that the work style of the union leaders is such that they (the leaders) put themselves above and outside the interests of the working class in Yugoslavia.   This closed and isolated leadership, occupied with its partial interests and personal political goals, has left the workers to the favour and disfavour of an increasingly powerful bureaucracy.   So, in the crucial, decisive battles for self-management (and in a changed class structure where bureaucracy confronts the workers instead of the bourgeoisie), workers are left without leadership and their own organisation. This significantly decreases the proletariat's power as it often loses battles and positions and becomes the easy plunder of a strengthened bureaucracy.

Some efforts towards returning the trade unions to the workers were made at the Eighth Congress of the Serbia Trade Union Confederation (19). After critical statements by worker delegates which primarily spoke of the trade union leadership's incompetence in carrying out its tasks (from the problem of organising work in the factory to organising workers outside the factory), the trade union leadership acknowledged its mistakes and made proposals towards improving the work of the trade union. So, in his closing speech N. Filipovic, the newly-elected president of the Serbia Trade Union Confederation, said that:

> it is high time that the trade union leadership responded to the requests of its membership and changed its style, method and manner of work. The working class is looking for an efficient trade union and leadership that will know how to oppose the invasion of bureaucracy and deformations within its own ranks. The revolutionary organisation of the working class cannot withdraw before the increasing impoverishment of the economic basis of self-management, nor reconcile itself with the domination of partial interests, high unemployment, inflationary economic policies, decreases in the standard of living and other negative phenomena in society (20).

This promise from the trade union leadership, if fulfilled, will return the trade union to the workers. However, we should mention that in recent years we have often heard such promises which, to the misfortune of the Yugoslav working class, remained mere promises.

We spoke earlier.of the fact that workers manifest their dissatisfaction at being deprived of their right to self-management by the bureaucratic structure through strikes. Such situations lead to a historical paradox: the trade unions do not set themselves on the side of the worker, but on the side of the strikebreakers who appear in the form of individuals, bureaucratic groups, party bodies and even the workers' council. Of course, trade unions justify their opposition to their own working class by the so-called 'democratic resolution of self-management conflicts'. Workers in Yugoslavia do, however, succeed in most cases in achieving their demands through strikes. A solution to the trade union's position in Yugoslav society should be sought in freeing the workers' organisation from the hands of the political bureaucracy and returning it to the workers.

THE RIGHT TO SELF-MANAGEMENT IN THE 1974 CONSTITUTION

The right to self-management was given to the working class in the Yugoslav Constitution of 1974. This right resulted from the right to work with socially-owned means of production which the Yugoslav workers received in the 1950 Basic Law on the Management of State Economic Enterprises and Higher Economic Associations by Work Collectivities.

The Basic Principles of the 1974 Constitution say that man's position in the Yugoslav self-management society is founded:

on the social ownership of the means of production, which precludes the return of any kind of system which exploits man and which, by ending the alienation of the working class and working people from the means of production and other conditions of labour, ensures self-management by working people in production, in the distribution of the product of labour and in guiding the development of society on self-management foundations... (21).

These Basic Principles, when they speak of expanding human rights and freedom, say that one of the basic rights is:

the right to self-management, on the basis of which every working man, on an equal footing with other working people, is in control of his own labour, his own and collective interests, in control of the planning of social development, and wields authority and manages public affairs... (22).

This theoretically specially given right is reflected in practice like a face in a distorted mirror. The right to work with socially owned means of production is increasingly turning into the right to non-work with socially owned means of production. This is happening for two reasons: first because the political bureaucracy is usurping the right to self-management, as we already mentioned, and second, because of the low level of work consciousness among the disillusioned working class. Furthermore, the right to self-management is often transformed into the right to do nothing but manage - a large number of people manage and only a few work. Yugoslavia is an example of a relatively small economy with an enormous administration. The classical separation of management from day to day executive functions has come about in many Yugoslav work organisations. Self-management bodies, often in conjunction with local political structures, create a typical self-management "management" which uses pressure to direct and deform the decisions of legitimate self-management assemblies. In such a situation, workers are left with no alternative but to manifest their self-management position by resorting to unpunished non-work, low productivity and absenteeism.

When the Yugoslav self-management system was being constituted, it was impossible to see that the entire institutional system was a big illusion, since its point of departure is that there are ideal producers who will create an ideal system if they are given ideal theoretical hypotheses. This was a system "made for angels, not men" (23). Such a utopian system started to develop and then the government appeared with its restrictive measures. It was believed in Yugoslavia that such a system could survive. The right to work with socially-owned means of production and the right to self-management led the Yugoslav working class into self deception. Beguiled by these formal rights, the working class did not notice that it was increasingly falling prey to administration and to the government, so that the 1974 Constitution and the 1976 Associated Labour Act are a "great ideological rationalisation of the system of state socialism" (24). It is a fact that if self-management is established by decree at the highest administrative level, then it tends to become merely administrative, i.e. it negates itself. Self-management can only be created by the workers themselves, but under much more developed socio-economic and cultural conditions. Therefore, every right given by the government through its Constitution (even the right to self-management) inevitably protects primarily the interests of that government and not the interests of those to whom the rights were given.

A WAY OUT OF THE CRISIS

In conclusion, we ask "what is to be done?" A way out of the crisis could be sought in the following:

First: idealisation in economic and social life should be repudiated once and for all, and problems should be solved at a practical level. In the same vein, some fundamentalistic Marxist assumptions should be repudiated and more exemplary developmental directions should be sought for Yugoslav society. Worn-out theoreticians of self-management should be replaced; for years they have not succeeded in finding new development paths for Yugoslav society. New people should be brought in to replace them, with new ideas and a long view to the future.

Second: the principles of recall from duty should be reaffirmed with resignations and sanctions for incompleted tasks, from the lowest party-political structures to the highest government structures. Clans at the highest political levels must be broken up and inept politicians should be replaced along with all those who behave like Louis XIV and believe "après moi le deluge".

Third: stabilisation of the country's economy by establishing market laws in business operations. This can be primarily achieved by uniting the atomised Yugoslav economy. When market laws start to function, an equilibrium will also be established between production and consumption; productivity would increase and the rate of inflation would decrease along with it. This will have a positive effect on people's standards of living, on their work motivation and responsibility in the work process.

Fourth: development of a modern society founded on science which will be included in international exchanges of scientific, technical and technological experience and discoveries. Economic professionalism should once and for all replace politicisation and a new creative spirit should be developed in the new generations.

NOTES

(1) The conversation was held on 21 January 1986, after midnight, during the third shift, during the course of research into work motivation.
(2) F. W. Taylor, The Principles of Scientific Management, Harper and Brothers Publishers, London, 1947, pp. 44-47.
(3) In April 1986, the conversion rate was 510 dinars to the pound (£).
(4) Zadar is a city on the Yugoslav coast about 350 miles south west of Belgrade.
(5) Labour productivity (growth rate) in the public sector in Yugoslavia was:

1954-1965	3.6%	1971-1975	2.1%
1960-1980	3.1%	1976-1980	2.1%
1963-1970	5.0%		

(6)   See R. Marinkovic, Economic Systems and Productivity, Belgrade, 1984.

(7)   The Yugoslav federation is composed of six equal republics which have become so independent that they have created their own autonomous economies and completely destroyed the unity of the Yugoslav economy and market.

(8)   Basic organisations of associated labour are the smallest production-work units in the Yugoslav economy. They independently decide on production, appearing on the market and distributing income.

(9)   Z. Pjanic, Samoupravni privredni sistem, Belgrade, Radnicka Stampa, 1983, p. 234.

(10) See E. Kardelj, Pravci razvoja politickog sistema socijalistickog samoupravljanja, Belgrade, Komunist, 1977.

(11) Basic organisations of associated labour must purchase apartments and give them to their workers to use. However, there are many more workers than financial possibilities in the basic organisations of associated labour. Therefore priority waiting lists are formed for receiving an apartment and this results in fierce conflicts between workers.

(12) The author of this work first used the term 'party state socialism' at the yearly gathering of Yugoslav sociologists, December 1984, in Subotica.

(13) The problems and dilemmas of the modern workers' movement were excellently analysed by R. Kalanj in the preface to the Yugoslav edition of H. Braverman's Labour and Monoploy Capital, Zagreb, Globus, 1983.

(14) H. Marcuse, One Dimensional Man, London, Abacus, 1972.

(15) See P. A. Baran and P. Sweezy, Monopoly Capital, London, Monthly Review Press, 1966 and P. Sweezy and C. Bettelheim, On the Transition to Socialism, London, Monthly Review Press, 1971.

(16) André Gorz, Adieux au prolétariat. Au delà du socialisme, Paris, Editions Galilée, 1980.

(17) Alain Touraine, L'après socialisme, Paris, Bernard Grasset, 1980.

(18) 'The Trade Union Confederation of Yugoslavia, as the integral and broad class socio-political organisation of the working class:
           - fights to carry out the constitutional position of the working class and its leading role in society; to develop socialist self-management socio-economic relations; the unity of working class interests; fellowship, equality ...
           - fights for unity in the socio-economic and political system; a united market in the uniform economic area of Yugoslavia; constant development of the productive forces of society; an increase in production and labour productivity; consistent application of the principles of distribution according to labour and the results of labour; equalising development as an entity and the faster development of economically undeveloped areas of Yugoslavia;
           - participates in establishing the country's development policy; builds political relations ...; establishes the basis for solving questions dealing with improving and equalising work conditions and the workers' life ...'

(19) The Eighth Congress of the Serbian Trade Union Confederation was held on 10-12 April 1986 in Belgrade.

(20) The speech was published in the daily newspaper Politika on 13 April 1986.

(21) The Yugoslav Constitution, 1974, Second Group of Principles, p. 39.

(22) Ibid., p. 40.

(23) J. Zupanov, from an interview given to a reporter from <u>NIN</u>
magazine, Belgrade, 2 February 1986.
(24) <u>Idem.</u>

PART III
DEVELOPING
COUNTRIES

7 Economic crisis and stability of employment in the Brazilian motor industry

JOHN HUMPHREY

INTRODUCTION

At the end of the 1970s, the trade union movement in Brazil appeared to be on the way to a renewal of its strength following over a decade of harassment and state control. The trade unions had suffered from a top-down and bureaucratic structure ever since the 1930s, when Getúlio Vargas had recognised and formalised the union structure, but at the expense of its subordination to the Ministry of Labour. For twenty years after the war the costs of bureaucratisation appeared to be out-weighed by the benefits of access to state finance and support, but after the 1964 coup these benefits were lost. The unions found that the military government imposed severe restrictions on union activities and used the Ministry of Labour's extensive powers of control and super-vision to the full. Towards the end of the 1970s, however, there were clear signs of a union revival. Strong growth in the consumer durables and capital goods industries, combined with a degree of political liber-alisation created the conditions for a renewal of union activity, whose emphasis was as much from the bottom up as from the top down.

The so-called 'new trade unionism' became prominent in 1977 during the campaign against the erosion of wages, and it was firmly established as a political force by the strike movements of 1978 and 1979 (1). In spite of this, the new movement's gains were precarious. A ground swell of militancy over wages had taken both government and employers by surprise in 1978, but the prevailing legislation on labour and wages was merely rendered temporarily ineffective. All the legislation and the powers it gave to the state remained operative, and in 1979 and 1980 there were signs that the government was willing to take a hard line in response to the challenge posed by the new unionism. Into this situation burst the debt problem and economic crisis. Generally speaking, unions are severely weakened by economic crisis, and there were some reasons for believing that the incipient resurgence of union activity and organisation in Brazil would be halted and reversed by mass redundancies and unemployment. However, the unions and workers at the heart of the new trade union movement - in particular the Metal Workers Union of São Bernardo do Campo in the Greater São Paulo region and the workers in the major vehicle assembly firms - survived the economic crisis and emerged stronger in 1985 than in 1980. This paper will try to explain why this happened. It will start by examining the impact of the economic crisis and then consider the labour movement response to it. The concluding section will discuss the reasons why the workers in the motor industry were able to enhance their organisation in period of crisis, even though workers in other industries were less successful.

THE ECONOMIC CRISIS

The Brazilian economy, and in particular manufacturing industry, showed strong and sustained growth from the mid-1950s through to the end of the 1970s. The industrial boom which started in the fifties was interrupted by a short recession in the sixties, but growth was resumed in 1967 with the boom of the 'economic miracle' period (2). This growth was slowed, but not halted, by the oil crisis in 1973, which caused some economic problems in 1974. The government's response was to continue growth at all costs, taking advantage of the free availability of international loans to finance a major development of heavy industry. In other words, the government postponed the need for readjustment to a much higher price for oil and a significant deterioration in the balance of payments. The motor industry survived the oil crisis without major problems, since the government's strategy for reducing the cost of oil imports was not a cutback in vehicle use, but rather renewed exploration for oil, the development of alcohol as an alternative fuel and incentives for motor industry exports, which were designed to help offset the import burden incurred through motor vehicle construction and use. While the twenty per cent per annum growth rate of the miracle period could not be maintained, vehicle production still grew by 4.5 per cent per annum in the period 1974-1979 (3).

The government's view was that in a country with a rapidly rising population (and one could also add, a failing agricultural sector which the government did not have the political will to tackle), manufacturing employment could not be allowed to stagnate. In terms of output and employment the government's strategy worked right up to the end of 1980. In the three year period, 1978-1980, industrial output grew at an average rate of 7.2 per cent per annum (4), and on the last day of that year, the industrial census registered employment in manufacturing industry as being double what it had been ten years previously, and thirty-five per cent higher than it had been at the end of 1975 (5). However, this success was bought at the price of a rapid increase in external debt, held mainly by commercial banks. In 1979 and 1980 this debt became increasingly difficult for Brazil to manage. A rising level of debt to be serviced, combined with declining terms of trade, a further rise in the price of oil, and a sharp upward movement in interest rates left the country's external finances in a precarious state (6). The combined effect of the deterioration in the terms of trade and the rise in interest payments was equivalent to a loss of roughly five per cent of gross domestic product in the period 1979-1983.

The Brazilian government was forced to face up to these problems at
the end of 1980. In 1979 and 1980 interest payments on the debt totalled US $10.5 billion and the deficit on trade and services was a further
US $10 billion. At the same time, loans to the value of US $13 billion
came due for repayment (7). In return for massive injections of fresh
money, the commercial banks demanded credit restrictions and control of
government expenditure. The result was an immediate recession. 1981
was a bad year for Brazilian industry, with output down by 10.1 per cent
compared to 1980, as can be seen in Table 7.1. In 1982 output was
maintained at its new lower level, but even this was only a respite.
Brazil was still in need of large net inflows of finance, and following
the Mexican default in August 1982, no money was forthcoming at all from
commercial sources. At the end of the year, the Brazilian government
was forced to have resort to the IMF, signing an agreement on economic
policy which guaranteed at least two further years of recession, even
though the government failed to reach most of the targets agreed. Industrial output dropped a further 6.3 per cent in 1983 (8).

Table 7.1
Brazilian manufacturing production by category of use
annual rates of real growth
1980-1983 (%)

Use category	1980	1981	1982	1983
Capital goods	+ 6.5	- 19.0	- 10.8	- 20.2
Intermediate goods	+ 8.3	- 10.6	+ 0.4	- 3.0
Consumer durables	+ 10.7	- 26.3	+ 8.0	- 4.0
(Transport materials	+ 9.0	- 27.2	+ 6.7	- 8.8)
(Mechanical engineering	+ 15.3	- 16.2	- 15.2	- 11.3)
Consumer non-durables	+ 5.2	- 2.9	+ 1.8	- 5.2
Total	+ 7.6	- 10.1	+ 0.1	- 6.3

Source: Relatorio do Banco do Brasil, 1982 and 1983.

The decline in industrial output was far from evenly distributed
across industry. While the output of consumer non-durables declined by
only 2.9 per cent in 1981, output of capital goods fell by 19.0 per cent
and consumer durables by 26.3 per cent. The crisis, therefore, was
particularly severe in heavy industry and in the Greater São Paulo
region, where such industries were disproportionately located. The fall
in output hit those industries, such as the motor industry (which forms
the major part of the transport materials sector) and mechanical engineering, where the new unionism had begun to flourish. The impact on
employment was immediate and severe. In the Greater São Paulo region,
employment in manufacturing industry continued to grow during the whole
of 1979 and up to October 1980, when it peaked at 162.0 per cent of its
December 1970 level (9). From this point on, it fell rapidly. By April
1981 it had fallen to a level of 151.0, and six months after that it
reached 139.4. During 1982, the decline stabilised somewhat, with the
index registering 135.0 at the end of the year, but the new round of

austerity measures adopted after the IMF was called in produced a further drop in employment to 121.1 by the end of 1983. This was twenty-five per cent below the peak reached thirty-eight months earlier (10).

In the motor industry, the fall in output and employment was much more sudden and violent, although once the initial crisis had passed the industry stabilised. In spite of a significant increase in the export of built-up vehicles, which rose by 56,000 units or 36 per cent, the industry faced a sharp decline in demand for vehicles. Domestic sales fell by 400,000 units in 1981, and as a result output fell by one third in 1981, a drop of 384,000 vehicles, although in 1982 and 1983 110,000 of this loss was recuperated (11). Employment in the major vehicle assembly firms located in the state of São Paulo (which means predominantly in the Greater São Paulo region) also fell sharply. Employment in the six major assembly firms dropped by nine per cent in the six months following the peak level registered in January 1981, and by a further fourteen per cent in the second half of the year. After this dramatic shake-out, employment stabilised in the following two years, rising gently in 1982 and falling equally gently in 1983 (12). However, 1981 was a traumatic time for the industry, and not least for its workers who had just begun to win some greater degree of power within the major plants and who had enjoyed a long period of near uninterrupted growth.

THE UNION RESPONSE

Would the workers and unions in the motor industry be capable of coping with the effects of the economic crisis? At the time of the crisis, a number of plausible arguments of both a structural and conjunctural nature were advanced which suggested that workers and unions in Brazil would be ill-equipped to cope with the effects of the crisis. In consequence, a retrocession in workers' organisation, particularly at plant level, might have been expected. Structurally, most unions in Brazil had had little time between the onset of liberalisation in 1977-1978 and the start of the economic crisis in 1981 to develop the kind of rank and file organisations which might survive mass redundancies. Historically, the unions had been tied to the state and financed by a levy on workers administered by the Ministry of Labour. Even in the Populist period prior to the military coup, they had been top heavy, bureaucratic organisations, and following the coup their welfare work had been encouraged while their organisational and representative work had been curtailed. In spite of the challenge to the union structure posed by the strikes in 1978 and 1979, no reforms had been introduced by the government.

In fact, Almeida's analysis of the strike movements of 1978 and 1979 led her to believe that the unions were not even moving in the right direction:

This decisive push from the rank and file (in 1978) led people to believe that even if workplace organisations which would transform the nature of the official trade unions did not actually exist, then they were at least a possibility. The pattern of strikes in 1979 went against these expectations in large measure. In relation to the labour movement, the strike movements gained in amplitude but were again centralised in the unions. The rank and file organisations did not develop as centres of command and decision, and the trade unions took up their central place again, even when the struggle took place largely without their presence (13).

In other words, the strike wave of 1978 had not proved a serious challenge to the centralised and bureaucratic structures of Brazilian trade unionism, and the strike wave of 1979 confirmed the importance of unions and union leaderships in strike activity. At the same time, the predominance of wage issues in both union demands during collective bargaining and in the final agreements made with employers seemed to indicate that the new strike movements after 1977 had not succeeded in enlarging the sphere of negotiated items (14). A widely held view of employers at the time was that unions were incapable of mobilising workers on matters other than wages (15), and it was felt that the widespread struggles and mobilisations of workers seen in 1979 had been due largely to the failure of the government's wages policy to accompany an acceleration in inflation. With the introduction of a new wages policy in 1979, which gave particular emphasis to realistic wage rises and extra pay for low wage workers, both the employers and the state expected worker mobilisation to be defused and militant leaders to be isolated from the rank and file. Without the wage issue, it was thought, unions would be poorly placed to develop demands at plant level, and in relation to redundancies and lay-offs no mobilisation would be possible.

For the workers in the motor industry, there were also conjunctural reasons for some pessimism concerning their ability to fight back in the face of mass sackings. With the long established labour system still intact, the Ministry of Labour had the right to supervise union finances, regulate their constitutions and suspend or dismiss leaderships which, in the Ministry's opinion, were not pursuing the interests of their members. Given that strikes were still illegal, the Ministry had the formal power to take over direct control of any union which supported or organised strike action. In 1978, taken somewhat by surprise by a sudden burst of strike activity which occurred mainly at plant level, the Ministry had not intervened, but as Almeida correctly noted (16), the Ministry of Labour began to resume a more interventionist and aggressive policy towards the unions in 1979. The most dramatic results of this change in policy were seen in the motor industry. The largest employers in the Brazilian motor industry were concentrated in the São Bernardo area of Greater São Paulo, and the metal workers union in the area represented workers in their plants. In 1979, the union's officials were temporarily suspended and its administration taken over by the Ministry of Labour after a fourteen-day strike (17). In 1980, the union came under Ministry intervention again after a forty-day strike in which the union and the government fought out a political battle. At the end of 1980, then, the union's elected leaders had been barred from office, and its affairs were in the hands of officials from the Ministry of Labour. The union was still waiting for the Ministry to appoint a committee of workers to run it until such time as fresh elections for an executive could be held.

Even worse, some of the major industry employers seemed to be taking full advantage of the union's difficulties. Some of them had sacked many rank and file militants and former union directors after the 1980 strike, while Volkswagen went a step further by announcing an employee representation scheme in September 1980. It was aimed at undermining

the union's support in the plant by providing an alternative framework
for employee-management relations, and it was explicitly designed so as
to keep it out of the control of union sympathisers in the plant (18).
The new employee representation committee had seventeen representatives
at Volkswagen's São Bernardo plant, of whom three were salaried and
fourteen hourly-paid. Seven of the hourly-paid were to be non-unionised
and seven unionised. Given the low rate of unionisation among salaried
staff and the restriction of candidature to workers with at least five
years seniority, a non-union majority on the workers' side of the committee was almost guaranteed. Even so, the firm took no chances. The
committee's role was defined as one of "co-ordinating the relationship
between employees and the firm" and it was primarily to inform management of worker opinion. Management had a majority on it, reserved the
right to call meetings and set agendas and the company had the power to
change or suspend the system at any time.

These circumstances were hardly the most propitious for confronting
the challenge of mass redundancies. The union's elected leaders had no
access to its funds or facilities, and the rank and file had been weakened by the employers' offensive following the 1980 strike. It might
have been reasonable to expect a very limited worker response to the
onset of the crisis. Big falls in employment could have led to the
total disarray of workers' organisation within the plants, the selective
dismissal of activists, a climate of fear and oppression within the
plants of a type not seen since the early seventies, and a major drive
to cut costs and increase productivity by management. The time could
not have been more favourable for management to do it. However, matters
turned out rather differently. The employers did manage to shed a lot
of labour in the course of 1981, but it was done with some difficulty
and with a rather different result for rank and file organisation at
plant level than might have been expected.

The first sign of resistance to mass redundancies came in April 1981
at Volkswagen. From January to March, VW had already cut back its
labour force from 46,000 to 38,000, and in April it proposed to reduce
labour costs further by cutting both hours of work and wages by twenty
per cent. Such a change required the consent of the union, as it meant
a change in employment contracts within the period of a legally binding
contract, and by this time the union had been handed over to a group of
workers appointed by the Ministry as an interim administration in advance of fresh elections. Not being able to find any group of workers
willing or able to take over the union which was not sympathetic to the
deposed leadership, the Ministry had been forced, in effect, the cede it
to that leadership. Although the newly formed employee representation
committee at VW produced a petition with 22,000 names in favour of the
company's proposals, the union organised a ballot which produced a two-
to-one majority against it. Volkswagen then threatened 5,000 redundancies, but it was forced to retreat following both opposition from the
union and a hostile reaction from the government. After a meeting with
the Brazilian President, the head of Volkswagen do Brasil announced the
suspension of the redundancies on 6 May (19).

Following trouble at the Fiat plant in Rio de Janeiro, the next major
confrontation took place at Ford's São Bernardo plant in July. This
plant had been a traditional centre of union militancy in São Bernardo
from even before the 1964 military coup, and it was considered to be the
best organised of all the major motor factories in the region. Ford had

124

cut its labour force by about 1,000 (or five per cent) in the first half of the year, and on 21 July a further 400 workers were summarily dismissed. Immediately, the whole plant went on strike, demanding the readmission of the sacked workers. The strike lasted for six days, and although the sacked workers were not taken back by the company, a number of significant gains were made. Firstly, a strike committee which was formed during the dispute was recognised provisionally by the company and its members guaranteed stability of employment. Secondly, the workers in the plant were given a guarantee that they would be paid up until the end of the year. Any workers sacked by the company before 31 December would receive pay up to 30 November and one month's pay in lieu of notice. Thirdly, the company agreed to open a list of voluntary redundancies so that those wishing to leave the plant could obtain enhanced severance pay. At first, this agreement did not prevent reductions in the labour force. The Ford work force (in the state of São Paulo as a whole) was cut by 1,200 in August, including 490 workers sacked at the São Bernardo plant and paid five month's wages, but late in August pressure from the work force obliged the company to stop this. From the end of August through to the end of the year the company's São Paulo labour force remained virtually constant (20).

July and August 1981 proved to be the turning point for the workers in the large vehicle assembly firms. From September onwards, mass sackings ceased, and in August the workers regained full control of their own union, when new elections produced an overwhelming victory for the candidates linked to the leadership deposed by the Ministry of Labour the previous year. At the same time, the recognition of the factory committee at Ford and the start of negotiations between the company and the new union leadership over the formation of an elected plant committee with strong union links marked a major extension of union organisation into the plants. The factory committee introduced at Ford early in 1982 was a major breakthrough for the union because it constituted a clear recognition by management of the union's right to be involved with the day to day running of the plant. In effect, management recognised that the plant could not run without some accommodation with the union, and this recognition involved the workers' elected representatives having an input in such matters as the disciplinary procedure. Compared to the situation in the seventies, when management had almost totally unbridled power, the new committee was a major advance. It allowed the union both to further extend its power within the plant and to establish a new base line for negotiations with other companies. After a considerable struggle, the union was able to force Volkswagen to abandon its own employee representation scheme late in 1982 and substitute it with a similar factory committee to that introduced at Ford.

These gains did not by any means signal the end of the difficulties facing the union. When the government was forced to have recourse to the IMF at the end of 1983, wage restraint was introduced in order to counter inflation and increase Brazil's export competitiveness. New legislation aimed to restrict rises in wages to twenty per cent below the rate of inflation, and with inflation running at about 200 per cent per annum, this would have meant falls in real wages of approximately thirteen per cent for most workers. There was considerable opposition to this legislation in Congress, and also by unions. In July 1983 the Metal Workers of São Bernardo again found themselves under Ministry of Labour intervention as punishment for the union's role in trying to organise a general strike against IMF policies, but in the larger firms strikes and disruption forced employers to concede larger wage rises than those allowed for by law in October 1983 and April 1984. The wage contention policy was neutralised, even though the unions could do little to offset the effects of mass unemployment on wage levels generally.

The development of factory committees meant a major gain for the union and a considerable advance in workers' power within the plants. At Ford, for example, the development of a formalised grievance procedure with factory committee and union representation secured one of the major demands of the late seventies, control over the arbitrary and repressive power of first-line supervisors. However, there were new demands to be pursued as well. Having recovered from the severest impact of the recession, the workers in the motor industry gave increasing attention from the end of 1983 onwards to the question of protecting levels of employment and creating new jobs. There were three main strands to this campaign. Firstly, the union and the factory committees remained firmly opposed to any fresh dismissals, and this forced a considerable degree of circumspection upon management. At Ford, for example, nearly 3,000 workers whose work had disappeared when the tractor plant in São Bernardo had closed at the end of 1982 were kept on the company payroll for over three months until the expansion of car production could absorb them into the main plant. In other companies, too, when work force reductions were required, firms asked for volunteers and offered enhanced compensation, rather than resort to sackings.

The second main strategy to protect employment was a campaign against overtime. The developing strength of factory committees in the larger plants such as Ford and Volkswagen meant that campaigns to stop overtime could be organised. With the slow recuperation of production in 1982 and 1983, the companies wanted to increase overtime so that production would be raised at minimal cost and without any hiring of workers who might be difficult to shed at a later date. Initially, the union negotiated higher overtime premiums in order to increase the cost to employers (21), but later workers in various plants tried to prevent overtime altogether through overtime bans and refusals to negotiate the shift changes necessary to accommodate increased overtime. At Ford's Ipiranga truck plant the company was forced to hire 500 assembly workers because of a ban on overtime. At the São Bernardo car plant, management spent a large part of 1983 trying to negotiate approximately thirty hours per month overtime in the engine plant, including working on alternate Saturdays. Failing to obtain no more than half the desired overtime, the firm hired 300-400 new workers working a six-day week (22). Similarly at Volkswagen a campaign against overtime by women sewing machinists forced the company to hire seventy new workers in August 1984.

The third main strategy adopted by the unions for reducing unemployment was to cut the working week, which stood at forty-eight hours in most factories. In August 1983, the founding conference of the CUT, the new union confederation, started its list of campaign priorities with unemployment, followed by stability of employment, the working week and a reduction in overtime. Only after these four items came items relating to wages, public sector workers and state companies (23). One year later, the demand for the forty-hour week was top of the list, followed by wage rises at three-monthly intervals and unemployment pay. At least some unions were capable of taking up non-wage issues, such as employment, sackings and hours of work. In the 1985 wage campaign the

Metal Workers of São Bernardo, together with other metal working unions, placed a reduction in the working week at the top of its agenda. The main demand was for a cut in the working week, without loss of pay. The auto industry employers refused to concede this, even though more than fifty smaller firms in the São Bernardo area signed agreements with the union which reduced the working week from forty-eight to between forty and forty-five hours. But even the motor industry employers began to make concessions after the strike had ended. Volkswagen signed an agreement in May 1985, shortly after the strike had finished, which reduced the working week and moved from two-shift to three-shift working. Those continuing to work two shifts would have their working week reduced by seventy minutes without loss of pay, while those transferring to three shifts (approximately two thirds of the work force by September 1986) would work 43.5 hours and be paid for 48. The result according to the union's leaflet for workers would be an increase in employment of 9,000 up to September 1986. The union stressed to workers that the 'sacrifice' of three-shift working was necessary to create jobs for those without work, and the new deal was approved in a ballot. In the course of 1985 other major employers in the motor industry entered into negotiations over shifts and manning.

THE BASES FOR WORKERS' RESISTANCE

By 1985, then, it was clear that workers' organisation in the motor industry had been strengthened rather than weakened by the crisis. Mass redundancies and the crisis had provided a major impulse towards increased organisation and an extension of the areas of negotiation in which significant successes could be gained. The fact that the onset of crisis appeared to give the struggle for workers' organisation at plant level a boost rather than set it back can be explained quite simply once the situation in the motor industry is examined carefully. In spite of the fact that this trend took some writers and also possibly some employers by surprise, the ability of some unions to mount sustained campaigns on non-wage issues was already apparent early in 1981.

Workers were certainly capable of organising and taking industrial action on the issue of redundancies. While wage questions were a major issue for Brazilian trade unions, in the course of the 1970s the unions began to raise other issues. In many cases, they were not able to win major concessions, and some issues were not suitable for the annual negotiations, but the items were placed on the agenda. Of particular importance in the motor industry were the struggle against so-called 'rotation' of labour, the policy of hire and fire used by the assemblers in the seventies (24), the demands for an increased union presence at plant level through union delegates and plant committees, and the campaign launched against the abuse of power by first-line supervisors. By 1980, these campaigns had gained considerable momentum, mainly through networks of union sympathisers in the plants and the extensive use of broadsheets and leaflets targeted at specific firms and departments.

Clearly, the large cut-backs in labour which began in the first half of 1981 provided a significant threat to the gains which had been made in all three of these areas. Labour turnover in the auto industry had been reduced after the first strike wave in 1978, and workers had begun to feel more secure, but in 1981 this security was threatened by mass redundancies. In terms of wages, this was the biggest threat possible to workers' wages and prospects. At the same time, large scale sack-ings threatened the union's organisation in the plants, because manage-ment could use cut-backs as a means of weeding out the workers who had been most troublesome, or most supportive of the union. Similarly, at a time of major work force reductions the scope for arbitrary and discrim-inatory use of power by the supervisors was quite extensive. When cut-backs are made, the supervisors usually indicate which workers in a particular section or department are to be sacked and which should remain, and when sackings are made by the thousand there is little control over their selection. This much was conceded by a personnel manager in a large electrical company, who said that when the firm sacked more than 3,000 workers in the space of six months it was imposs-ible to check the criteria used by the supervisors (25). For all these reasons, unemployment and mass sackings were crucial issues for workers in the motor industry. The basic gains of the previous three years appeared to be under attack. In the short term, some mobilisation could have been expected.

However, it was less clear that such mobilisation could be translated into a permanent strengthening of the union and its rank and file base. While the continuation of the political liberalisation process and the emergence of new political parties provided a climate which was more helpful to unions than that existing for most of the seventies, the ability of unions and workers in large plants to survive the impact of the crisis was by no means a foregone conclusion, as is shown by an evaluation of three strikes over redundancies in the city of São Paulo (26). It shows that in three large plants in one of the industrial zones of the city in 1982, strikes in response to sackings did not lead to long term gains for workers, either in terms of organisation or in terms of employment. Strikes and stoppages over dismissals could pro-duce temporary gains, such as stability of employment for three months, but sackings were renewed later and the factory committees which emerged from the initial struggles were victimised and then forced out of exis-tence. The militants did not have a strong enough base within the plants or enough support outside to survive.

Comparing São Paulo with the success of the Metal Workers' Union in São Bernardo, three reasons seem to account for the difference. First-ly, and probably most importantly, the plants in São Paulo had little history of worker organisation, and so the workers had to start almost from the beginning. The Metal Workers' unions in São Paulo had not actively organised workers in the plants prior to 1981, partly because of the size and diversity of the category. The workers in São Paulo were geographically distant from the union's nearest office and had little contact with it. What little organisation existed in the plants was not linked to the union at all. In São Bernardo, the union was still well placed to oppose the 1981 sackings, in spite of the Ministry of Labour's intervention in the previous year. Instead of disappearing into limbo after the intervention - the normal fate of deposed union leaderships - the executive had set up a strike fund and continued to organise from temporary premises, using the networks created from 1977 to 1980. The shift in the focus of strike activity in 1979 noted by Almeida (27) did not signify any let-up in the development of rank and file organisation in São Bernardo, either before or after the 1980 intervention. Bulletins, pamphlets and meetings remained frequent. There was no alternative leadership for the union, and the Ministry of Labour recognised this fact early in 1981, when they appointed an interim executive whose allegiance to the deposed leaders was made explicit from the start. During the Ford strike in July 1981, the firm negotiated with Luis Inácio da Silva (Lula), the former president of the union, even though he had no official position whatsoever. The employee representation scheme at Volkswagen should also be seen in this light. It was a tribute to the continuing strength of the union that after a failed forty-day strike in April 1980 and the Ministry's intervention, the largest firm in the industry should feel obliged to find a positive alternative to the union's influence within the plant itself. As one of the firm's senior personnel managers made clear, the union's campaign against the supervisors had seriously eroded their authority, and a counter to the union's in-plant organisation was required (28).

Secondly, the union leadership in São Paulo had been in conflict with many of the activists in the plants, who represented conflicting political and union positions. Throughout the seventies, the leadership had been resisting attempts by the Metal Workers Opposition in São Paulo to depose it, and the main power base of the opposition was in the southern part of the city. Much of the organising in the larger plants had been done independently, or in opposition to, the leadership, which had little interest in devoting resources to build up a rank and file organisation which would be hostile to it. In São Bernardo, in contrast, the leadership retained strong links with the rank and file militants in the plants, which meant that there was no serious gulf between the first waves of protest against sackings which occurred within the workplace and the de facto leadership of the union. The São Bernardo union had managed to incorporate many of the leading militants into its ranks during the course of successive struggles. For the 1978 union elections, the President, Luis Inácio da Silva (Lula), renewed the union's executive with a winning slate of candidates which included some of those active in the 1977 wages campaigns. In preparation for the 1980 strike, efforts had been made to widen the group in charge and create much stronger and enduring channels of communication between the leadership and the militants in the larger plants.

Thirdly, the resistance to mass sackings and the success with which the union built up its in-plant organisation in São Bernardo was facilitated by the nature of the crisis in the motor industry. In the capital goods industry, output fell in 1981 and continued falling, while in the consumer non-durables sector output fell slowly at first but continued to suffer through to the end of 1983. In the motor industry, the collapse was sudden and sharp, but soon over. The worst had passed by September 1981, and although there was no significant recuperation of employment, the underlying situation was not too bad. The industry had invested heavily in the late seventies and the general strategy was to increase competitiveness and model ranges in the domestic market and export more parts and complete vehicles. At Ford, for example, this meant over US $300 million in investment, the introduction of the Escort model and an increase in plant capacity of nearly 100 per cent. Volkswagen, Fiat and General Motors also extended their model ranges significantly, introducing such models as the Santana, Uno and Cavalier. In the case of the São Paulo factories, the decline in employment was more pronounced and long term. As well as the effects of the economic crisis, the workers in two of the firms (in the electrical industry) had to deal with a partial shift in production from São Paulo to Manaus, which further undermined their bargaining power.

129

The economic crisis in 1981 might have led to a retrocession in rank and file organisation in the motor industry, and the events in São Paulo show how this might have happened. However, because of the underlying strength of the union, the centrality of the issues raised by mass sackings, the economic situation of the industry and continuing political liberalisation in Brazil, the workers in the motor industry had stronger plant organisation in 1985 than in 1980, before the crisis. This did not mean that their problems had ceased, as the Ministry of Labour's intervention in 1983 and the 1985 strike showed quite clearly, but neither event was a serious set back for the union. It remains to be seen, however, to what extent other unions can gain ground while the recession lasts.

NOTES

(1) For accounts of these strikes see John Humphrey, Capitalist Control and Workers Struggle in the Brazilian Auto Industry, Princeton University Press, 1982, chapters 6 and 7; José Álvaro Moisés, 'Current issues in the labour movement in Brazil' in Latin American Perspectives, no. 23, 1979; Maria Herminia Tavares de Almeida, 'Tendencias recentes da negociação coletiva no Brasil', paper presented to the seminar 'Movimientos Sociais e Relações de Trabalho', Belo Horizonte, December 1980.

(2) Accounts of economic development in post-war Brazil can be found in Francisco de Oliveira, A economia da dipendência imperfeita, Rio de Janeiro, Graal; Paul Singer, 'Evolução de economia brasileira: 1955-1975' in Estudios CEBRAP, 17, 1976.

(3) These figures are taken from the monthly bulletins of the National Vehicle Producers Association, ANFAVEA.

(4) Relação do Banco Central do Brasil, 1982.

(5) Censo Industrial, Brasil, 1970, 1975 and 1980.

(6) For a general account of the debt crisis in Latin America, see Martin Honeywell, 'The world debt crisis' in Latin American Bureau, The Poverty Brokers, London, Latin American Bureau, 1983. For more specific accounts of Brazil, see Albert Fischlow, 'Latin American external debt: the case of uncertain development' in M. Syrquin and S. Teitel (eds.), Trade, Stability, Technology and Equity in Latin America, New York, Academic Press, 1982, and also Paulo Davidoff Cruz, 'Notas sobre o endividamento externo brasileiro nos anos setenta' in A. Kageyama et al. (eds.), Desenvolvimento capitalista no Brasil, Rio de Janeiro, Brasiliense, 1983.

(7) Cruz, art. cit., p. 64.

(8) Relação do Banco Central do Brasil, 1982, 1983 and 1984.

(9) In the same month, transport materials sector employment peaked at 180.4 per cent of its December 1970 level.

(10) These figures are for manufacturing industry in the Greater São Paulo region. They were collected by the employers' federation, FIESP, collated by the state statistical agency, SEADE, and published in the Anuário Estatístico de São Paulo, 1981, 1982 and 1983.

(11) These figures on motor industry output were provided bu ANFAVEA and collated by SEADE.

(12) These figures on employment in the major vehicle assemblers were provided by the employers to the Ministry of Labour. They were collated by SEADE and published in the Anuário Estatístico de São Paulo. All subsequent employment figures for the large motor firms

130

are taken from the same source.

(13) Almeida, _art. cit._, p. 17.
(14) Ibid., pp. 26-30.
(15) Humphrey, _op. cit._, p. 196.
(16) Almeida, _art. cit._, p. 17.
(17) For a full account, see Humphrey, _op. cit._, chapter 6.
(18) Further details can be found in Humphrey, _op. cit._, pp. 202-203, and in John Humphrey, 'Changing patterns of industrial relations in the Brazilian auto industry', _Actes de GERISPA_, 6, 1984.
(19) Further details can be found in Humphrey, _op. cit._, pp. 205-206.
(20) Events were described in newspapers at the time, and also in José Carlos Aguiar Brito, _A tomada da Ford_, Petropolis, Vozes, 1983, pp. 39-59.
(21) According to the union's handbook on the settlement supplied to workers, up to thirty hours per month overtime on weekdays would receive a premium of thirty per cent, while more than thirty hours per month and any Saturday working would be paid at 150 per cent of the normal rate. Sunday working would be paid a double time.
(22) Information on Ford São Bernardo was provided by the industrial relations management, while for Ford Ipiranga the factory committee provided the information.
(23) Jornal do CUT, September 1983
(24) See Humphrey, _op. cit._, pp. 87-100.
(25) This much was openly admitted by the personnel manager of a large electrical firm in São Paulo, who said in an interview with the writer in 1982 that causes of apparent favouritism had been found when dismissals had been made, but that it was impossible to check properly.
(26) The information on the plants in São Paulo is taken from a discussion document prepared with and for some of the militants involved as part of their evaluation of the experience.
(27) Almeida, _art. cit._, p. 17.
(28) The manager made this statement in a seminar to the Associação Paulista de Administração de Pessoal in 1982.

8 Labour, the oil boom and economic recession in Ecuador

DAVID CORKILL

In common with trade unions in both the developed and developing worlds, Ecuadorian labour has been confronted with a new set of economic circumstances and political realities during the 1980s. Economic recession, the debt crisis, a decline in living standards and attempts to restructure the economy through the application of neoliberal, free market policies threatened to undermine the progress made by the Ecuadorian labour movement during the preceding decade. It will be argued that the impact of the economic crisis has been particularly damaging for labour in Ecuador because the trade union movement is still in the formative stage of its development and struggling to come to terms with rapid economic development, accelerated social change and long standing internal and organisational weaknesses.

The Ecuadorian labour movement ranks as one of the smallest and weakest in Latin America, a situation attributable in large part to the lack of industrialisation and the pre-capitalist, artisanal forms of economic organisation and activity. It is no coincidence that when revenues from the oil boom of the early 1970s began to be channelled towards the expansion of the industrial sector, the emergent working class found a political voice and attempted, as an interest group, to influence government policy-making. Nevertheless, despite the short-lived favourable economic and political circumstances, the advances made by the labour movement were circumscribed by factors which relate both to the nature and timing of the late industrialising process undergone by the Ecuadorian economy and the accumulated problems of factionalism, corruption and poor organisation which are features of its recent history.

This analysis of labour in Ecuador adopts, as far as possible given the exiguous literature and absence of monographic studies of particular industries (1), the 'multivariate approach' suggested by Ian Roxborough to account for the differences among Latin American labour movements (2). Consequently I shall focus on a number of variables which help to explain the weakness of labour in Ecuador: the role of the state in the economy, the structure and composition of industry and the labour market, the degree of homogeneity among the working classes and relations between the unions and the political parties. The focus will be on endogenous variables, which is not meant to imply that external factors are of secondary importance. Clearly the evolution of the Ecuadorian economy has been conditioned by its insertion into the world capitalist system, which has determined the character and extent of its 'dependent industrialisation'. The intention here is to underline the specificity of Ecuadorian development and the role of labour in that process.

THE STATE AND ECONOMIC DEVELOPMENT

Prior to the 1970s, the state played a minor role in the regulation of the predominantly agricultural economy dominated by the agroexporting interests of the coastal region and the landowners of the highlands whose production was oriented towards supplying the domestic market. The economic model, based on free trade and integration into the world market, limited state intervention to infrastructure development and the provision of incentives for export sectors. Favourable international market conditions in the 1950s and 1960s encouraged the state to promote agricultural production (bananas, cocoa, coffee and rice accounted for ninety per cent of export revenues in 1960) and begin a modest programme of import substitution industrialisation. The bureaucratic activities of the state began to expand under the military junta (1963-66) which introduced agrarian reform legislation and credit policies which stimulated agriculture-related industrialisation, especially milling, packaging and processing (3).

It is only when Ecuador enters the ranks of the oil exporters in the early 1970s that the revenues become available to pursue a concerted industrialisation strategy. From the outset of this new phase of development the state assumed a central role in the exploration, production and export of oil and the redistribution of the proceeds. The absence of an autonomous industrial bourgeoisie, the restricted internal market, the low productivity of labour and the high levels of unemployment and underemployment were all factors which obliged the state to invest heavily in the industrial sector. State policies were designed to provide protection for industrial enterprises and stimulate the development of new industries associated with the second phase of the ISI model (chemicals, electrical goods, motor car assembly, metals, etc.). Revenues from oil exports were channelled directly into industrial development: of the 1,416 million sucres invested by the CFN (Corporación Financiera Nacional) in 1978, ninety per cent went into the manufacturing sector. Foreign capital, attracted by the larger national and Andean markets, contributed US $325 million (1972-78) over sixty per cent of which was destined for industry, especially the food, drink and chemicals sectors (4). The stimulus afforded to industrial activity can be gauged from the following statistics: the total value of manufacturing output quadrupled during the first six years of the decade and 508 new firms were registered under the Industrial Development Law between 1970 and 1979 as a direct result of changes which encouraged the import of machinery and equipment, the export of industrial goods and new investment through a programme of tax exemptions and subsidies on credit provision and oil consumption (5). The manufacturing sector registered annual growth rates of ten per cent in real terms between 1972 and 1980 and employment in manufacturing grew at an average rate of 11.5 per cent between 1974 and 1978 (6).

The economy soon began to exhibit some of the negative effects of export-led late industrialisation and the contradictions inherent in the development model. The industrial sector manifested a high dependence on foreign inputs of capital and technology along with an overreliance on government protection in the form of tariffs, subsidies and prohibitions. The capital intensity of much of the investment meant that very little extra employment was generated in a labour-abundant economy and consequently the model demonstrated a low propensity to improve the living standards of the mass of the population (7). The new industries had been established at a time when optimism about the continued flow of oil revenues and the potential of the Andean Pact market was at its height. Unfortunately, little attention was paid either to the cost and quality competitiveness of the industrial exports or their vulnerability to fluctuations in external demand. The new investment also reinforced the tendency towards the concentration of manufacturing act'/ity in the two growth poles of Pichincha province (Quito) and Guayas province (Guayaquil) - in the mid-1970s 81.8 per cent of modern industrial enterprises were located here (8) - and therefore contributed to the acceleration of rural-urban migration trends which were imposing such severe pressures on the urban infrastructures (9).

By the second half of the 1970s, the economic model came under increasing strain. Inflation, escalating government expenditure and a downturn in the world economy exposed the anomalies and shortcomings in the military government's economic strategy. Only by borrowing heavily from abroad and thereby increasing external indebtedness and incurring crippling debt service repayments (22.9 per cent of total expenditure by 1980) could the extensive panoply of subsidies be sustained. In fact, by 1978 nearly half the central government budget was swallowed by tax exemptions and subsidies on domestic oil consumption, basic foods and credits (10). In any case, the subsidy programme of the 1970s favoured modern, capital intensive industries at the expense of small industry/ artisan production and benefited the urban middle and upper high income groups with a penchant for expensive imported goods, rather than addressing the problem of internal market constraints and social justice. This became even more overt as the mildly redistributionist aims of the first phase of military government (1972-76) became subordinated to the needs of the modern industrial/export sectors and concentrated on investment in the physical infrastructure: energy, communications and the development of natural resources.

By the late 1970s, Ecuador had confirmed the experience of many developing countries where industrialisation has not been matched by an equivalent expansion in employment. The concentration of investment in the capital intensive manufacturing and petro-mining sectors, to the detriment of artisanal and small scale industrial activities, which still contributed 66.7 per cent of total manufacturing employment in 1975, created a serious deficiency in employment creation (11). (See Table 8.1)

Table 8.1
Production and employment in manufacturing industry
by technology level (%)

	value of production		employment	
	1975	1980	1975	1980
Large firms	39.2	52.4	18.1	20.9
Small firms	42.1	32.4	15.1	21.0
Artisan	18.7	14.1	66.7	58.2

Source: Rob Vos, Industrialización, empleo y necesidades básicas en el
Ecuador, ISS-PREALC Working Paper no. 7, Quito, July 1984, p.60.

Inevitably the excess supply of urban labour added to unemployment and underemployment rates. Estimates vary as to the exact levels, but all the available evidence points to the magnitude of the problem. The National Development Council (CONADE) calculated unemployment at 8.7 per cent of the work force (180,000) and underemployment in urban areas at 45 per cent. In the rural areas the percentage of underemployed may be as high as 75 per cent, producing a combined urban/rural total of 1,300,000 (12). The unavailability of remunerative, productive employment has contributed to the rapid growth of the urban informal sector i.e. those working in petty services, domestics and the self-employed. Indeed the low level of labour absorption has increased the informal sector share in total urban employment from 45 per cent to over 55 per cent in 1980 (13). The situation is particularly acute in the marginal suburbs of Ecuador's largest city, Guayaquil, where perhaps as much as three-quarters of the occupied population is engaged in the informal sector.

MIGRATION AND THE LABOUR MARKET

The supply of labour was affected dramatically by the economic changes that followed the exploitation of oil reserves in the Oriente region of the country. The high population growth and accelerating rate of internal migration has transformed Ecuador into the most rapidly urbanising society in Latin America. Nevertheless, Ecuador still has one of the largest rural populations in the region and one of the highest annual population growth rates at 2.6 per cent. While the rate of population growth is declining (down from 3.3 per cent for 1962-74), urban areas have been growing at a rate of 4.8 per cent per year as migrants are attracted by higher income levels and job opportunities and 'pushed' by rural poverty and property concentration (14). One study estimated the average annual number of migrants at 73,000 for the 1974-82 period - more than double the figure for the 1960s - and another calculated urban population growth at 140 per cent in the two decades from 1960 to 1980 (15). Only as late as 1983 did urban population levels pass the 50 per cent mark. (See Table 8.2)

Roxborough has stressed that the previous experiences of the labour force - in this case an agrarian or provincial small town, non-industrialised background - affects the organisability of workers and circumscribes the possibility of collective action (16). Indeed the chief characteristic of both the rural and recently urbanised work force in Ecuador is its heterogeneity. The rural labour force was divided between the pre-capitalist (highland) and capitalist (coastal) sectors of

Table 8.2
Population
Urban/rural and literacy levels

	Total population (millions)	Urban %	Rural %	Illiteracy (age 15+, %)
1950	3.2	28.0	72.0	43.7
1962	4.6	35.6	64.4	32.5
1974	6.8	44.4	55.6	25.7
1982	8.3	48.7	51.3	16.7

Source: Jorge V. Alarcón, Transition, Growth and Basic Needs in Ecuador, ISS-PREALC Working Paper, no. 31, The Hague, October 1985, p.24.

agriculture and further segmented by ethnic, linguistic and regional differences which delayed the breakdown of traditional forms of social control. The belated penetration of capitalist relations of production into the countryside as a result of the Agrarian Reform and the modern- isation of agriculture in the 1960s did not convert the peasantry into a homogeneous rural proletariat. Some were proletarianised but others became marginal 'campesinos' and large numbers became temporary migrants working in the urban services and construction sector but maintaining their links with the rural economy (17).

While the oil boom of the 1970s generated temporary employment oppor- tunities in services and construction, labour absorption rates in the dynamic mining and manufacturing sectors remained low (only 0.4 per cent and 10.4 per cent of the work force was employed in these sectors in 1982 [see Table 8.3]). In fact, job creation has been most significant in the service sector: out of 490,000 jobs generated between 1972 and 1984, 280,000 were in services and the highest growth has been in the public sector where the expansion of public administration, state enter- prises, banking and education has provided opportunities for the ed- ucated and skilled and enlarged the middle income groups (18). Public

Table 8.3
Economically active population
by economic activity (%)

Sector	1962	1974	1982
Agriculture	63.0	52.9	42.5
Mining	0.2	0.3	0.3
Manufacturing	9.4	10.2	10.4
Electricity, gas, water	0.2	0.4	0.5
Commerce	5.8	8.5	9.6
Transport	2.5	2.5	3.7
Financial services	0.6	0.9	1.4
Services	13.2	14.8	21.9
Other	1.6	4.2	2.0
New workers	0.9	1.4	2.1
Total	100.0	100.0	100.0

Source: A. Gutiérrez, Labour Market Functioning, Employment and Basic Needs in Ecuador, ISS-PREALC Working Paper no. 13, Quito, August 1984, p. 2.

sector employment more than doubled between 1971 and 1975 to over 150,000 and totalled 271,966 or 22.9 per cent of the urban work force in 1982. Once again, the two metropolises of Quito and Guayaquil have benefited disproportionately from the growth of public sector employment (19).

WAGES AND LIVING STANDARDS

Despite the high economic growth rates registered during the 1970s, Ecuador has continued to suffer one of the highest concentrations of incomes in Latin America. Indeed the evidence suggests that growth has strengthened income disparities and led to a fall in the living standards of low income groups making Ecuador a country with "one of the highest incidences of non-satisfaction of basic human needs" (20). An urban household budget survey conducted in 1975 found that 38 per cent of income earners received less than the minimum wage which was, in any case, fixed below the poverty threshold (21). Demonstrably, minimum wage legislation has not benefited those employed in the sizeable informal sector and the self-employed. While the economy grew at an average rate of 7 per cent annually between 1970 and 1982 real wages increased at only 3.3 per cent and the minimum wage ('salario mínimo vital') registered only a 1.5 per cent annual rise in real terms (22). Productivity increases stayed ahead of wages in every year except 1979 and 1980 and wage costs as a component in the total cost of exported goods actually fell. (See Table 8.4) Such evidence can only lead to the conclusion that economic growth failed to augment the domestic market for manufactured goods and aggravated the inequalities between the richer segment of Ecuadorian society and the poor.

Table 8.4
Minimum living wage
1972-1983

| | Minimum wage Nominal | | Real terms | Wages as % | Inflation |
	Increase (sucres)	Index	Index	of GDP	rate %
1972	750	125.0	106.0	31.7	7.7
1973	750	125.0	94.4	29.2	12.0
1974	1000	166.7	102.1	27.0	22.7
1975	1250	208.3	111.3	31.2	14.4
1976	1500	250.0	121.0	31.8	10.1
1977	1500	250.0	106.9	30.0	12.9
1978	1500	250.0	94.3	29.8	13.1
1979	2000	333.3	113.2	29.0	10.1
1980	4000	666.7	202.9	33.3	12.8
1981	4000	666.7	176.8	31.5	14.7
1982	4600	766.7	158.2	29.1	16.4
1983	5600	933.3	121.8	24.1	48.1
1984	6600	1100.0	n.a.	n.a.	31.2

Source: Edgar de Labastida and Rob Vos, Los niveles de vida en los barrios populares de Quito y Guayaquil y la fijación del salario mínimo, ISS-PREALC Working Paper no. 8, Quito, August 1984, p. 31.

It should be pointed out that the economic elite and the agroexporting interests in particular have traditionally shown little interest in the creation of a modern consumer market in Ecuador. During the 1970s, expanding internal demand and the possibilities associated with the Andean Pact held out the prospect of continued growth without redistribution (23). This helps to explain why wages have declined and the political class has discouraged popular participation and mobilisation as a means of achieving economic and social change.

UNIONISATION AND LABOUR MILITANCY

In the past, the Ecuadorian labour movement has been noteworthy only for its sectionalism and ineffectiveness, which has enabled successive governments to ignore, coopt or coerce the union leadership. Many of the difficulties surrounding the unification process begun in the 1970s stemmed from past divisions and rivalries within the union movement as three major national confederation competed for members among the work force. The oldest confederation, CEDOC (Central Ecuatoriana de Organizaciones Clasistas [24]), was founded in 1938 under Catholic auspices and recruited a predominantly artisan membership from the conservative highlands, although by the early 1970s it had enrolled a large contingent of peasant organisations. A split occurred in 1975 between the Marxist and Christian Democrat wings which led to the formation of CEDOC Socialista. A second 'central', the CTE (Confederación de Trabajadores del Ecuador), founded in 1944, became the largest of the confederations, drawing its strength from industrial and service sector unions and maintaining close ties with the Communist and Socialist parties. CEOSL (Confederación Ecuatoriana de Organizaciones Sindicales Libres) was founded in 1962 with CIA and AFL-CIO support and it is affiliated to ORIT (25).

Estimates of union membership are notoriously unreliable as the 'centrales' tend to inflate the figures which have fluctuated from year to year. Some idea of the relative strength of the 'centrales' can be gleaned, however, from Table 8.5. The most striking feature of the figures is that only half the unionised work force is organised by CTE-CEDOC-CEOSL, the remainder belonging to the independent sector. Even accepting the overall total of 220,000 unionised workers, this represents a very small proportion of the economically active population

Table 8.5
Trade union membership 1973

| | Affiliated unions | | Members | |
	Number	%	Number	%
CTE	800	18	40,000	18
CEDOC	750	17	37,500	17
CEOSL	600	14	32,500	15
Independents	2,200	51	110,000	50
Total	4,350	100	220,000	100

Source: Osvaldo Hurtado and Joachim Herudek, La organización popular en el Ecuador, Quito, Inedes, 1974, p. 89.

138

(approximately 12.5 per cent in the early 1970s). A later estimate puts the expansion of the unionised work force ('centrales' and independents) for the whole decade at 146,300, at an annual growth rate of 9.5 per cent (26). Yet despite an impressive rate of union formation (40 per cent of the total for Pichincha province were established between 1971 and 1979 - see Table 8.6), the percentage of the work force organised by trade unions never exceeded 19 per cent and averaged 16 per cent for the 1970s. Indeed, the capacity of manufacturing industry to absorb labour lagged behind traditional sources of employment (food, drinks, textiles, etc.) (27). Even by 1980, according to Gilda Farrell, the working class proper accounted for approximately 15 per cent of the urban economically active population in the three most industrialised cities in Ecuador and only five per cent of the total work force (28).

Table 8.6
Unionisation
Pichincha Province

Period	Number of unions formed	%
1925-60	160	35.1
1961-70	106	25.2
1971-79	190	41.7
Total	456	100.0

Source: Marco Velasco, Insubordinación y conciencia de clase, Quito, CEN, 1983, p. 71.

The existence of three rival confederations and the proliferation of independent unions points to one of the major difficulties facing Ecuadorian labour. Ideological and personal rivalries among union leaders precluded cooperation and inclined them to expend their energies in competition for new recruits rather than advancing the interests of the membership. As a consequence, many workers preferred to join the smaller occupational unions such as the FNChPE (transport workers) and FNTP (petrol workers) which both disaffiliated from the CTE during the mid-1960s and are noted for their independent action. As these two unions represent strategically important sectors of the economy - transport and energy - they are vital components in any coordinated industrial action. Their attitude to the call for a national stoppage can prove vital to the success or failure of the action.

The modern Ecuadorian trade union movement has inherited a long tradition of hostility and interest conflict between artisan and wage labourer. Many artisans are small capitalist industrialists who, encouraged by conservative political interests, regard themselves as employers vis-à-vis the wage labour they employ. Consequently they have established their own representative organisations, which have become extremely splintered, and resisted integration into the national federations dominated by workers in manufacturing industry. The distinctive character of this group was recognised in 1976 with the creation of the CTE inspired National Association of Artisanal Associations (FNAA) but this federation encountered much hostility from many artisans who feared absorption and a loss of identity (29).

The low levels of industrialisation and unionisation created a further problem. While the unions were able to organise and win some economic and social security benefits for the numerically small, factory-based working class, the great mass of the urban poor or sub-proletariat remained unorganised. The low penetration of unionism is reflected in the growth of non-union forms of association, particularly artisan guilds, peasant and worker cooperatives and neighbourhood associations. Even when these organisations are added to the total of unionised workers, Osvaldo Hurtado calculated that only some 452,000 Ecuadorians belonged to any form of popular organisation in the early 1970s (30).

ORGANISED LABOUR UNDER MILITARY RULE

Although internal divisions within the armed forces ensured that the economic model lacked the necessary coherence to be successfully implemented, organised labour did stand to benefit from the mildly redistributionist and pro-industry policies of the Rodríguez Lara government (1972-76). However, the reformist and developmentalist project had a distinctly pre-emptive character in that it sought to minimise and control working class mobilisation.

The second phase of military rule (1976-79) reflected the growing crisis in the economic model. Rising inflation, escalating government expenditure and the downturn in the world economy induced a recession which the military triumvirate confronted by abandoning the internal market oriented industrialisation strategy in favour of a model of growth based on the export sector, a closer alliance with foreign capital and anti-labour policies. The employers reacted to the economic problems of the second half of the decade by blaming the unions and looking to the military junta to discipline the work force. The President of Pichincha's Industrial Chamber spoke in March 1976 of "the profound concern among industrialists over the serious situation of anarchy and disrespect afflicting worker-employer relations, as a result of the overt political campaigning of the union federations..." (31). Such statements expressed the concern being felt about the upsurge in labour activity and the trade unions' ability to organise national strike action on a scale hitherto unforeseen.

Evidence of labour's new combative mood was provided by the first nationwide strike, held on 13 November 1975 when the three trade union 'centrales' demonstrated their ability to mobilise mass support behind a nine-point programme which articulated political as well as economic

Table 8.7
Ecuadorian governments
1972-1984

Military
February 1972 - January 1976   General Rodríguez Lara
January 1976 - August 1979   Vice Admiral Poveda Burbano
                                (head of a military triumvirate)

Democratic
August 1979 - May 1981   Jaime Roldós Aguilera
May 1981 - August 1984   Osvaldo Hurtado Larrea
August 1984 -   León Febres Cordero

demands. The workers' minimum programme, while prioritising demands for an increased minimum wage, a fifty per cent rise in wages and regular indexing of pay, also included calls for the repeal of anti-labour decrees, the nationalisation of strategic sectors of the economy, a more radical agrarian reform, labour participation in state organisations, increased social spending and the elimination of foreign influences (32). This quantum leap in union solidarity and political awareness had been underlined by the creation of a 'comité unitario' (August 1975) which played a coordinating role in the November strike action.

While 1975 can be regarded as a watershed for the Ecuadorian labour movement, the momentum could not be sustained and a second national strike (18 May 1977) was disadvantaged by a combination of official disapproval and harassment and the resurfacing of splits within the labour confederation, the FUT (Frente Unitario de Trabajadores). Troops were sent in to remove strikers whenever they occupied their factories and police afforded protection to workers who did not wish to heed the strike call. A confrontation between the teachers' union (UNE) and the government in 1977 resulted in the dissolution of the organisation and the gaoling of its President for two years (33). By far the most serious incident took place in October of the same year at the El Aztra sugar mill where over one hundred people may have died (24 according to official sources) as police forcibly removed protesters who had occupied the premises. The junta's anti-labour offensive also included strong Ministry of Labour backing for the employers' side in the wage negotiation machinery and 'divide and rule' tactics which sought to exploit the personal and political rivalries among the union leadership by according official recognition to less militant breakaway factions like Jorge Cuisana's CEDOC group.

The right-wing phase of military rule amounted to nothing less, according to one observer, than a "systematic offensive" to "disarticulate" the mass movement as a prelude to the demilitarisation of the state (elections had been scheduled for 1978) and the reassertion of "bourgeois hegemony" (34). The government did succeed in stifling labour unrest - in 1978 the number of disputes registered a 50 per cent fall over the 1975 figures - but it must also be acknowledged that the union movement contributed greatly to its own problems during this period. Two processes were at work during the 1970s which had a profound impact on labour politics: the acceleration of union recognitions and the influx of new recruits. In the wake of this expansion, a new, more militant leadership gained control of the trade union movement. Peasant unionism gained ground steadily and came to play an important role in the radicalisation of the movement's political positions. The segmentation of the economy, and in particular the increase in the number of state employees (employment in the state bureaucracy grew at a rate in excess of 10 per cent per year between 1976 and 1980), placed strains on a union movement which had to absorb an ever greater number of competing demands and interests.

The advances that were made during the 1970s must be weighed against the debilitating in-fighting and sectionalism which threatened to sap the effectiveness of the movement. Splits appeared in CEDOC between a Marxist wing allied closely with the CTE under Emilio Velasco and a Christian Democrat wing under the old conservative leadership. The struggle for power also affected CEOSL where the new leadership under José Chávez took the federation into closer cooperation with the CTE and

CEDOC. Nor has the Marxist CTE been immune to internal power struggles. Its Pichincha division, the FTP, fell occasionally under the control of the MPD, a Maoist group which is perennially at odds with the national leadership (35).

The struggles inside the three federations mirrored, to some extent, the fluctuating political context. As Ecuador edged slowly towards democracy the question of the labour movement's political role came into sharper relief. The majority of labour leaders supported the democratisation process and sent delegates to the commissions set up to draft the new constitutional arrangements, but some leaders began to express concern at the overtures being made to them by the political parties who were anxious to cultivate union support. In fact, the return to democracy with the elections of 1978-79 and the legalisation of the political parties opened up a new era for the union movement. Under the dictatorship, when partisan political activity was proscribed, the unions, which were legally recognised organisations, could present themselves as the unrivalled spokesmen for and defenders of the working classes. Indeed, trade union development has to be seen in the context of the formation of a gamut of interest groups - cooperatives, business organisations, etc. - which emerged as a response to the growth of state power and regulatory activities during the 1970s.

The return of open competitive party politics and a democratically elected government confronted the labour leadership with a set of uncomfortable realities and contentious problems. While the union leaders are usually militants in the PCE, PS, FADI or MPD (36), these left wing parties have never succeeded in mobilising any significant electoral support. In the 1979 Congressional elections, the MPD and the UDP won only two of the 69 seats (respectively, 4.79 and 3.11 per cent of the total votes cast). Clearly there is little correlation between the level of unionisation and disciplined voting for left-wing candidates in national elections. No labour leader has ever been elected to Congress. For the great majority of workers and peasants, democratic politics dominated by oligarchic, populist and latterly middle class reformist parties have effectively excluded them from the decision-making processes and denied them access to a forum in which to air their grievances and influence policy-making.

The dilemmas facing the labour movement in a democratic system became apparent during the administrations of Jaime Roldós and Osvaldo Hurtado (1979-84). Given a choice in the contest for the presidency between a conservative representative of the oligarchy and a young, reformist candidate, the unions threw their weight behind Jaime Roldós who at least offered the prospect of democratic consolidation, a measure of social justice and developmental economic policies. While the Roldós programme fell short of labour demands for major structural reforms and an anti-oligarchic programme, pledges to raise wages, create jobs and improve training opportunities convinced the moderates in the union leadership that the government was at least preferable to a military dictatorship.

The tacit cooperation between the government and the unions did not endure long. The programme of development and reforms, enshrined in the Development Plan (1980-84) was quickly derailed by a combination of political obs tructionism in Congress and a det eriorating economic climate. The Hurtado government chose as its priorities economic stabilisation and the preservation of democracy: a course of action which in practice meant the abandonment of measures inimical to Ecuador's creditors and the opposition. The imposition of economic austerity in order to combat inflation, the debt crisis and falling oil revenues sparked off five general strikes in the space of eight years. (See Table 8.8) Although the government could not be blamed for the disastrous floods of 1982 which forced up the price of basic foodstuffs, the 'realistic' pricing policy, the elimination of subsidies and the devaluations of 1982 and 1983 convinced the unions that the poorer sections of the community were being made to bear the brunt of the crisis.

Table 8.8
The incidence of general strikes
1975-1985

13 November 1975	18 March 1983
18 May 1977	31 October 1984
17 February 1981	9-10 January 1985
13 May 1982	27 March 1985
14 October 1982	

The FUT responded to the stabilisation plan by demanding a price freeze, wage and salary increases, job security guarantees and the nationalisation of strategic industries. With only a minimal voice in Congress and little or no influence within the centre-right cabinet, the labour movement felt compelled to take its protest into the streets and use the only political weapon at its disposal: mass mobilisation and the general strike. The five national stoppages organised during the deepening economic crisis were accorded an important educative function in consciousness raising, politicising and propagandising the FUT membership and its unorganised sympathisers (37).

While the frequency of FUT-organised nationwide strikes demonstrated a growing militancy and an ability to mobilise substantial mass support, it did not indicate a diminution in the debilitating factionalism within the labour movement. The strikes under the Roldós-Hurtado governments took the form of somewhat tardy responses to emergency economic packages which included devaluations, price rises and the removal of subsidies on basic foodstuffs. The protests only served to highlight tactical disagreements among the 'centrales' and independent unions and split moderates from militants over such issues as the duration of the strike or the advisability of maintaining a dialogue with the government. While Hurtado might criticise disruptive action, his ministers were always willing to enter into negotiations in order to reach a compromise with the strikers. The demonstrable inability of the unions to sustain an indefinite strike or to maintain solidarity for more than 24 or 48 hours weakened their bargaining position and increased the pressure to compromise. Moreover, both sides had a common interest in the preservation of democracy which, given the ever-present threat of military intervention, inclined the union leadership to pragmatism.

When the union militants dismissed the government-union dialogue as a divisive tactic, the Ministry of Labour could point to its pro-labour record and willingness to reverse the dictatorship's anti-labour legislation. Four increases in the minimum salary, amounting to 330 per cent over a five year period, had been enough to keep pace with price rises even during the period of high inflation. Wages were now reviewed biannually by over one hundred sectoral commissions, comprising labour, government and employer representatives, rather than annually as was the case prior to 1979. In fact the Ministry had encouraged the consolidation of union finances by authorising regular deductions from members' salaries, and ensured that redundant workers received a dismissal payment (38). The existence of such a favourable climate had encouraged the creation of some 1000 new unions between 1979 and 1983 and a corresponding increase in the unionised work force from 343,850 (1978) to 446,956 (1983) (39). Certainly the employers' organisations and right wing political parties poured scorn on the government for its encouragement of labour and its supposed 'socialist' tendencies.

It would be wrong to conclude that the progress made since democratisation in 1979 is irreversible. The vulnerability of the labour movement can be ascribed to a number of factors. The qualified success with which the FUT has presented a united front in state-union relations is not replicated in negotiations with individual firms in the private sector which are still largely uncoordinated and atomised. Only in the larger firms have the unions consolidated their position; precisely those sectors in which job stability, competition for skilled workers and an ability to concede improvements in pay and conditions is a reality. Indeed, as Table 8.9 demonstrates, a fairly high level of penetration exists in the sectors created by import substitution industrialisation and substantial foreign investment. Similar levels have been achieved among the expanding white collar work force in the bureaucracy and in education where the teachers' union (UNE) has a long history of solidarity and effective action.

Table 8.9
Unionisation levels in manufacturing industry
1980

Provinces of Guayas, Pichincha and Azuay

Industry	Unionisation %
Food, drink and tobacco	45.9
Textiles, clothing and leather	40.5
Furniture and timber	33.0
Paper and printing	33.6
Chemicals, plastics and rubber	36.6
Non-metallic minerals	46.9
Metallurgical industries	31.7

Source: Jorge Fernández, "Un decenio de industrialización en el Ecuador: un balance crítico" in Cristian Sepúlveda, El proceso de industrialización ecuatoriano, Quito, IEE-PUCE, 1983, p. 110.

Any optimism regarding the ability of the FUT to defend the economic interests of its members and articulate their political demands must be tempered by the realisation that the Ecuadorian labour movement has steadily lost members as a result of unemployment and lay-offs during the 1980s. The labour movement faces a monumental task in organising the majority of the working population who comprise the informal sector.

Under the Labour Code, temporary workers, domestic servants and other casuals are not subject to unionisation. In spite of the Code's prohibitions concerning the employment of children under 14 years of age, estimates put the number of youths and adolescents obliged to earn a living this way at over one million.

The election of León Febres Cordero, the candidate of conservative political and business interests, in August 1984, confirmed the political weakness of the left in Ecuador. Evidently many FUT members preferred Febres' populist slogan of 'Bread, housing and jobs' to the discredited centre-left option or the appeal of the traditional left. Febres polled particularly strongly in the working class areas on the coast and in his home city of Guayaquil. Once again the election provided evidence of the electoral weakness of the left. The Communist, René Maugé, standing as the FADI candidate, polled just over 4 per cent of the vote in the first round of the Presidential election, the maverick far left Jaime Hurtado (MPD) 7.3 per cent and the Socialist Front candidate picked up a minuscule 0.8 per cent (40).

The free market, monetarist economic model set in motion by the new President signalled the end of the government-union dialogue and its replacement by open confrontation. Further price rises, the dismantling of tariffs and protection for domestic industry and the unwillingness to grant substantial wage increases in line with inflation provoked a militant response from the unions. During the first six months of the Febres administration, the FUT organised three general strikes to protest against the government's programme. The first stoppage (October 1984) focused on the austerity measures linked to the IMF's refinancing of Ecuador's foreign debt. Febres declared the strike "illegal and subversive" and sought with some success to undermine its effectiveness. Although FUT president José Chávez claimed the involvement of 600,000 workers, the non-participation of transport and oil workers meant that the response was far from universal (41).

The FUT had more success with its second, two-day strike in January 1985, called in response to petrol (66 per cent), public transport (50 per cent) and other price rises. The unpopularity of the package ensured that the union demand for a 100 per cent increase in the minimum wage and the repeal of the price rises would mobilise substantial support and receive the backing of the opposition parties in Congress. Nevertheless, the strike could not be regarded as a resounding success. The bus drivers' union (FNChPE) did not take part and the strike call evoked a far stronger response in the Andean region than in Guayaquil and the coastal provinces which suggested that the regional dimension had entered into FUT labour politics. Nor could the unions take much comfort from the government's tough response to the strike. Febres declared the action illegal and threatened to deduct two days' wages for every working day lost during the stoppage. In addition the government sought to discredit the unions by identifying the leadership with international terrorism following the discovery of arms and explosives near Quito (42).

The third general strike against the Febres government (March 1985) underlined the extent to which political, constitutional and economic issues had begun to overlap. The ostensible reason for the union action had been to press the demand for a 15,000 sucre minimum wage and to continue the protest over the rising cost of living. Febres decreed an

8,500 sucre minimum wage following a protracted Congressional battle during which the opposition accused the President of undermining democracy and seeking to establish a 'civilian dictatorship'. The FUT President, Froilán Azanza, made no attempt to disguise the overtly political content of a strike called in defence of the constitution as well as higher wages.

The dilemmas confronting the Ecuadorian labour movement were neatly encapsulated in the growing militancy of 1985. The politicisation and frequent mobilisations of the membership held the danger that the rank and file would weary of regular strike calls. The close identification with the opposition parties threatened to undermine the hard-won unity of the past decade. Faced with an unsympathetic government willing to use all the repressive and propaganda means at its disposal and which had, by mid-1985, secured a majority in Congress, the labour movement has been compelled to react defensively. The initiative now rests with a government hostile to the interests of organised labour.

CONCLUSION

In this article it has been argued that the trade union movement in Ecuador, while making undoubted progress over the past decade and emerging as a significant interest group, has become a victim of intra-elite conflict, the economic crisis and the factionalism that has traditionally plagued its internal politics. Although the appropriation of oil revenues enhanced the relative autonomy of the Ecuadorian state, no consensus existed concerning the economic project and the Rodríguez Lara government's plans to promote 'national capitalism' by forging an alliance between the state, private capital and foreign investment was soon blown off course. That no new class of progressive-minded industrial entrepreneurs emerged is primarily attributable to the fact that many of those who responded to the new industrial opportunities were landowners or wealthy exporters who had diversified their interests. Ecuador, therefore, lacks an independent industrial bourgeoisie with the political weight to introduce a modern, capitalist labour relations structure. The new political parties that did appear, like Izquierda Democrática for instance, espoused developmentalist policies but basically represented the new urban middle classes and have been unable to displace entirely the traditional parties and economic power groups who were able to regain power in 1984.

The new social forces created by the development process of the 1970s (government employees, wage earners and workers in the informal sector) have not been mobilised effectively in an alliance that could implement a coherent programme of structural reforms. The reformist Sixth Development Plan (1980-84), containing impressive proposals for agrarian reform, industrialisation and popular participation in decision-making, lacked a clear political and social basis and commitment to implement major changes, i.e. tax reform, which could have provided the financial resources for the fulfilment of the plan's objectives. The preference for foreign borrowing to fund development resulted in a severe fiscal crisis as economic recession and high interest rates undermined the strategy. The government cuts of 1982-83 as part of the IMF adjustment package meant that the burden of the economic crisis fell most heavily on the poorest sections of society. The backlash against the measures caused the narrow defeat of the reformist ID candidate in the 1984

Presidential elections.

Organised labour in Ecuador, already weakened by the measures taken to combat the recession, has, since August 1984, found itself under attack from an antagonistic government. The removal of industrial subsidies has led to a contraction in the manufacturing sector and the mass dismissal of workers has driven up unemployment at the time when the dismantling of subsidies on food and other essentials has cut living standards dramatically. The effectiveness of the strike weapon in such circumstances has diminished as workers fear for the loss of their jobs and anticipate the inevitable violent police response to militant action (43). Ecuadorian labour now confronts an uncertain future. Economically, the collapse in the price of the country's main export, petroleum, threatens a further contraction in the economy at a time when an internal union debate is taking place about the efficacy of the general strike as a political weapon to protest austerity measures. Opposition to the present government's policies has shifted from the streets to Congress, a forum in which the weakness of labour is most apparent and where the absence of a political party to act as an effective representative of working class interests is an enduring handicap (44).

NOTES

(1)   Exceptions are Elías Muñoz Vicuña and Leonardo Vicuña Izquierdo, 'Historia del movimiento obrero del Ecuador' in P. González Casanova (ed.), Historia del movimiento obrero en America Latina, Mexico, Siglo XXI, 1984, and Nick D. Mills, Crisis, conflicto y consenso, Ecuador 1979-1984, Quito, Cordes, 1984, especially chapters 7 and 8. I am extremely indebted to the Institute of Social Studies in The Hague for providing me with copies of the Working Papers which form part of a joint study with PREALC under the title 'Planning for basic needs in Latin America' which includes an indepth study of Ecuador.
(2)   'The analysis of labour movements in Latin America: typologies and theories', Bulletin of Latin American Research, vol. 1, no. 1, October 1981, pp. 81-95.
(3)   Jorge V. Alarcón, Transition, Growth and Basic Needs in Ecuador, ISS-PREALC Working Paper no. 31, The Hague, October 1985, p. 15.
(4)   Marco Velasco, Insubordinación y conciencia de clase, Quito, CEN, 1983, pp. 39-40.
(5)   Fabio Villalobos, La utilización de la capacidad instalada en la industria manufacturera ecuatoriana, ISS-PREALC Working Paper no. 10, Quito, August 1984, p. 26.
(6)   Mills, op. cit., p. 128.
(7)   Rob Vos, Industrialización, empleo y necesidades básicas en el Ecuador, ISS-PREALC Working Paper no. 12, July 1984, p. 6.
(8)   M. Bastiaenan, J. Solf and Rob Vos, Urban Poverty, Access to Public Services and Public Policies. A Case Study of the Marginal Suburbs of Guayaquil, Ecuador, Working Paper no. 7, Quito, January 1983, p. 33.
(9)   Some new industrial centres did emerge, e.g. Manabí on the coast and Azuay and Cotopaxi in the highlands. J. V. Alarcón, op. cit., p. 79.
(10) Rob Vos, Access to Basic Services and the Public Expenditure Incidence, Ecuador 1970-1980, ISS-PREALC Working Paper no. 4, Quito, October 1982, p. 9.

(11) Manuel R. Agosin, 'An analysis of Ecuador's Industrial Development Law', Journal of Developing Areas, April 1979, p. 269.

(12) Washington Macías, Problemas socioeconómicas del Ecuador, Guayaquil, Ecuatextos, 1983, p. 172.

(13) M. Bastiaenan, op. cit., p. 54.

(14) A. Gutiérrez, Labour Market Functioning, Employment and Basic Needs in Ecuador, ISS-PREALC Working Paper no. 13, Quito, August 1984, p. 2.

(15) W. Armstrong and T. G. McGee, Theatres of Accumulation, London, Methuen, 1985, p. 113.

(16) Roxborough, op. cit., p. 90.

(17) For an interesting discussion of this process: S. Commander and P. Peek, 'Oil exports, agrarian change and the rural labour process: the Ecuadorian sierra in the 1970s', World Development, vol. 14, no. 1, 1986, pp. 79-96.

(18) Alarcón, op. cit., p. 46.

(19) Catherine M. Conaghan, 'Democracy by attrition: parties, civil society and political order in Ecuador', paper delivered to the Conference on Redemocratisation in Latin America, University of Pittsburgh, March 1985, p. 28.

(20) Lidia Barrientos, Ecuador's Development Profile and Basic Needs Performance, ISS-PREALC Working Paper no. 24, The Hague, 1985, p. 7.

(21) Gutiérrez, op. cit., p. 17.

(22) Rob Vos, Industrialización, op. cit., p. 151.

(23) Catherine M. Conaghan, Industrialists and the Reformist Interregnum: Dominant Class Behaviour and Ideology in Ecuador, 1972-1979, unpublished PhD thesis, Yale University, 1983, p. 8.

(24) CEDOC changed its name from the original Central Ecuatoriana de Organizaciones Católicas in 1976. The right-wing faction created CEDOC de los Trabajadores. James Dunkerley and Chris Whitehouse, Unity Is Strength. The Trade Unions in Latin America. A Case for Solidarity, London, Latin American Bureau, 1980, p. 92.

(25) ORIT: Organización Regional Interamericana de Trabajadores. A pro-US regional labour organisation.

(26) Mills, op. cit., p. 129.

(27) Jorge Fernández, 'Un decenio de industrialización en el Ecuador, un balance crítico' in Cristian Sepúlveda, El proceso de industrialización ecuatoriano, Quito, IEE-PUCE, 1983, p. 104.

(28) Gilda Farrell, 'El movimiento sindical frente a la segmentación tecnológica y salarial del mercado de trabajo', in Sepúlveda, op. cit., p. 194.

(29) Alan Middleton, 'Division and cohesion in the working class: artisans and wage labourers in Ecuador', Journal of Latin American Studies, 14, 1982, p. 193.

(30) Osvaldo Hurtado, Political Power in Ecuador, University of New Mexico Press, 1980, p. 236

(31) Ecuador Debate, Quito, 4 December 1983, p. 18.

(32) Muñoz Vicuña, op. cit., pp. 252-3.

(33) The Guardian, London, 6 October 1977.

(34) Alejandro Moreano, 'La tautología del poder y lenguaje del pueblo', in Ecuador: passado y futuro, Quito, El Conejo, 1983, cited in Mills, op. cit., p. 140.

(35) Weekly Analysis, Guayaquil, 18 May 1981, p. 3.

(36) PSE: Partido Socialista Ecuatoriano; MPD: Movimiento Popular Democrático; FADI (Communist dominated left alliance) and UDP: Union Democrática Popular.

(37) Mills, op. cit., pp. 170-1.
(38) Ibid., p. 185.
(39) Ibid., p. 186.
(40) Howard Handelman, 'The dilemma of Ecuadorian democracy III', UFSI Reports, no. 36, 1984, p. 5.
(41) Latin America Weekly Report, London, 30 November 1984.
(42) Latin America Weekly Report, London, 25 January 1985.
(43) Nueva, 123, Quito, February 1986. Interview with FUT leader, José Chavéz.
(44) María Arboleda, Raúl Borja and José Steinsleger, Mi poder en la oposición. El primer año del gobierno de León Febres Cordero, Quito, El Conejo, 1985.

9 Trade unionism on the periphery: the case of the Bolivian mineworkers 1965-1985

GAIL MARTIN

INTRODUCTION

The history of Bolivian labour in this century has been dominated by the struggle of the tin mining unions for social justice. This chapter will suggest that this epic era may be coming to a bitter end. Since its foundation in June 1944, the National Federation of Bolivian Mineworkers (FSTMB) has been a major political force, providing not only a vice-president and several ministers of state, but even assuming responsibility for the management of the state-owned Bolivian Mining Corporation (COMIBOL). Such close political involvement reflects not only the overwhelming contribution mining has made to export earnings, but also the historic vanguard role played by the miners in resisting oligarchic monopoly of economic and political power, in the process of which they won for themselves and other sections of the population major social advances. The high point came in 1952 when miners backed the National Revolutionary Movement (MNR) insurrection, thereby beginning the Bolivian National Revolution, the first such social revolution in Latin America since the Mexican revolution in 1910. The middle-class MNR was stiffened at every point by the militant demands of the miners and their representatives, and between them major reforms were pushed through, including the nationalisation of the large mines, workers' control, universal suffrage and agrarian reform. The MNR-labour alliance was formalised via the system of 'co-gobierno', or co-government, under which until 1956 trade unionists occupied leading ministries such as Mines and Petroleum and Labour. The watchdog of the workers was the newly created (Bolivian Workers Congress (COB), and at the heart of the COB was the FSTMB, which took up its role as political vanguard of the Bolivian masses. The newly created COB would share with the FSTMB a commitment to anti-imperialism, political pluralism with Leninist anarcho-syndicalist and populist elements represented in its members, and a determination as far as possible to pursue genuine proletarian interests and the realisation of socialist objectives by maintaining nationally and internationally their political independence (1).

During the first phase of the Revolution which coincided with the presidency of Víctor Paz Estenssoro, 1952-56, the miners, despite agonised debates and misgivings about the MNR's true political character, supported the MNR by mobilising repeatedly to thwart counter-revolutionary coup attempts; by maintaining the profitability of the newly created COMIBOL despite the fall in their real wages and the inevitable disruption caused by the mass exodus of foreign technical staff after 1952; and by trying to promote higher standards of efficiency and morality in management via the workers' representatives in the face of the MNR practice of applying political rather than professional criteria in appointments to top managerial posts. Miners and their leaders continued to support the agrarian reform programme and the creation of a national social security system, and advanced progressive policies such as the building of a smelter in Bolivia to reduce the country's vulnerability to world markets, or the diversification of export markets to include the socialist bloc economies. Despite this committed support the MNR was unable to overcome the multiple problems facing the economy once the price of tin began to decline following the end of the Korean War in 1953. Falling export revenues quickly translated within Bolivia into scarcities, roaring inflation and an expanding black market. Faced with these difficulties, the MNR fell increasingly under the conservative influence of the United States administration of President Dwight D. Eisenhower, 1953-61, leaving the worker ministers up to 1956, and the pro-MNR COB leaders generally after that date, in the anomalous position of trying to mediate an increasingly free-market government strategy to their members.

The new government plan after 1952 had been to use mining profits to promote economic diversification and social development. It was a strategy which ultimately misfired: it left the Bolivian economy more indebted in 1964 (when a military coup ended civilian government) than it had been in 1952, and it divided the labour left from their centre-right allies in the MNR once it became clear that the decapitalised mining sector was expected to shoulder the burden of the deflationary policies adopted after 1956 to correct the results of earlier incompetence and mismanagement. Not until the return of civilian government in October 1982 with the presidency of Hernán Siles Zuazo (himself a former MNR leader and president from 1956-60) would labour again have any significant opportunity to influence policy formation and decision making at government level. During the hectic years that followed (1982-85), Communists were appointed as Ministers of Mines and Labour and the FSTMB assumed responsibility for the management of COMIBOL (2). However, after twenty years of military misrule there were no magical solutions: the Bolivian economy floundered in debt, and against a background of falling international mineral prices Siles decided to abandon the presidency with a year still to go. Following elections in June, the veteran Víctor Paz Estenssoro was inaugurated as president on 6 August 1985. This chapter will briefly review the process of this last quarter of a century in order to assess, in historical perspective, the ability of the FSTMB to defend the jobs and living conditions of its members in the current political situation, and particularly in the face of new problems created by the unparalleled crisis in the international tin market.

THE ECONOMIC CONTEXT

Bolivians are the poorest people in a poor continent, only Haitians excepted, and they are getting poorer. The population of six million is scattered across a country twice the size of France in one of the lowest density distributions in Latin America. Although half of the population works in the rural economy the four per cent who work in the mining sector produce more than half the export revenues (3). Yet this 'labour aristocracy' with access to the capitalist economy has at its core the COMIBOL face workers with a life expectancy of 37 years due to the prevalence of silicosis and tuberculosis in the mining communities.

The nation has a GDP per capita of US \$400, and a recently established minimum wage of US \$18 per month (4). The total national debt is US \$4.8 billion and interest repayments are equivalent to 57 per cent of export revenues (5). Over 30 per cent of these revenues come from the sale of tin which Bolivia, as the highest cost producer in the world, delivers at about twice the international selling price (6). Moreover the general decline in the relative value of minerals and metals in the international market, together with falling production in Bolivia, reduced the value of the country's mineral exports from US \$663 million to US \$354 million between 1981 and 1984, and to US \$280 million in 1985 (7). COMIBOL, the foundation of which was perhaps the greatest achievement of the 1952 revolution, has only one out of eighteen of its units operating at a profit, and accumulated losses over the last decade are estimated at US \$200 million (8). Expensive attempts at the vertical integration of the mining economy planned in the 1970s such as the Vinto smelter at Oruro, the tin volatisation plant at La Palca and the lead-zinc plant at Karachipampa have been hampered in the 1980s by falling production which means that these plants have no hope of running at economic levels (9).

The Bolivian economy, in short, has been overwhelmingly dependent historically on the export of minerals and metals; its chief mining export remains tin which has played a dominant role in the economy since the first years of this century; it is a commodity for which global demand is falling due to substitution by aluminium and plastics, and whose market is dominated by the existence of a huge United States stockpile accumulated in the 1940s and 1950s through cheap purchases of Bolivian tin and now estimated to equal total annual world production (10). More than other third world producers, Bolivia faces an almost hopelessly difficult situation because of high production costs and the failure of earlier generations both before and after the 1952 revolution to use the profits generated by mining either to regenerate mining or to promote an alternative export sector with long-term growth prospects. The breadth and depth of the national predicament have undermined all efforts by successive regimes of different political hue in the 1950s, 1960s and 1970s to diversify and develop the economy. The miners therefore find themselves hopelessly trapped in a decapitalised, and now possibly redundant, industry which has some of the worst working conditions in the world.

THE FSTMB, 1965 TO 1985

In Bolivia it is trade unions rather than political parties which provide fundamental leadership for the workers. There are many reasons for
this in the particular geographical, social and economic reality of the
country where huge physical distances, the predominance of traditional
cultural and social patterns amongst the Indian majority and the
repeated recourse by conservative elements to the military as a means of
imposing their will have prevented the establishment of a democratic
environment in which political parties could develop a national framework.

However, the failure of left parties such as the Revolutionary Workers
Party (POR Trotskyist) and the Bolivian Communist Party (PCB) to build a
strong national platform independently of the FSTMB has encouraged those
parties to shelter within the Federation and regard the considerable
influence they exercise there as the basis for their existence as national political forces. This serves the interests of some union leaders
- the veteran Juan Lechín Oquendo is the most obvious example - who have
been able with consummate skill to exploit the political rivalries
within the Federation to preserve their own executive positions. Lechín
has occupied the post of Executive Secretary of the FSTMB in an unbroken
run since 1945. The desire to preserve the overall political independence of the Federation (and indeed of the COB) is also nurtured by a
residue of the anarcho-syndicalism of the early twentieth century, by a
collective memory of the tutelage imposed by the MNR during the period
of co-government between 1952 and 1956, and by a realistic appraisal
that in the volatile Bolivian context, as in other third world countries
where authoritarian regimes frequently occur, the union is ultimately a
more durable form of working class defence than the political party.
Despite successful attempts to mobilise the people on numerous occasions, no one party since the MNR has been able to win enough national
support for long enough to overcome the problems of militarism, economic
dependence and political factionalism: indeed, in the late 1970s there
were no fewer than 70 political parties in Bolivia.

The inability of political parties to offer coherent leadership to the
workers therefore places an especially heavy responsibility on the COB
and individual unions to defend the interests of their members and their
dependants. Unfortunately the miners, the most militant section of the
national labour force, are for the most part isolated from the urban
centres (except for those in San José or Potosí), being located high on
the Altiplano at 14,000 feet or more above sea level. The focal centre
of the solidarity which develops in these communities as a result of
harsh working and living conditions is the Catavi-Siglo XX complex,
which is Bolivia's largest single enterprise with 5,000 workers. The
militancy of the Bolivian mining proletariat, legendary throughout Latin
America, has also been consolidated by successive acts of repression and
violence such as the massacre of 400 men, women and children at Catavi
on 21 December 1942, the bombing of the mining towns in 1965, the murder
of dozens of workers during the Night of San Juan in June 1967 and more
recently the ruthless onslaught on communities such as Corocoro during
the dictatorship of General Luis García Meza, 1980-81.

Undoubtedly the historic vanguard role of the miners has been based
not only on their heightened political consciousness, but also on an
awareness of their central role in the export sector. Yet the formation

of unions in the mines was a lengthy process. Extreme isolation, an over-supply of labour and the hostility of successive conservative regimes prevented the formation of the national federation until June 1944, when the government of Major Gualberto Villarroel provided the conditions for the foundation of the now celebrated FSTMB. It was the Miners Federation which provided the vital physical and ideological support for the national revolution of 1952 before the complete dependence of the economy on the uncertain world market for tin exacerbated the strains of the multi-class MNR coalition and ultimately divided worker from worker as well. When the crucial conjuncture developed in 1956-57, with the implementation of an IMF 'stabilisation plan' underlining the growing influence of the US over Bolivian government decisions, the COB divided, as the railwaymen backed the government's deflationary package against the call of the COB executive, led by the miners' leader Juan Lechín Oquendo, for a general strike. This was to prove to be a turning point not only in the development of the revolution but also in the subsequent history of the country. The FSTMB itself also split over the stabilisation plan, when the second largest mine, Huanuni, supported President Siles Zuazo's economic strategy and his attempt to form a rival federation. This initiative eventually failed after deaths had occurred in the fighting between Siglo XX and Huanuni, and both the COB and the FSTMB rebuilt unity around the struggle to defend workers against the worst effects of the deflationary policies. Nevertheless it had been demonstrated that, in the short term at least, there were competing interests amongst sectors of labour as a whole, between different mines, and also within labour groups at individual mines (11). In November 1964 a military coup led by Generals René Barrientos and Alfredo Ovando Candia removed the MNR from power.

The left in general and the miners in particular were to pay heavily in the decades following 1965 for the failure to preserve civilian government and keep alive the hope of a project based on the building of an expanding Bolivian economy based on productive cooperation between labour and government. Although there were brief interruptions to this sustained era of repressive military rule, some of which brought major political innovations such as the Popular Assembly of 1971 (see below), it would be October 1982 before a return to civilian and democratic government was achieved. In the intervening years the FSTMB bore the brunt of the repression of the Barrientos regime up to his death in 1969, and of the Hugo Banzer regime between 1971 and 1978.

Following the imposition in the mines in 1965 of what was called the 'May System' (which in practical terms meant 30 per cent wage reductions, layoffs, deportations of leaders and military occupation of the mines), it became impossible to sustain either the COB or the FSTMB at their national levels. The victory of Barrientos at the polls in 1966 indicated the value of his earlier courting of the peasant vote and highlighted the political isolation of the miners, who remained opposed to his regime to its end. It was in this period that miners lost their most dedicated militant leaders such as César Lora (1965), Federico Escóbar (1966) and Isaac Camacho (1967). However, the establishment in Bolivia in 1966-67 of a guerrilla 'foco' under Ernesto Che Guevara promised to end this isolation and open up a second front only 150 kilometres from the main mining areas. The decision to hold a clandestine meeting of the FSTMB in Siglo XX to coincide with the important festival of San Juan in 1967 may or may not have been intended to stimulate support for the guerrilla war (12). It was at any rate used by the military as a pretext to invade the camp and unleash an assault on the unprepared miners and their families that left at least 80 dead (an event which has been vividly recreated and brought to world-wide attention through the work of Bolivian film director Jorge Sanjines) (13). The FSTMB responded to this murderous attack with a two-week strike, but the assault meant that not until 1969 would the Federation be able once more to rally its activists and re-establish a national organisation.

The severe reduction of living standards, the assassinations and deportations, and the denial of any genuine democratic rights encouraged the emergence of a new phenomenon in the political environment of the Bolivian mines, namely the radicalisation of the Oblate priests based particularly in Siglo XX, who in the 1950s and early 1960s had devoted their energies to combating Communist influence in the mines. This emphasis now gave way to the work of priests such as Gregorio Iriarte and Mauricio Lefevre who saw it as their duty to defend those who could no longer defend themselves (14). This attitude, already foreshadowed in 1965 in the personal role played by Iriarte in smuggling union militant Federico Escóbar out of the area and away from the army which was encircling the camp, became more generalised via Siglo XX's Radio Pío XII which now offered itself as the "voice of the voiceless". The role of the Bolivian union radio transmitters has achieved continental impact for their efforts to build union solidarity, integrate their local communities and maintain contacts among isolated mining camps, and between those camps and the capital. During time of military attack such transmitters become a crucial weapon available to the miners to combat the spreading of disinformation and to coordinate the resistance against military advance, whose first objective inevitably becomes the elimination of the radio station itself. In 1965 the 23 transmitters in the different mines were all destroyed, but Pío XII survived due no doubt to its clerical status, its conservative reputation and the literacy campaign it ran in the surrounding areas. The transmitters were returned in 1969, only to be destroyed again in 1971. During the Banzer dictatorship even Pío XII experienced long periods of enforced silence, for example from 1971 to 1973 (15).

The death of Barrientos in a mysterious helicopter crash in April 1969 brought General Ovando Candia to the presidency a few months later, with a progressive civilian element in his cabinet which included young rising politicians such as Marcelo Quiroga Santa Cruz. This was a government supposedly dedicated to revolutionary nationalism under military rule, undoubtedly influenced by similar trends in the recently installed Peruvian regime of General Juan Velasco Alvarado. Not only was the political climate liberalised to allow both the 14th FSTMB Congress in April 1970 and the 4th COB Congress in the following month, but also the US Gulf Oil Company was nationalised and diplomatic relations with the Soviet Union were established. However, right-wing forces in the military were alarmed by the vigorous political debates in these congresses, which led to the elaboration by miners of a radical political thesis adopted by COB after some modification of the dominant Trotskyist line by Communist delegates (16). There was also the apparent return of the guerrilla threat with an offensive by the Army of National Liberation (ELN) at Teoponte in July. A right-wing coup was launched on 7 October, but a daring counter-response by General Juan José Torres, and rapid support furnished by the COB, created the conditions for an unprecedented sequence of events during the following ten months. Between October 1970 and August 1971 Bolivia was ruled by a combination of forces: on the one hand the left-leaning Torres in the government palace keeping the rest of the military sullenly at bay, and on the other the labour-left coalition organised in the COB and FSTMB responding to the opportunity which now presented itself by creating a new institution called the Popular Assembly. Once again the miners would play the leading role in this major innovation. Although some writers discuss this period in terms of the possible existence of "dual power" (17), the Assembly managed only one full session of ten days before it was swept away by the Banzer coup on 21 August 1971. It remains however to date a high point of proletarian consciousness and achievement, albeit short-lived.

At the 1970 April and May Congresses of the FSTMB and the COB, the long established leadership of Juan Lechín Oquendo had been challenged by Víctor López. This was more than a personal challenge, since it represented an attempt to bring the power of both bureaucracies more fully under the control of the mass membership. Lechín defeated López on both occasions, as indeed he would defeat him again in the election for the presidency of the Popular Assembly (by 103 votes to 58), monopolising the top three national labour posts in his own hands. However, the COB had established a Political Command with representatives of both the unions and the parties and it was this body which called for the meeting of the Popular Assembly in April 1971. The first full session met, symbolically, on the eve of 24 June, the night of San Juan, and lasted for ten days.

The Assembly declared itself an independent working class institution whose function it was to defend working class interests and set guidelines for government policies. Collaboration with Torres via the resurrection of the old co-government device of the post-1952 period was already rejected since the Political Command had refused, on 8 October, Torres' offer of one third of the cabinet posts, and when this offer was increased to one half the Command hedged their suspicious acceptance about with so many impossible caveats that the proposal died an inevitable death (18). Opinions differ on the wisdom of this refusal: the PCB and important non-Communist mining leaders such as Víctor López, Sinforoso Cabrera and Alberto Jara had argued in favour of acceptance, but had been unable to overcome the opposition of Lechín, the POR and the majority to a return to what was seen as the poisonous embrace of co-government. It was argued instead that the Assembly should be used to define and advance a genuine proletarian position. Therefore whilst Torres, uneasily and indeed insecurely lodged in the government palace, pursued his own policies - reinstating miners' wages to the pre-1965 levels, cutting the salaries of over-paid state bureaucrats, touring the mines and promising to arm the miners should the military turn on them, decreeing worker participation in the National Oil Corporation (YPFB), renationalising the Matilde mine and expelling the US Peace Corps - the Popular Assembly devoted its first session to the vexed but crucial question of worker participation in the management of COMIBOL.

The composition of the Popular Assembly gave the workers a major voice: 132 delegates went to industrial unions; 53 to the organisations of the 'middle classes'; 23 to the peasants; and 13 to the left parties. The most striking feature of this pattern is the under-representation of the peasants, whilst the left parties fared better than their 13 delegates suggested, since some of their members reached the Assembly via other sections. René Zavaleta lists at least nine distinct political organisations at work in the Assembly, and he attributes the under-representation of the peasantry to the desire of the PCB and the POR to deny access to the rival left (19). Whether this or merely the old reluctance of the urban-industrial proletariat and its leaders to share power with the rural majority was responsible, it proved as damaging in 1971 as it had in the 1950s and 1960s when the COB statutes were heavily biased towards the representation of urban and mining workers. Not until the 1970s and the emergence of independent Indian groups such as the Revolutionary Movement Tupak Katari led by Genaro Flores would this fundamental obstacle to working class power be tackled. Nevertheless, the military-peasant pact of Barrientos survived to support Banzer until 1974 when the massacre of over 80 peasants finally ended it (20).

Zavaleta criticises the Popular Assembly for ignoring the real issue - power - and for concentrating too exclusively on the question of the management of COMIBOL. For him, this is symptomatic of the overdevel-oped role of the union in Bolivian politics, and of the ideological confusion reigning in the Assembly. He writes that the Assembly may have been the "most developed phase of the masses' populism", but that it was not "the first stronghold of the socialist revolution" (21). Cayetano Llobet Tabolara too argues that the Assembly demonstrated a 'workerist' mentality both in the time spent on this question and also in the way that Communist and Trotskyist party members amongst the miners' delegates chose to support the Federation's official candidate Lechín rather than Víctor López, another top miners' leader, who had the official endorsement of the two parties. For Llobet this demonstrates that in Bolivia the vanguard of the people is the union, the Federation (22). However for the miners the management of COMIBOL was at the very heart of the struggle for state power and therefore the achievement of genuine worker control in COMIBOL was a major national as well as a sectoral objective. The scheme for equal co-participation in management offered by Torres was rejected in favour of the scheme of majority co-participation worked out in the Assembly which gave the Federation equal representation on the board of directors, the right to appoint the general manager, who would not have a casting vote, and the supervision of the worker representatives by the rank and file in their union assem-blies. By this means the FSTMB sought to establish workers control based on the collective rather than the individual representation of workers, as had been the case in the period 1952-63, and because of Bolivia's continuing dependence on the export of minerals to bring the working class closer to the control of the state (23). The achievement of an efficient and accountable system of workers control was a goal which dated back to the adoption of the famous Pulacayo Thesis in 1946 when the miners, only two years after the foundation of their Federation and in the face of an implacably hostile regime, accepted for themselves an essentially Trotskyist view of their role in the building of social-ism in Bolivia. Although the thesis has been supplanted in subsequent congresses, it remains a powerful point of reference for leaders and rank and file alike (24).

Many observers are in agreement, then, that 1971 was a high point in the efforts of the Bolivian working classes, led by the miners, to begin the building of socialism in their country. Indeed, their success may be measured by the repression that followed the Banzer coup of 21 August 1971 which swept Torres into exile and began a seven-year dictatorship broken only by the 'auto-coup' of November 1974 when the earlier support of the civilian parties such as the MNR-Paz Estenssoro and the Bolivian Socialist Phalanx (FSB) was discarded by Banzer himself in favour of an exclusively military regime, and a complete ban on all political and union activity was imposed. Torres' ultimate loyalty to the army prevented him from arming the people when the test came, and a web of interests stretching from Washington to Brazil via Santa Cruz would keep the new regime in power until 1978, sustained as it also was by rising prices for tin and oil. Internally the labour-left had to face the return of the death penalty, the assertion by the state of the right to hold prisoners indefinitely, and the operation of a brutal police system. Between 1971 and 1977 an estimated 200 people were killed, 14,750 gaoled and 19,140 exiled (25).

In such conditions, so widely paralleled in other parts of South America at this time, the FSTMB managed, defiantly, to hold its 15th Congress at Potosí in November 1973 and re-elect its exiled leaders to their executive posts. However, only once were they able briefly to assert a national challenge to the military regime following the 16th Congress held in Corocoro in the first week of May 1976. The government-imposed labour coordinators in the unions were denounced, old loyalties reconfirmed, and the regime was given 30 days to respond to the demand for a wage increase from the prevailing US $1.75 per day to US $4.00. Before the promised strike date news arrived in Bolivia on 2 June of the assassination of Torres in Argentina. The refusal of Banzer to allow the repatriation of the body for burial in Siglo XX, as his widow requested, exacerbated an already tense situation and on 9 June the Federation's headquarters in La Paz were occupied, six leaders exiled and the following day the army was sent to Siglo XX and the other camps. The miners held out for between two and three weeks before the enforced return to work. Thomas Greaves and Javier Albó, two social scientists, happened to be carrying out field research in one of COMIBOL's mines at the time and they have left an eye-witness account of how difficult it proved to be to pursue the strike effectively once the leaders were dismissed and the mines occupied. These observers situate the problem at the local level, within the general context of multiple dependence in which Bolivian miners find themselves:

> The miners' strike illustrates powerful dependencies that controvert miners' efforts to improve their lot through collective action. These dependencies severely limit their capacity to pursue a strike of extended duration, in fact the loss of steady wages and consumer credit almost preclude striking at all. Second, the loss of jobs entailed hardships of such magnitude that to invite dismissal was almost foolhardy. And third, the channels of communication, essential to united action, are mainly in the hands of their adversaries, blocking workers' efforts to coordinate action amongst mines, and serving as an incisive tool to advance the strategy of the government. At the local level, this is the texture of dependency (26).

There were however forces at work in Latin America in the late 1970s which would allow a return to a more liberal political climate, and Bolivia was one of the first republics to experience the return to constitutional rule - briefly, as it turned out - in 1978. The unrestrained use of force by the Banzer dictatorship had engendered a new kind of support for the Bolivian people and particularly for the miners who bore the main burden of the economy and of political repression. New organisations such as the Commission for Justice and Peace, the

Jesuit Centre for Peasant Research and Development and the Permanent Assembly of Bolivian Human Rights (APDHB) took up the challenge of documenting and publicising the abuses of the regime. For example, in 1978 the APDHB published a <u>Study of the Purchasing Power of Miners' Wages</u> in which it was demonstrated that although the value of mining production had increased dramatically in the period 1971-78, real wages in the mines had fallen by 13.8 per cent; and that whilst a small minority of skilled workers might earn relatively decent wages by working 16-hour shifts seven days a week in the most dangerous locations, the vast majority of miners were unable to feed and clothe their families adequately. These subsistence levels were contrasted with the opulent salaries enjoyed by those who administered the mines (27).

Internationally, the British National Union of Mineworkers took the initiative in supporting this work of documentation and information with the report they produced in 1977 following the clandestine visit of three of their Executive to the mines in Bolivia. By drawing attention to the complete denial of political and trade union rights in the mines the NUM was able to secure the withholding of a £19 million grant by the British government to the Banzer regime for the rehabilitation of the mines, thereby seriously weakening its position (28). Undoubtedly, too, the human rights policy of US president Jimmy Carter was a further encouragement to Banzer to vacate the government palace. Equally important was the fact that the economy was facing problems: although the value of tin exports (still accounting for some two-thirds of export earnings) had risen spectacularly in the period 1972-78 from US $113 million to US $374 million, production had actually fallen from 30,277 tons to 29,697 tons. At the same time the foreign debt of this poor country had risen from an already difficult US $782 million to a staggering US $3.1 billion (29). Given these pressures, Banzer agreed in December 1977 to a limited amnesty and within a week the wives of three excluded exiled miners were on hunger strike in the offices of the Archbishop of La Paz. By the time the strike finished a wave of support coordinated by organisations like the APDHB and the Union of Bolivian Women had brought over 1,000 out on hunger strike in support across the country. On 20 January all demands were met: a general amnesty was decreed, sacked miners were to be reinstated and the military would withdraw from the mines. If this was the symbolic end of the Banzer dictatorship, it was also the prelude to a confused two-year period in which three general elections, six presidents and three successful coups flickered across the Bolivian political scene (30).

The confusion as newly liberated political forces jostled for position and priority, and whilst new alignments were tried out in the military, was not conducive to the serious pursuit of workers' demands, yet there was worse to come when the emergence of a more solid political core in the shape of the Popular Democratic Union (UDP) - an alliance of left and radical political parties led by the seemingly irrepressible (or perhaps incorrigible) Hernán Siles - provoked a coup of unprecedented savagery on 17 July 1980 led by General Luis García Meza, and doubly condemned for its well documented links with the growing cocaine mafia. The irruption of the García Meza regime brought a return to the worst excesses of the Barrientos-Banzer eras, and indeed a new low in political depravity was reached by the leading members of this group of 'gorillas', of whom García Meza and his Minister of the Interior, Colonel Luis Arce Gómez, are only the most notorious. It required a major international effort before the last vestiges of the regime were removed in October 1982 in favour of the accession of the UPD and Hernán Siles, three years after they had been first elected. The FSTMB leadership, exiled once more during the 1980-82 period, had collaborated fully in the campaign against the dictatorship, publishing documentary proof in 1981 of the crimes being perpetrated in Bolivia and reinforcing the efforts of the APDHB to bring international odium down upon the generals responsible (31). Thus not until 1982 was the Miners Federation able to return to the fundamental issues raised by the experiences of 1952-65 and briefly resurrected in 1971. Inevitably, however, events had moved on and the situation had been transformed by almost two decades of unbroken military rule and by an unnerving decline in the national economy in the face of rising indebtedness. As the miners and workers began to consider once more the pressing problems of the mining economy and the directly related issue of industrial democracy, their leaders could hardly have been unaware of the fact that the mass membership and the mining communities in general were emerging from a period of dictatorship which for a substantial element of the labour force represented not just a major part of their working lives but indeed almost half their total life expectancy. These matters would therefore be discussed with renewed urgency.

James Dunkerley and Rolando Morales view the period 1982-85 as one in which the left failed "to overcome the the contradictory heritage of 1952 or to provide anything remotely resembling a coherent answer to the gravest economic crisis in Latin America". This of course begs the question of how much freedom of manoeuvre the left really had during this time, but these authors do give the statistical evidence for what they describe as a "terminal state of political and economic decomposition" - a debt of US $5 billion and a fall in GDP of 25 per cent between 1981 and 1984 (32). It was in this genuinely catastrophic context that the labour movement struggled once more to protect the interests of the workers and their families. Tumbling world prices for tin, falling production in the mines and a man in the presidency who was more associated with the disastrous experiences of the 1956-57 'stabilisation plan' than any other single individual in Bolivia did not augur well for the ability of the leaders of the COB and the FSTMB to be able to salvage some positive benefits from the accumulated experiences of labour during the previous three decades. Yet it also seemed that the privations of the military regime had tempered Siles' conservative tendencies, and his refusal to use the military against the workers in this period, which was in part at least a recognition of the miners' contribution to the effort to restore democratic rule, guaranteed labour leaders the political space to formulate their demands. The fact that miners at Huanuni, COMIBOL's most profitable mine, gave Siles 45 days to meet their wage demands indicated that they intended to pursue their claims with renewed energy.

However the mishmash of economic initiatives which flowed from the Siles administration in its first months did nothing to resolve the desperate problems facing the most impoverished elements in the country, and reflected instead the mixed composition of the government in which centre-right, Communist, radical and independent elements struggled together in an uneasy co-existence. The inability of Siles' two Communist appointees in the Ministries of Mines and Labour to solve the the pressing problems confronting these two sectors was to rebound on the party at the national level in the COB and the FSTMB when in the 6th COB Congress in September 1984 Communist leaders Simón Reyes and Oscar

Sanjines were removed in favour of the independent Víctor López, the peasant leader Genaro Flores, and the Trotskyist leader of the factory workers Eduardo Siles (33). Shortly after this, the communists left the government and in 1985 the party split (34). In April 1983 workers at La Palca, in a spontaneous action, took over their plant in response to a two-week strike by SITCOM, the engineering union, thus spearheading the action that led to the Federation's takeover of the COMIBOL headquarters in La Paz at the end of the month, an unequivocal action led somewhat uncharacteristically by Lechín (35). Long negotiations finally resulted in a July agreement with Siles to establish equal co-participation in COMIBOL giving the Federation equal representation on the board of directors. The Federation accepted this compromise in order to regularise the Corporation's legal position and facilitate a loan of US $27.5 million that was pending. The miners' first representatives on the board would be Víctor López, José Pimentel, Símon Reyes and Daniel Ordoñez, all of whom were established Federation leaders used to operating at the national level (36). Given the parlous state of the national mining corporation at this time, miners argued that their imposition of workers control should be viewed as the assumption of a national obligation rather than the seizure of a political conquest (37).

On the question of co-government the workers presented their programme to Siles in August 1983. Lechín had expressed the view that "the COB cannot join the government to act as Siles Zuazo's tail, and simply to legitimise his past and present mistakes. If it joins, it must carry out its own programme" (38). This programme, as it turned out, included rejection of negotiations with the IMF, an end to debt repayments, control of private banks, sale of gold reserves to meet the current emergency, workers' control in private industry and majority worker participation in COMIBOL and all other state decision-making bodies. (39). The presentation of such maximalist demands was reminiscent of the Torres era in 1970, and of course such demands would not be met by Siles: indeed, the inevitable conclusion must be that Lechín never intended to find himself in close political partnership once more with his veteran opponent of the 1950s. However, Siles did agree to majority worker participation in COMIBOL in September 1983, through a system that gave the Federation four directors and the major voice in the appointment of both the vice-president and general manager of the Corporation (40). The presidential decree establishing this system indicated its possible extension to other state enterprises.

The extent of the problems facing the mining economy in the general state of economic collapse which threatened once more proved beyond the abilities of the miners' leaders to resolve in the short term. As the miners took charge, COMIBOL was still producing two-thirds of Bolivian tin and mining provided 48 per cent of total exports and one quarter of government revenues. Mining and related activities occupied 80,000 workers or 4.5 per cent of the active labour force. In September the miners of Comibol's most profitable and best financed unit at Huanuni began what turned out to be a two-moth strike over the failure to implement agreed wage deals, the lack of food in the 'pulperas' (commissaries) and the inadequate supplies to the mine. Similar problems in San José, Potosí and Catavi led to 12,000 of the 27,000 labour force supporting the action. Strikes and stoppages multiplied - in December 1983 and February 1984 - and culminated in a major demonstration in La Paz in March 1985 when 10,000 miners travelled to the capital. None of their complaints were new, and the practices developed by men in the mining districts for surviving in these conditions merely increased the problem. For example, the manager of Huanuni mine estimated that he was losing up to 100 tons or one third of his monthly production in theft at this time. Yet the new management structure allowed the Federation to bring forward their idea for an expanded role for the state mining corporation which had long been their objective. During 1983-84, the Bolivian Gold Deposits Corporation (YAB) was established to draw on some of the huge profits available from gold. It has been calculated that the nation was losing up to US $280 million in smuggled gold in 1982, equal to the value of tin exports at that time, whereas official exports of the precious metal were US $5 million (41). The opening of a new plant at Karachipampa in January 1984 brought COMIBOL a new role in the refining of silver and lead, and led to the reopening of the Pulacayo mine, and COMIBOL also took over the marketing functions of the badly run state smelting company, ENAF. Thus although the mining economy was beset by the general national predicament and buffeted by an unsympathetic international market, nevertheless some efforts were made towards imaginative management in this unprecedented experiment in workers control. At this time however the political tide began to engulf the government as Siles Zuazo staggered from one financial and political crisis to another, even undergoing a self-imposed hunger strike and a brief kidnapping, and ultimately being forced by church leaders, in the light of a rapidly deteriorating political and social situation, to agree to bring the 1986 election forward by a year. Faced with a discredited government with no answers to give to its citizens, the fractured left could only watch as the right regrouped around Paz Estenssoro and Banzer, whilst they themselves had no credible alternative to propose.

THE CURRENT POLITICAL CONTEXT

On 6 August 1985 Víctor Paz Estenssoro, at the age of 77, was inaugurated for the fourth time as president of Bolivia, one more surprising chapter in a long and chequered political career which had begun in the late 1940s and 1950s when, as leader of the MNR, he successfully launched the National Revolution of 1952-1964. However in 1985 the immediate aftermath of Paz Estenssoro's inauguration appeared in most respects the antithesis of the earlier triumph and more in keeping with the style of the same Paz Estenssoro who had tried to remain in power in 1964 despite the opposition of the workers and who later collaborated with the repressive dictatorship of General Hugo Banzer in the 1970s. On 29 August 1985, President Paz announced with decree number 21060 his 'New Economic Policy'. Its 166 clauses represented a determined plan, characteristic of the era, to expose the Bolivian economy with its inflation rate of 14,000 per cent to the full rigours of market prices: the Bolivian peso was set free to find its own level; price controls were abolished and a wage freeze decreed for four months; subsidies on food and transport were either lowered or removed altogether; the special commissary shops in isolated industrial enterprises were to be closed and state corporations such as COMIBOL decentralised with a view to their later privatisation; and statutory employment guarantees for state employees were also removed (42). In short, Bolivia was to be exposed to the full blast of monetarism so ruthlessly applied in other parts of Latin America since the 1970s.

The reaction to such draconian measures was swift. On 30 August the FSTMB declared a 24-hour strike in all mines, and their traditional adversary the military responded on 31 August by declaring their support for the government's action. On 4 September, the COB began a general strike which would last for 30 days, involving miners, teachers, factory workers and bank employees, and culminating in a hunger strike of 700 trade union leaders in protest at the arrest of 350 comrades and their deportation to jungle prison camps following the imposition of a 90-day state of siege on 19 September. As a result of the repression major figures such as the veteran Juan Lechín Oquendo (still leader of both the FSTMB and the COB) were removed from the political arena, in flagrant violation of the hard-won 'fuero sindical' or right to immunity from prosecution for activities associated with trade union office. The executive committee of the COB was reformed in clandestinity and led by Edgardo Vásquez (43).

Despite sit-ins in the mines and hunger strikes by miners and their wives, the strike failed after three weeks and constituted a major defeat for the workers, although some mines had stayed out for five weeks (44). This setback for the COB arose in part from the unexpected alliance between the MNR led by Paz Estenssoro and National Democratic Action (ADN) led by his erstwhile rival for the presidency, General Hugo Banzer. Despite their bitter competition during the election, they reached an informal agreement to cooperate in the Congress to support the declaration of the state of siege, and this was later formalised on 16 October with the publication of a 'Democratic Pact' in which power sharing was envisaged (45). The ending of industrial action on 2 October was a clear defeat for the COB, since the government agreed merely to free those arrested during the strike and to participate in a mixed commission to review the New Economic Policy. Other reasons for the defeat were not hard to find: a general weariness and despair amongst workers who had supported two indefinite strikes in the recent past (November 1984 and March 1985), neither of which had achieved major results; the lack of coordination once leaders were taken; the failure of peasants to join the action; the fear of dismissal amongst state employees; and capitulation in the face of repressive moves by the government. Within weeks of this major setback for labour the position of the miners would be dramatically - and perhaps decisively - weakened by the crisis which overtook the international tin market.

THE TIN MARKET CRISIS

The unprecedented events of 1985, involving the complete collapse of the international market for tin, would once again demonstrate, only two months after Paz's proud declaration of his new economic plan, the power of the international market to relativise internal Bolivian measures to deal with the financial and economic crisis facing the country. On 24 October, a telephone call from the office of Pieter de Koning, manager of the Buffer Stock of the International Tin Council (ITC), signalled that the tin market was facing its biggest crisis since 1929. The ITC operates what has generally been agreed to be the most successful of the UN-sponsored commodity agreements. The organisation, to which 22 producing and consuming countries belong, finances a buffer stock mechanism to regulate the international price of tin within a previously agreed floor and ceiling price range. The sixth agreement concluded in 1982 was not ratified by Bolivia, which still produces about 10 per cent of world tin, since the floor price was too low to guarantee profitability to its high-cost mines. Although a physical market in tin operates in Kuala Lumpur, indicating Malaysia's important role as the major producer, the acknowledged centre of world trade is still the London Metal Exchange (LME), which operates the futures market.

The inability of the Buffer Stock manager to continue to sustain the price of tin above £8,140 per ton (approximately US $12,000), and the suspension of LME dealings was not unforeseen due to clear over-production in recent years, but the inability to resolve the crisis has raised fundamental issues: what legal obligations do ITC member states have to honour the debts run up by their manager in pursuit of the agreed price; how are differences of opinion between consuming nations such as the United Kingdom and West Germany to be reconciled, quite apart from those between producer and consumer; what can be done to ensure that members such as Thailand control smuggling, which undermines the whole strategy of commodity arrangements; what is to be done about new producers like China and Brazil who have refused to join the ITC, and about the US stockpile; and finally, what implications are there for the LME in terms of its future structure in view of the widely held view that such a crisis would never have occurred had the LME operated a clearing house for its deals such as are standard in other commodity trading systems? (46) On 4 February 1986 came the news that the Kuala Lumpur market had re-opened in desperation over the failure to renegotiate a resumption of trading in London, and that the selling price for tin was, at £5,500 per ton, almost £3,000 lower than the closing price in October, thereby increasing the liabilities of the ITC by one third and threatening some of the 13 LME brokers with bankruptcy - just desserts, some have argued, for the irresponsible behaviour of these brokers in the previous months (47).

These events assume disastrous proportions for Bolivia, selling in an increasingly competitive market with the highest production costs in the world. A graphic indicator of its disadvantageous position is neighbouring Brazil, which in recently becoming a tin exporter has ended Bolivia's monopoly of the strategic metal in the American hemisphere. From nothing Brazil has built up an export level of 18,877 tons in 1984, making it the world's fourth producer and a supplier of tin to the USA, Western and Eastern Europe, and Latin America. With estimated reserves of 250,000 tons, most of it alluvial, Brazil's future as a tin producer is secure, yet tin plays a minimal role in the Brazilian export profile. Tin produced for Brazil's biggest export company, Paranapanema, in the area north of Manaus, is estimated to have production costs as low as US $3,000 - 4,000 per ton, and even the more expensive tin of Rondonia costs only US $8,000 a ton (48).

Even before the present crisis reports were circulating of the parlous state of the Bolivian mining economy, and with an inflation rate of 14,000 per cent in 1985 little serious hope existed of attracting the capital needed to open up promising new developments such as the gold deposits known to be available in the remoter parts of the republic. However, from the point of view of labour, any further exploitation is likely to be double-edged. Interviewed recently, Sr Raúl España-Smith, president of the private Medium Mine Owners Association, spoke of the considerable scope for "highly mechanised, low labour-intensive operations to be set up on a number of sites offering the prospect of quick returns on a tolerably small initial development" (49). This will do little to alleviate the conditions in which the vast majority of the people of the country live, nor help those workers whom COMIBOL finds it increasingly difficult to employ or to care for once they become sick from silicosis and tuberculosis. The recently sacked Minister of Mines, ex-FSTMB leader Sinforoso Cabrera, is now being criticised for granting unauthorised permission to the Pioneros de Río Madera Cooperative to prospect in Pando where large companies such as International Mining Corporation are seeking concessions (50).

CONCLUSIONS: THE PREDICAMENT OF LABOUR

What are the political, social and economic prospects for miners, struggling within the context of this weak economic base? The problems which pre-dated the ITC crisis were already sufficient pretext for Paz Estenssoro to impose a state of siege and effect a political rapprochement with Banzer, the man who had subjected the country to military dictatorship between 1971 and 1978. Now the ITC crisis has exerted a further squeeze on the Bolivian economy. In these circumstances three possible scenarios present themselves: either a major social uprising in which the workers and peasants seize power and attempt to reverse the neoliberal policies of the present government; the continuation of the deflationary policies of the Paz-Banzer alliance; or the re-imposition of military rule so recently suspended when Siles came to power in 1982.

The immediate impact of the collapse of the international tin market has been to strengthen the government of Paz Estenssoro, at least in the short term, in his struggle with the Miners Federation. The 27,000 employees of COMIBOL now face mass redundancies with perhaps as many as 9,000 jobs in peril. At the national level the FSTMB has mobilised the influential housewives committees of the mining centres to focus public attention on the social consequences of failing to provision the mines with food and medical supplies, and promised in March 1986 to produce within 60 days a rehabilitation plan for COMIBOL based on a rejection of Paz Estenssoro's economic strategy and a diversification into gold mining over a ten-year period. At the local level, miners in Huanuni responded in January by electing a Communist leadership in the annual union ballot (51). At Catavi-Siglo XX where 800 had already been laid off by the start of January, workers led by long-time unionist militant Filemón Escóbar have refused to accept Paz Estenssoro's judgement that the era of tin is over and have committed themselves to work an uninterrupted spell of 45 days (despite the fact that no wages had been paid out in the mines for three months), hoping to raise production to 240 tons and to lower costs to US $3 per pound of fine tin and so demonstrate the mine's continuing viability (52). The immediate task for the Federation is to preserve regular jobs since the most advantaged workers are those 27,000 employed directly by the state corporation COMIBOL, or the 7,000 working for the larger private mining companies which now produce 25 per cent of tin and 50 per cent of other mineral exports. Permanent employment brings with it access to housing, health, education, subsidised shops and sometimes recreational facilities too. Full-time employment is particularly highly prized in Bolivia because of the guarantees it provides in terms of severance pay and compensation for accident or illness. Wages for unskilled labour are not high (perhaps as little as a dollar a day), but the value of access to the above benefits, however poor in practice, can only be understood when set against the inability of a weak and impoverished state to provide such facilities for the mass of the population. The worker is encouraged to seek dependence on the enterprise that employs him rather than on the state.

Yet the conditions won by the Federation are threatened by the presence in the mines outside this favoured category of a wide range of types of informal employment such as the 'veneristas' who rent alluvial deposits from the company and work for piece rates that are directly tied to the international price of tin; 'locatarios' who work abandoned shafts, buying their own equipment and shouldering all the prospecting and marketing risks; 'lameros' who work the tailings or waste dumps; 'palliris', women who chip away by hand at the accumulated piles of rejected ore; and 'jukus', illegal workers who enter the mines after the shift workers finish to collect ore to sell to the 'veneristas'. It has been calculated that during the 1970s up to one fifth of COMIBOL's production came from marginal miners such as these (53). The advantages to the company are obvious, since these workers shoulder alone and individually the risks and burdens of their dangerous and unhealthy labours and relieve the enterprise of the financial responsibility for them and their dependants. To the unions, however, they represent an alternative, usually non-unionised, cheap labour supply. The growing inability of the mining economy to employ full-time labour has acute implications in the private sector where as many as 2,000 small firms are run on part-time peasant labour, offering work to between 20,000 and 30,000 (54). Richard Godoy, after a recent study in the Norte de Potosí, concludes that this can be quite profitable in narrow cost terms:

> Peasants who are paid a set price for each pound of, say, clean antimony concentrate (regardless of its costs or of the time invested) will save on timber, coca leaves, carbide, and other material inputs. Despite the danger of 'roof falls', they will eschew timbering, despite exhaustion they will chew coca modestly, despite darkness they will work under the flicker of only individual carbide lamps, despite the threat of accidents they will not buy helmets, gloves or iron-tipped boots. To take time to make a tunnel safer is to perform an unremunerated service for which the cost is decline in output. To chew more coca, to purchase a lamp or a helmet is to nibble away at their small profits (55).

The author then contrasts this situation with that operating in the COMIBOL mines or the large private mines, where "management must build camps, schools, hospitals, movie houses, sports facilities and churches". The FSTMB is now facing a situation in which their struggle will not be to advance, but actually to prevent the widespread return of conditions reminiscent of the pre-1952 era, when private capital dominated the mining sector.

The magnitude of the economic and political challenge now facing Bolivian workers in general and the miners in particular prompts with even greater urgency the resolution of the long-standing problem of how to secure a meaningful political alliance with the peasantry. Before 1952 this was impossible due to the semi-feudal conditions prevailing in the rural areas, but after the revolution and the implementation of agrarian reform the opportunity to link up with the newly forming peasant unions was missed and the MNR was able to control the peasants through local political bosses ('caciques') who continued to dominate

the rural areas, although they might now sport MNR colours. This failure to follow up their early efforts and to respond to the exhortations
of individual trade unionists such as Federico Escóbar, miners' leader
at Siglo XX in the MNR period, was to cost the movement dear in the
period 1957-74 when Siles, Paz Estenssoro, Barrientos and Banzer all
benefited from peasant support in their confrontations with the miners.
Since then several attempts have been made to increase peasant participation in the COB and to associate peasant leaders more closely with the
national leadership of the workers' unions. Despite being crippled
during the regime of García Meza, Genaro Flores of the CSUTCB (Confederation of Bolivian Peasant Workers, founded in 1979) has been at the head
of this movement. The news in early October 1985 that Paz Estenssoro
was forming a new rival peasant confederation under a similar name may
indicate that these efforts are promising to bear fruit.

The participation of the peasant majority is a prerequisite for
success in any attempt to resist right-wing government policies where
the military is giving unified support to that government. The urban-
industrial workers and middle sectors are not strong enough alone to
overthrow the state. The situation has changed since 1952 when an urban
insurrection backed by the miners swept the oligarchy from power and all
but destroyed the armed forces despite a long history of militarism in
Bolivia. Following the 1952 revolution the army was reduced to minimum
levels and only revived when the labour-MNR alliance began to collapse
and the United States urged the restoration of the military and the
disarming of the workers' militias. The adoption by the MNR in 1964 of
a military vice-presidential candidate was perhaps the inevitable first
step towards the military's return to power in November that year.

Since 1964, as we have seen, Bolivians have suffered a long period of
military rule culminating in the García Meza regime, whose involvement
in the drug smuggling trade discredited his government internationally
and finally committed the United States, so often a supporter of military regimes in Bolivia, to his removal from power. The crimes of the
regime have been well documented, from the assassination of leading
politicians such as Marcelo Quiroga Santa Cruz, to the hiring of ex-Nazi
Klaus Barbie to help Arce Gómez coordinate the activities of para-
militaries brought in especially from Argentina. For the COB and the
FSTMB this latest military regime meant the bulldozing of their headquarters, the exiling of their leaders, and the exposing of their rank
and file to unrestrained violence. Whilst international pressure helped
a return to constitutional rule in 1982, the continuing growth of the
drug business is a constant reminder of the dangers of the new situation
in which the country finds itself, where the old problem of militarism
has become fused with the new one of drug smuggling on a vast scale.

Coca cultivation is widely practised in Andean America and coca leaves
are freely available in most Bolivian markets. The chewing of the dried
leaves mixed with lime is a traditional device for staving off hunger
and exhaustion. However, the demand for the processed drug in the US
and Europe has turned production based on peasant cultivation into a
booming industry. Climatic conditions and geographical isolation lend
themselves to clandestine production, so that despite the declared
opposition of successive regimes extensive areas are given over to coca
in the Beni, Chapare and Santa Cruz. Huge financial sums are involved.
Chief drug boss Roberto Suárez is reputed to have a personal fortune of
US $400 million and to be ready to finance the national debt repayments

if his conditions are met. The estimated value of the trade annually in Bolivia alone is US $2 billion, which is more than twice the entire legal economy. More than 500,000 people are involved (56). The impor- tance of this for Bolivian workers and the miners who have traditionally led them is evident. There exists within the state an activity which is prosperous and expanding. It has close links with the military estab- lishment. Being illegal, it is impossible for the state to tax this source of fabulous profits which have made the reserves of the Santa Cruz banks larger than those of the Central Bank in La Paz. Yet this activity threatens the state itself when its gangster methods become prevalent within the military, a threat demonstrated recently by the difficulties in bringing García Meza to trial after nine successive judges removed themselves from his case (57).

Meanwhile the mining sector continues to decline, unable to find sufficient capital to break out of the downward spiral, leaving the labour force and its leaders to contemplate the probable disappearance from Bolivia of old-style mining and with it the opportunity to organise large numbers of workers for their mutual defence and advancement. Top FSTMB leaders, many of whom have been active in the Federation since the formative years of the 1940s and 1950s, can look back on four decades of almost unremitting struggle. Since its foundation in 1944 the FSTMB has played a crucial role in ousting the oligarchy and creating the politi- cal opportunity for the modernisation of the state, by means of the enfranchisement of the entire adult population, the granting of agrarian reform and the nationalisation of the mines: the major national re- source. It has not, however, succeeded in its more fundamental object- ive of dramatically improving the living and working conditions of its members, and instead has suffered repeated assaults from successive military regimes. It may be possible to argue that the miners bear some responsibility for this, having been unable to preserve the labour-MNR alliance of the 1952-64 era. Yet clearly, the preference of the middle- class MNR party for capitalist solutions to the pressing problems caused by acute economic dependency led inexorably to a clash with labour and to a defeat for the miners, which may be considered inevitable given the the declining role of tin and the shadow of the military, advised and armed by the United States, waiting in the wings. Except for the brief and highly charged period 1970-71, it has not been possible since 1964 for the FSTMB to regain the initiative which had, in 1952, forced the even then reluctant MNR into radical reform. Undoubtedly then, as now, the most serious impediment to a sustained and coherent programme of socialist reconstruction was the absence of a firmly established party of the left which would be able to draw upon the strengths of the Bolivian labour movement, and of the FSTMB in particular, to begin to tackle the enormous economic and social problems facing the country.

Should the miners, confronting without doubt their most serious pol- itical and economic challenge since 1944, now lose their position as the most strategically placed labour group in the republic, it may well mean that the working class as a whole will be leaderless in a way that has not been true for nearly forty years. Local observers already detect in the labour movement an uncharacteristic defeatism and an apparent reluc- tance to raise issues from the sectoral to the national level, when this had for so long been the hallmark of the FSTMB (58). The tragedy for the miners in this new situation, where the whole basis of the Fed- eration is threatened, is that they have acquired through struggle the consciousness to allow them to understand their predicament, but they are further than ever from finding the means to overcome it.

NOTES

(1) For a review of the achievements of the revolution, see R. Alexander, The Bolivian National Revolution, New Jersey, Rutgers University Press, 1958, and J. Dunkerley, Rebellion in the Veins. Political Struggle in Bolivia 1952-1982, London, Verso, 1984. On recent developments in Bolivian trade unionism, see Y. Le Bot, 'Le mouvement syndical bolivien à la croisée des chemins (1978-1980)' in Problèmes d'Amérique Latine, 62, 1981, pp. 111-158. Numbers of union members are very hard to calculate in countries where such affiliation attracts the attention of military-authoritarian regimes. Added to this is the difficulty of paying union dues regularly where great poverty exists. In these case a rough guide to the strength of a union may be gained by looking at the employment figures by sector, although these too are often approximations. The 1984 ILO Year Book of Labour Statistics gives the following figures for Bolivia in 1982: 70,000 in mining, 94,000 in manufacturing, 6,000 in electricity and gas, 56,000 in construction, 91,000 in transport, 11,000 in finance, 58,000 in trade and hotel services, and 214,000 in urban community services. Of course the majority are peasants who work in agriculture - given as 676,000 (p. 267).

(2) In November 1983 FSTMB General Secretary Víctor López became vice-president of COMIBOL, presiding over a board of directors in which the Federation had 4 out of 7 members. See Latin American Weekly Report, 11/11/83.

(3) The total value of mining exports in 1985 was US $280 million; in 1984 the value had been US $354 million. See Latin American Commodities Report, 24/1/86, p. 2. In the period 1977 to 1983 minerals had contributed between 43 and 70 per cent of exports depending on the price of tin. See Latin American Monitor: Andean Group, August 1985, p. 65.

(4) Informe 'R', La Paz, November 1985, p. 15.

(5) The Guardian, 14/12/85, p. 8.

(6) For example the average cost of a pound of tin produced at Huanuni is US $6.80. The cost at Catavi-Siglo XX is US $12. The resulting price per ton at each mine is US $15,000 and US $26,000. See Latin American Commodities Report, 6/12/85, p. 3.

(7) Latin American Commodities Report, 24/1/86, p. 2.

(8) Latin American Monitor: Andean Group, November 1985, p. 219.

(9) Tin production has fallen from 33,000 tons in 1977 to 15,000 in 1985. In 1985 Bolivia also produced 2,240 tons of wolfram, 125 tons of silver, 8,600 tons of antimony and 800 kilos of gold. See Latin American Commodities Report, 24/1/86, p. 2.

(10) House of Commons, Second Report from the Trade and Industry Committee, Session 1985-86. The Tin Crisis, vol. 1, Report and Proceedings of the Committee, London, 1986, p. ix.

(11) For a general historical review of Bolivian trade unionism, see G. Lora, A History of the Bolivian Labour Movement, Cambridge, Cambridge University Press, 1977.

(12) See C. Llobet Tabolara, 'Apuntes para una historia del movimiento obrero en Bolivia' in P. González Casanova (ed.), Historia del movimiento obrero en América Latina, tomo 3, Mexico, Siglo XXI, 1984, pp. 307-358. See p. 343 for comments from Víctor López that

the planned meeting at Siglo XX was to deal exclusively with union matters.

(13) Noted Bolivian film maker Jorge Sanjines has devoted his major works to depicting the struggles of the Bolivian working classes. His masterpiece El coraje del pueblo (The Courage of the People), 1971, deals with the massacre of San Juan.

(14) See the book published by G. Iriarte in Buenos Aires in 1976 (Tierra Nueva), Los mineros bolivianos. Other dramatic descriptions of the daily lives of the mining communities can be found in J. Nash, We Eat the Mines and They Eat Us. Dependency and Exploitation in the Bolivian Tin Mines, New York, Columbia University Press, 1979; and National Union of Mineworkers, Report of NUM Delegation. Trade Union and Human Rights in Bolivia and Chile, London, NUM, 1977.

(15) See H. Schmucler and O. Encinas, 'Las radios mineras de Bolivia. Entrevista con Jorge Mancilla Romero' in Comunicación y Cultura, (UNAM, Mexico), 8, July 1982, pp. 69-86.

(16) Lora, op. cit., pp. 360-361.

(17) Idem., and R. Zavaleta, El poder dual en América Latina, Mexico, Siglo XXI, 1974.

(18) Lora, op. cit., and a personal communication from Víctor López, Lima, September 1981.

(19) R. Zavaleta, 'Bolivia. Military nationalism and the Popular Assembly' in New Left Review, 73, May-June 1972, pp. 63-82.

(20) Between 80 and 200 peasants are estimated to have died in January 1974 following clashes with the army near the village of Tolata. See the church account, Comisión de Justicia y Paz, La masacre del valle, La Paz, 1974.

(21) Zavaleta, 'Bolivia ...'. p. 72.

(22) Llobet, op. cit., p. 351.

(23) Lora, op. cit., p. 365.

(24) For an English translation of the Pulacayo Thesis, see North American Congress on Latin America (NACLA), 'Bolivia: the war goes on', NACLA Report , 8:2, February 1974.

(25) Dunkerley, op. cit., p. 208.

(26) T. Greaves and J. Albó, 'An anatomy of dependency. A Bolivian tin miners strike' in M. A. Seglison and J. A. Booth (eds.), Political Participation in Latin America, vol. 3: Politics and the Poor, New York, Holmes and Meier, 1979, pp. 169-182.

(27) Asamblea Permanente de los Derechos Humanos de Bolivia, Estudio sobre el valor adquisitivo del salario de los mineros, La Paz, APDHB, 1978, p. 26.

(28) See footnote 14.

(29) Dunkerley, op. cit., p. 36.

(30) There were three general elections in this period: July 1978, July 1979 and June 1980. There were six attempted coups of which three were successful: General Juan Pereda Asbún in July 1978, General David Padilla in November 1978, and General Luis García Meza in July 1980.

(31) See FSTMB publication, Un año de la infamia. Apuntes para la historia del movimiento obrero boliviano, La Paz, FSTMB, 1981, and Asamblea Permanente de los Derechos Humanos de Bolivia, La heróica resistencia de los mineros de bolivia, 17 Julio - 6 Agosto 1980, Lima, APDHB, 1981.

(32) J. Dunkerley and R. Morales, 'The crisis in Bolivia' in New Left Review, 155, 1986, pp. 86-106. See p. 89.

(33) Latin American Weekly Report (LAWR), 14/9/84.

(34) Dunkerley and Morales, op. cit., p. 104.
(35) LAWR, 29/4/84.
(36) LAWR, 12/8/83.
(37) For an interesting and well-informed discussion of this period, see
     Y. Le Bot, 'L'expérience de co-gestion à majorité ouvrière en
     Bolivie (1983-1984). Entre l'utopie ouvrière et le déclin du
     secteur minier' in Problèmes d'Amérique Latine, 73, 1984, pp. 105-
     119.
(38) LAWR, 12/8/83, p. 7.
(39) Idem.
(40) LAWR, 16/9/83, pp. 8-9.
(41) D. Fox, 'Bolivia' in Mining Annual Review 1984, London, Mining
     Journal, 1985, pp. 302-307. See p. 304.
(42) Informe 'R', August 1985. See also The Guardian, 14/12/85, p. 8.
(44) For an interesting insight into the development of the Housewives
     Committees in the mines, see Domitila Chungara, Let Me Speak,
     London, Stage I, 1976.
(45) Informe 'R', October 1985, pp. 4-5. In the elections Banzer won
     28.57 per cent of the votes compared to Paz's 26.42 per cent, but
     the congressional vote went to Paz by 94 to 51.
(46) See Financial Times, 21/11/85, and Sunday Times, 3/11/85.
(47) Conservative MP Robin Maxwell Hyslop, a member of the House of
     Commons Select Committee (see note 10), commented: "LME dealers who
     continued selling on credit to the ITC Buffer Stock Manager when in
     their own judgement he was trading beyond his means, gambled and
     have lost" (quoted in 'The tin disaster' in International Labour
     Reports, 15, May-June 1986, p. 8).
(48) Financial Times, 15/11/85, and Latin American Commodities Report,
     6/12/85, p. 2
(49) Financial Times, 17/10/85.
(50) Idem, and Latin American Commodities Report, 7/2/86, p. 2.
(51) Note for example the election reported in Hoy, 13/1/86, of
     Communist leaders Ruffo Rivera and Jaime Ramos by a large majority.
(52) Presencia, La Paz, 19/3/86.
(53) Ricardo A. Godoy, 'Technical and economic efficiency of peasant
     miners in Bolivia' in Economic Development and Cultural Change,
     34:1, 1985, pp. 103-120.
(54) Le Bot, 'L'expérience ...', p. 107.
(55) Godoy, op. cit., pp. 114-115.
(56) Latin American Monitor: Andean Group, November 1985, p. 232. See
     also A. Henman et al., Big Deal. The Politics of the Illicit Drug
     Business, London, Pluto Press, 1984.
(57) Time Magazine, 19/5/86, p. 64.
(58) Informe 'R', April 1986.

10 The crisis of trade unionism in Turkey

HÜSEYIN RAMAZANOGLU

In this essay I shall attempt to examine the development of Turkish trade unions in order to clarify events leading to the crisis of trade unionism in the 1980s. I shall not attempt a detailed analysis of the role of labour movement in the transformation of the Turkish social formation since the foundation of the Republic in 1923.

As the capitalist mode of production became established in Turkey, a fierce struggle developed for the monopolistic control of state power between the fractions of the Turkish ruling classes. I have analysed these struggles in depth elsewhere (1). In this paper I want to argue that with the development of a wage labour force, trade unions became important agents in these struggles for power, but agents which could be manipulated in different ways by competing interests.

According to Marxist theory, one would expect to find that in a social formation dominated by the capitalist mode of production, the major contradiction is between capital and labour. Given the uneven levels of capitalist development in Turkey, however, the struggle between capital and labour has not so far been the dominant struggle in determining the outcome of class struggles in Turkey. This situation is likely to change following the economic and political restructuring of the 1980s, since Turkish capitalist development is firmly dominated by an alliance of monopoly/industrial and financial capital. After their long struggles, commercial and landed capital have at last been defeated and put in a subordinated position to this alliance. The Turkish state is in the process of being restructured to meet the needs of this alliance of monopoly/industrial and financial capital and Turkey is also being opened up to international markets. These developments came to a head in the military intervention of 1980. As a result, the contradictions between capital and labour will inevitably become much clearer than before, and the future of Turkish capitalism will be affected by the nature and development of labour's continuous struggles against capital. The role of trade unions in this struggle is likely to increase and become influential despite the current limitations on trade union political and economic activities which were imposed by the 1982 constitution.

Although trade unions always were politically active throughout the period leading to the last military intervention of 1980, the economic, political and ideological framework in which they operated was always given to them. They themselves did not and could not at any stage set their own political agenda. I will argue that trade union struggles have been primarily of benefit to those to whom the unions were economically, politically, and ideologically opposed.

Although the Turkish case is clearly determined by the specificity of that social formation, this general analysis could raise questions which are applicable to other cases in the newly industrialising countries today.

CAPITALIST DEVELOPMENT AND TRADE UNIONS

Trade unions are the creations of industrialisation and particularly of capitalist development. When the industrial revolution created new needs for increasing numbers of people to work in the manufacturing sector, the short-fall of labour power in the cities could only be made up by migration from the countryside. This process led to the growing separation of small direct producers from their land and rural communities, and forced them to be transformed into wage labourers working in the factories which were located in the cities (2).

Whenever a wage labour force is established early attempts by the workers to organise and defend themselves against blatant and savage exploitation have been met by shows of force from employers, backed by the state security forces. Workers only slowly and partially gained rights to collective bargaining and to strike, while employers retained their right to lock out troublesome workers.

Generally these rights have been gained as a result of long, bitter and often bloody struggles. They have to be seen as **political rights,** which are administered and controlled by the state on behalf of society. They are not **natural rights** which are sacrosanct and cannot be taken away. Even where full political rights to trade union activity are achieved, there is no guarantee that a change in economic, political, or ideological conditions will not undermine or destroy them.

Today, in many countries of the world trade union rights are guaranteed by international agreements. The International Labour Organisation (ILO) exists to monitor and where possible to protect the rights of working people all over the world. But the existence of these rights depend (a) on the extent to which the integrity of the state is secure, (b) on the nature of the capitalist transformation and the need to restructure the state, and (c) on the ability of the working classes to fight and defend them. The Turkish example is no exception to this rule.

THE GROWTH OF TRADE UNIONS IN TURKEY

The first signs of workers' movements in Turkey can be dated back to the 1870s when some workers associations were established as a result of the introduction of 'Tanzimat' policies and the liberalisation of the Ottoman economic system (3). It is not, however, fruitful to concentrate on this period too much as these workers associations were not well organised and they did not really play any marked role in the development of the Turkish labour movement. These associations came together around a single issue, and did not have any continuity. The only time there was a significant development was when the dockyard workers in Istanbul went on strike in 1871. Otherwise, the conditions under which the workers had to work were appalling, and their wages were very low, indeed. In 1909 the right to form workers associations was abolished. After World War I, the workers movements started again. During the War of Independence (1919-23) these associations played a very important and supportive role.

The period following the War of Independence and the foundation of the Republic in 1923 created the conditions for the workers to organise in trade unions, which had continuity. Their existence was the end result of the populist ideology of the Kemalist regime, but they were not expected, nor were they allowed, to attain any real economic and political importance (4). But the trade unions did become politically important after 1961. During the period 1961-80, trade unions came into full being and took an active part in Turkish politics.

It is possible to divide the history and the development of trade unionism in the Turkish Republic into four periods: 1923-46, 1946-61, 1961-80 and 1980 to date.

The 1923-46 period

This period was dominated politically by a single-party regime of the Republican People's Party, which was formed by Mustafa Kemal Atatürk. The populist and etatist (5) nature of the Kemalist regime ostensibly allowed an open political and economic system where the people of Turkey could participate in the decision making process regardless of their social, economic, political and ideological positions. The phrase used to describe the new composition of the social order was "classless, advantageless and integrated mass". In fact, this was a period dominated by an unswerving drive to establish the foundations of an industrialisation programme under the auspices of the state in the face of bitter opposition from landed and commercial capital which dominated the political and economic relations of the newly formed Republic. The stark realities of the situation could not be covered by the rhetoric for long. The working people of Turkey found to their cost that there was no such thing as power sharing by all for all under a system increasingly dominated by capitalist relations of production. It was, nevertheless, an important, albeit frustrating, period for the trade unions because they were able to establish an organisational base upon which they could build in the future.

After the foundation of the Republic in 1923, workers were able to organise in a more effective manner. Their new political consciousness and organisation showed a remarkable difference from that of the previous period. Whereas before, labour protests were based on spon-

taneity, after 1923 workers became much more conscious of their role in
society. They organised in trade unions rather than in workers' associations, which did not have any political direction or set objectives.
By use of the rhetoric of Kemalism and the populist single-party regime
of the RPP, working people were proclaimed to be integral partners in
the building of new Turkey. In 1923, at the Izmir Economic Congress,
where the new Turkish economic development strategy was determined, the
right of workers to form trade unions was recognised and it was also
decided to modify the legislative structure to incorporate working
people's rights into society (6). But these rights were never implemented, because they were abolished in 1925 as a result of an uprising
instigated by the trade unions which were organising in the Eastern
provinces.

In 1927, Turkey started sending observers to ILO meetings and automatically became a full member in 1932 when she joined the League of
Nations. Contrary to the appearance presented to the outside world and
to Kemalist rhetoric, there was wide ranging oppression of the workers
and of union activities during the 1923-46 period. Union attempts to
organise under a single national body of a trade unions' confederation
were directly blocked by the government. The real blow came in 1936 in
the form of a new Labour Law, which prohibited the right to strike, and
also imposed "compulsory arbitration" for the resolution of labour
disputes.

The 1946-61 Period

The legitimacy of the single-party regime was tested by the formation of
a new political party, the Democrat Party (DP), in 1946. The DP was
formed by a group of politicians who had broken away from the RPP and
who represented the interests of landed and commercial capital. In this
period landed capital and commercial capital were struggling to re-
establish their ascendancy over the nascent industrial capital. The
interests of industrial capital were fostered by the Kemalist Republican
People's Party government, and in particular by the regime's etatist
strategies. Success for landed and commercial interests came in the
1950 general election when the DP won a land-slide victory over the RPP.

Trade unions faced these new political developments without the benefit of an organised and struggle-hardened movement. With the introduction of multi-party politics in 1946, the trade unions wanted to
capitalise on the instability of the new situation and concentrated on
organising all over the country. RPP was not only worried by the new
threat posed to its rule by the DP, but it was also concerned at these
initiatives taken by the trade unions. Demands made by the unions and
by the DP were perceived to be similar, and to prevent further deterioration of the situation the government declared martial law. In December
1946, the martial law authorities banned the newly formed trade unions
on the pretext that they were connected to socialist parties.

In February 1947, the government passed a new law regulating trade
unionism. According to this law, employers were also given the right to
form unions. Unions could be formed without official permission, but
they were liable to be monitored by the authorities. This law did not
cover all wage earners. Collective bargaining and strikes were not
allowed. Trade unions were banned from taking part in political activity, joining the unions was made voluntary.

The opposition party (DP) was at odds with the party in power (RPP) who were totally opposed to granting collective bargaining and strike rights to the unions. DP in order to strengthen its position vis-a-vis RPP defended the trade unions and supported their claims. This led to mass defections to DP from the labour movement, and in February 1950, the Free Federation of Trade Unions came into being.

The DP victory in 1950 and the ensuing discussion on the issues of collective bargaining and strikes provided long-needed encouragement to trade unions. There were a number of trade union federations formed covering a wide range of industries. Despite initial promises the new DP government did not pass reforming trade union legislation. There was no mention of collective bargaining and strikes in the government programme published in October 1951.

In spite of this discouragement, the trade unions managed to achieve a confederation which was to gather all the disparate and wide spread unions under a single framework. The new confederation (Türk-Is) was formally constituted in July 1952. This new body neither generated sufficient support from its members nor was effective in influencing the government to grant it collective bargaining and strike rights.

The DP years were also marked by the growing influence of the USA on Turkish affairs. Turkish troops were sent to Korea to fight side-by-side with the UN troops. American trade unionism was taken as the model for Türk-Is to follow. The Marshall Plan and the Truman Doctrine gave rise to the development of a situation where everything American came to be seen as good. Trade unions were helped financially and educationally by their American counterparts, and several trade unionists were sent to the USA to learn American methods and practices. Americanisation of Turkish trade unionism led to a regression of the working class struggle at an ideological level, as the goals were redefined in purely economistic terms.

The effects of the boom years of the Korean War were felt by the Turkish economy, too. Turkish (primarily agricultural) goods were highly sought after because of the high demand generated by the Korean War. Turkish landed and commercial capital made huge profits, and the interests of industrial capital received low priority. The unions also benefited from the war situation because the government had established a method of cooperation which provided jobs and benefits to workers without providing rights to collective bargaining and strikes. Furthermore, the government divided the trade unions by offering material support to those who supported its policies at the expense of the others who were actively advocating full trade union rights. The close cooperation between the government and Türk-Is came to a halt in 1953, and especially after 1954, with the withering of the war economy and the tightening of the world economic markets.

Despite some bitterness and legal proceedings against some trade unionists, the links between the DP and the labour movement continued until 1957. During the 1946-60 period the labour movement had acquired the right to organise but not the right to exercise full trade union functions. This situation was further exacerbated by the very low level of industrialisation. The unions were primarily seen as power bases upon which politicians could build their political careers.

Events did not help the DP government to regain the popularity it once enjoyed among the people. After a brief flirtation with liberal economic policies in the early 1950s, the fortunes of the government gradually worsened as the demand for Turkish products abroad waned and the liberal trade regimes became detrimental to the future of Turkish capitalism. Lack of clear economic objectives and increasing desertion from the DP ranks by supporters and political activists did not give much to cheer about. The breach driven between the pro- and anti-government unions instead of meeting old promises contributed to the further erosion of popular support (7).

The DP government found it increasingly difficult to ignore the demands made by the etatist politicians to revert to old policies which favoured industrial interests. Some of the merchants were rapidly transferring their allegiances and long-term support over to the rejuvenated industrial interests as the gains made by commercial capital during the boom years were rapidly being invested in industrial projects. The alliance between landed and commercial capital was being challenged as the political base of the government came under increasing pressure both from within and without. The government's solution was to increase anti-democratic practices and to use the military and the police to deal with the growing unrest. It attempted to pass legislation to make the constitutional base of the regime redundant by giving itself powers to rule by decree.

This situation ended in the military intervention of May 1960, which restored the principles of democratic rule, banned the DP from political life, and punished the leaders of the DP regime by sentencing three of their senior ministers (one being the Prime Minister) to death, and the rest to gaol sentences of various lengths.

The new 1961 constitution, which guaranteed the establishment of a liberal political order, also secured the right to form trade unions, thus granting, in Article 47, full trade union rights including the right to take part in collective bargaining and to strike.

The 1961-80 Period

This period introduced hitherto unknown political and ideological freedom to Turkey. The military returned to their barracks, a coalition government was formed under the direction of the RPP, and its leader, Inönü, became prime minister. Again, the unions had to put pressure on the government to listen to their demands and to include trade union legislation into its programme. New political parties of all persuasion came into being, and the legislative work of giving trade unions full political status started in earnest in 1962.

At this time trade unions were still few in number and small in size. There was only one confederation, which had rather diluted objectives. In addition, the employers also started forming their own organisations, e.g. the Confederation of Turkish Employers' Unions (its Turkish acronym is TISK), which started pressing the government to delay the granting of full trade union rights to workers.

This struggle continued until 1963 when the government could no longer resist union demands. The Employment Minister, Ecevit, introduced Law 274, which granted trade union rights to all wage earners, and Law 275, which gave trade unions the right to take part in collective bargaining and the right to strike as prescribed in the constitution.

What distinguishes the 1963 trade union legislation is that, contrary to previous historical experiences of various labour movements, the Turkish labour movement gained these rights without any real struggle. The state acceded to the demands of the workers without challenging their rights to make these demands. Union rights were seen to be purely political rights granted as a result of the prevalent conditions in Turkey at the time. They could, therefore, be taken away or modified later because the working class had not gained the necessary experience to defend them. In addition to this weakness, the organisation of the trade unions was left completely to the state. As a result the unions were organised in ways in which the state deemed necessary, and which in later years turned out to be not in the best interests of the working class.

By the early 1960s, the level of industrialisation in Turkey was still very low. Capital accumulation was just gaining momentum, and economic development was taking place in a closed economy. Although economic objectives were clearly laid out, political and ideological practices were not in congruence with these objectives. State power was shared uneasily by landed, commercial, industrial, and financial capital. In order for industrial and financial capital to restructure the accumulation of capital and the distribution of surplus and surplus labour in their own favour, changes had to be made to the distribution of political power which favoured industrial and financial interests.

The struggle that had started in 1923, in the aftermath of the War of Independence, was about to move up to the next stage of rapid industrialisation in the context of the peculiarities of the distribution of state power among the fractions of Turkish capital.

The labour movement joined in this battle with great energy neither necessarily understanding the nature of the struggle nor having the relevant political experience or organisation to benefit from it. Türk-Is published a twenty-four point document praising the virtues of rapid development and industrialisation, and of arriving at the stage of modernity with haste. In the process, the document argued, all barriers must be crushed, and any reactionary mentality to progress must be eradicated. Workers thus espoused the interests of their employers.

After a brief encounter with parliamentary politics, Türk-Is took a position which put it above party politics. This non-partisan policy led to the eventual erosion of the Turkish trade union movement and the political split that inevitably occurred amidst shouts of betrayal and American lackeyism. A new confederation broke away from Türk-Is in February 1967. It was called the Confederation of Revolutionary Trade Unions (its Turkish acronym is DISK).

DISK adopted a more directly political attitude to Turkish politics. It supported revolutionary and left wing political activities in general, and in particular, the socialist Workers Party of Turkey (WPT) during the parliamentary elections of 1969. DISK started fulfilling the long awaited and necessary role of raising the political consciousness of the working classes, developing strategies and tactics for the working classes to adopt in their struggle. This role was, however, marred by difficulties inherent in the Turkish system and lack of experience on the part of DISK itself.

Trade unionism expanded very rapidly in the 1960s. Unions began to be effective in collective bargaining with employers. Strikes began to be used as weapons to fight employer power. Türk-Is gradually took over the unions in the public sector whereas DISK controlled the unions in the private sector.

1968-9 were also the years when the struggle for the monopolistic use of state power between the fractions of capital reached new heights. Industrial and financial capital were making inroads into the power base of commercial and landed capital. In 1969, a general election was held as a result of the RPP leader Inönü's loss of the vote of confidence in Parliament. The Justice Party (JP) won with a comfortable majority, and its leader, Demirel, became the new prime minister. Although the electoral base of the JP government was primarily in small towns and the rural areas dominated by landed and commercial interests, its ideology in practice was to promote industrialisation and to support the development of industrial and financial capital. This contradiction inherent in the JP and exemplified in the person of its leader, played a crucial role in shaping the politics of Turkey until 1980.

The economy was also coming rapidly under the domination of capitalist relations, and all sectors were becoming increasingly integrated into the market economy. Halting the tide of generalised commodity production, the expanded reproduction of capital and the migration of small direct producers from the countryside to the cities and abroad was proving very difficult for the landed and commercial interests. These interests were still able to resist the continuous attempts of industrial and financial capital to assert their domination of state power when their domination of the economy was completed.

Industrial and financial capital were being challenged firstly by the landed and commercial interests, and secondly, but to a much lesser extent, by the growing trade union movement. DISK was proving to be the only effective trade union organisation to be taken seriously by the ruling classes. The irony of the situation was that DISK was too weak to have had any chance of success had it not been for its 'usefulness', as perceived by some fractions of Turkish capital.

This 'usefulness' appeared to be particularly apparent to industrial and financial interests who were after the monopolistic use of state power but who needed to restructure the state before they could realise their aims. By exaggerating the power of trade unions, using the threat of revolution, and the spectre of secessionist movements in the East (especially Kurdish) they set about inflicting irreparable damage to the democratic system as laid down by the 1961 constitution. Their representatives argued that the constitution was not suitable for Turkey because it was allegedly not accepted by the people.

These interests saw their chance in the instigation of a military intervention that could lead to the progressive restructuring of some of the state apparatuses. Lack of political understanding, low levels of theoretical knowledge of capitalism, and lack of experience on the part of the left in general and the labour movement in particular contributed to the development of such a situation. The situation was further endangered by the effective deployment of agents-provocateurs among the left groups and fear of secessionism in the East among the population at large. They achieved this aim by stimulating the left wing organisations to pursue policies which could be interpreted as revolutionary and/or secessionist.

DISK came under continuous provocation from the state and state-bred right wing organisations. The actions of the state reached their climax in 1970 when Laws 274 and 275 were replaced by a new Law 1317, which limited trade union rights. When DISK and its supporters protested, there was bloodshed on 15-16 June 1970. As a result of appeals made to the Constitutional Court by some political parties, some of the amendments of Law 1317 were overturned.

This did not stop the agitation and the degeneration of left wing politics. Gradually the demands of the labour movement, socialist parties, and progressive organisations were all merged into the spectre of revolution, secessionism and anarchy in the country. Whereas previously the labour movement had argued for nationalist policies coupled with anti-Americanism and the creation of a national democratic front to resist the rise of 'fascism', the mantles of nationalism and democracy were taken away from them and, this time, donned by the right wing parties and neofascist organisations. The labour movement and the socialist organisations were totally helpless when the military intervened in March 1971, overthrew the Demirel government and stated that it was doing so in order to save the country from anarchy and to restore constitutional democracy and law and order.

This second military intervention brought with it a whole range of punitive measures directed against the left and particularly against the labour movement. The justification for the intervention was "to save the country from anarchists and secessionist movements". This meant the introduction of new legislation which was meant to restrict general democratic rights and, specifically trade union rights. People who had taken part in the development of left wing and progressive politics, and those who had been active in the trade union movement, were identified as "communists", and the whole might of the military regime came down on them. Socialist organisations were crushed, left wing political parties were banned, people were killed or given long-term gaol sentences, lives were ruined, and the bases of the 1961 constitution were totally undermined.

The effects of this period of military dictatorship on the labour movement were serious. Collective bargaining rights and the right to strike and lock-out were suspended. There was a decrease in real wages, and living conditions of wage earners worsened. Martial law authorities acted ruthlessly and without recourse to law in crushing the opposition to capitalist rule. There were, however, serious difficulties encountered by the military rulers and their civilian allies because people at large were not willing to accept the legitimacy of the military intervention and to forfeit the rights given by the 1961 constitution. There were also further problems created by the cracks in the power block which had urged the military intervention. Competing interests, i.e. industrial/financial versus landed/commercial, could not agree on a formula which would have made the restructuring of the state possible, thus changing channels of access to the use of state power.

As the struggle within the power block continued, and interminable discussions about an acceptable solution to the problem drew on, it became very difficult to sustain a military regime without a mass support base. During this time the trade unions were hampered in their activities by a hostile environment, lack of political direction, and also lack of leadership. Still the educational activities continued under adverse conditions. The trade union movement could not be criticised for failing to develop political consciousness. The problem was in the content of their teaching, which was not entirely relevant to a labour movement that had to come to grips with the realities of a rapidly changing environment where capitalist development could not be stopped. What was being taught was how to stop capitalist development by reading the Marxist classics without necessarily relating their teachings to the specificity of the Turkish social formation. Theory reading was substituted for a concrete analysis of concrete conditions in the Turkish case.

The left managed to continue, although to a reduced extent, with their 'revolutionary practices'. Usually, their idea of a 'revolutionary practice' was to bomb the buildings where American companies were located, or to kidnap American servicemen and in general to fight American imperialism, i.e. they identified their struggle as against imperialism rather than Turkish capitalism (8). These activities were more dangerous and more threatening to the integrity of the Turkish left than anything else. These actions could have possibly given some short-term success, but they could not substitute for long-term strategic development of the struggle of the Turkish left within Turkish capitalism. Indeed, before the military intervention the state had used the excuse of 'fighting the anarchists' for the launching of a coup. After the coup, they continued to provoke the remnants of the left to armed struggle so that they could justify the continuation of the military dictatorship.

Despite its efforts the military regime could not sustain its faltering image, and agreed to hold a general election which signalled the end of this unhappy and cruel phase of Turkish politics. It was difficult to say who had won, but it was certain that the left and the trade union movement learned a great deal from it. After the 1973 elections, the newly revamped, social democrat RPP, under the new leadership of Ecevit, formed a coalition with the reactionary and religious National Salvation Party (NSP). Trade unions rapidly came under the growing influence of the RPP attracted by its populist and social democratic slogans. Class struggle was to a large extent to be replaced by people's power, and the contradictions of capitalism were to be suppressed by the creation of a People's Sector. The future of the trade union movement was mortgaged to the success of social democracy, and the future of left politics was extensively identified with this development. The lessons taught by the Allende experience in Chile were not learned by the Turkish left, although they sent fraternal messages to the Chilean people and totally condemned the action when the military overthrew the democratically elected government and instituted a military dictatorship instead. The Turkish left did not learn the crucial political lesson of the difference between the state and the government until much later. They were quite happy to substitute one for the other in their analysis of Turkish capitalism, the state and the RPP government.

181

Trade unionism gained momentum after the 1973 general elections. More public sector unions joined DISK, and Türk-Is lost credibility and support among its trade unions. The long-standing divisions between the social democrats and right wingers within Türk-Is became more pronounced. Public sector unions were not really involved in any struggle under Türk-Is. The situation in the private sector, dominated by unions belonging to DISK, could not have been more different. The failure of the 1971-73 military regime and the people's increased awareness of the contradictions of capitalist development, contributed to the politicisation of the public sector unions. The membership of the unions belonging to DISK increased rapidly as large numbers of workers left unions belonging to Türk-Is.

The intensification of the struggle among the trade unions and also the worsening of the economic situation added to the growing politicisation of daily life. Workers started choosing their unions according to their political positions, and the unions started choosing their political allies according to their positions. Political parties of the right quickly established their own confederation of trade unions (MISK, linked to the neofascist National Action Party, and Hak-Is, linked to the National Salvation Party). The main parties of the period, the Justice Party and the Republican People's Party, did not have confederations formally associated with them, but they had extensive influence in Türk-Is and DISK respectively.

Workers belonging to any of these trade union organisations could not work in a workplace if it was dominated by a rival trade union. Battle lines were clearly drawn, and compromises were a thing of the past. The motto of the day was, "you are either with me or against me".

DISK continued to be active in collective bargaining negotiations and where the workers could not obtain satisfaction they frequently resorted to strike action. Outbreaks of strikes led to bloody clashes with the police and with the army. Lock-outs by the employers became a common method of keeping the rise of workers' power at bay. The state gave active support to employers organisations. The first Nationalist Front government, which replaced the RPP-NSP coalition in 1975, was a coalition of right wing parties (including the NSP) and was dominated by the JP. Demirel as leader of the JP, became prime minister of this new government. His deputy was Ret. Colonel Türkes, the leader of the neofascist National Action Party. This government openly used and protected right wing and neofascist movements (especially activists of the National Action Party known as the Grey Wolves) to crush and intimidate workers engaged in struggles against their employers and the police. State apparatuses, especially the security forces, were opened to recruits from the right wing parties which formed the coalition.

Whilst the political situation was getting gradually worse, the representatives of Turkish capital were continuing with their unresolved struggle over how to undermine the political framework laid down by the 1961 constitution so that the dominant fractions, monopoly/industrial and financial capital, could monopolise the use of state power. Landed and commercial capital had seen the writing on the wall long ago, and were chiefly involved in damage control. Since firstly, their interests were irreconcilable with the interests of the working class, secondly, they could not be separated from the power block, and thirdly they could not leave the ideological and political struggle solely in the hands of the monopoly/industrial and financial capital, they had to act in tandem with the latter in using the trade union movement and the left wing organisations to undermine the integrity of the Turkish democracy. The ruling classes managed to capitalise on the lack of medium and long-term strategies in the trade union movement and on the workers' misunderstanding of the specificity of the transformation process of Turkish capitalism. That is, workers were using a crude interpretation of Marxist theory which stressed the uniformity rather than the diversity of capitalist development. This made it difficult for unionists to understand, let alone to anticipate, the struggles for power between fractions of capital. They could not then defend themselves from the many-sided assaults on any show of workers power.

The ideal solution for the ruling classes would have been to bring RPP and JP together to form a coalition which would have at least given them room to manoeuvre. This dream did not come true, and the politicisation of all levels of Turkish society continued unabated. The situation was further exacerbated by the growing world economic recession and its impact on the Turkish economy. Measures to promote effective economic growth which were urgently needed were not taken, because of the unresolved struggle among the fractions of capital. The Turkish state in this period was still organised to function in a closed-economy and a closed-society. The new need, however, was to open the economy to world markets, to encourage foreign investment, to establish money markets and stock markets and to change the production process so that it became export-orientated rather than reliant on import-substitution. All these changes were ultimately political in essence because they would have meant both changing the distribution of political power and also restructuring the allocation of resources. These measures would have required a fundamental restructuring of the Turkish state.

The fragmented class struggle into which the trade unions were drawn was not clearly directed at taking over the state. That struggle had to wait until Turkish capitalism had matured and capitalist state power was effectively monopolised by the monopoly/industrial and financial capital. The main struggle prior to 1980 among the fractions of the ruling classes was over achieving this monopolistic control of state power. The struggle between capital and labour at this time was fragmented by the violence of the domestic struggle, during which the trade union movement was divided and manipulated. Union activity, however, was still important because it was affecting capital accumulation and aggravating the economic difficulties faced by the Turkish capitalists as a result of shrinking export markets and rapidly dwindling foreign currency reserves. Labour remained politically weak, however, and there was no danger at any time of the capitalist state being overrun by left wing revolutionaries or the unions.

The struggle with the unions and the left was proving to be highly advantageous to the ruling classes, because the blame for the growing economic crisis could be attributed to the activities of the Turkish left and the unions. The Nationalist Front government openly provoked the left further and pushed it into corners out of which it could only escape by armed struggle. In 1976, the government also introduced State Security Courts (SSC) to try the 'anarchists', who invariably turned out to be the left wing activists, trade union members, and intellectuals.

During this period, the differences between DISK and Türk-Is widened further. DISK was supporting the retention of the May 1 as Workers' Day, and Türk-Is was opposing it. DISK was totally opposed to the establishment of SSCs, while Türk-Is qualified its opposition. As it more clearly represented workers' interests in a declining economy, DISK came to dominate the trade union movement. In 1977, the call for a May Day meeting was answered by hundreds of thousands turning out to give their support to DISK and to show their opposition to the government and its blatant use of violent fascist practices. Unidentified people, who were widely suspected to be members of security forces, opened fire on a peaceful protest, and forty people died either by gun shots or by being trampled on in the subsequent panic (9). This year was also the election year. DISK supported RPP and a RPP win was seen as the last chance the country would have before it plunged further into chaos and nearer to the next military intervention.

The RPP won the majority of the votes but did not have sufficient number of seats in the Parliament to form a majority government. The accepted political formula was for Ecevit to form a minority RPP government which would be supported by small right wing political parties and independents in the Parliament. This unstable government won DISK's support on the understanding that its right wing support did not go so far as to dilute the RPP's labour policies. Türk-Is, on the other hand, did not really extend its support to the new government, but the situation was far from clear. The ruling classes again argued for a JP-RPP coalition and failed. Not only did Demirel and Ecevit not trust each other, but their parties represented quite different interests. The configuration of political forces could not allow the formation of such a coalition, which could not have given unconditional support to monopoly/industrial and financial capital. Some people among the Istanbul section of the Association of Turkish Industrialists and Businessmen (its Turkish acronym is TUSIAD) argued for supporting the RPP government, but were quickly disassociated from the organisation.

The economic, political and social situation turned from bad to worse. As the conditions for the workers worsened and inflation increased, trade unions became more and more active. State apparatuses, which had been penetrated earlier by the parties who had formed the first Nationalist Front government, refused to work with the RPP government. Government policies were rendered ineffective when key officials refused to implement them. The government, for example, could not control the police which was thoroughly penetrated by supporters of the National Action Party. In many cases it was the police and other security forces who were the real instigators of violence and anarchy. They openly condoned violence by neofascist activists and protected them. They had trained paramilitary troops who operated with impunity side-by-side against the left and the unions. The SCCs were working full-time in sentencing those trade unionists and left wing activists who had managed to escape alive from the clutches of the security forces and the so-called 'patriotic' civilian forces. The left and the unions were declared to be full of anti-Turkish, anarchists and 'communists', and the right wing organisations, such as Grey Wolves, were, on the other hand depicted to be the custodians of Turkish nationalism and unity.

This curious political situation continued until 1979 when the RPP government fell and the second Nationalist Front government was formed by virtually the same partners as the first one. Only one very small right wing party had disappeared from the scene and therefore was not in the second coalition. Demirel, again was the prime minister, and Turkes, now much more overt in his politics, with an increased parliamentary share, was his deputy.

1979 and 1980 saw the escalation of strikes by increasingly desperate workers leading to armed struggles with the state security forces and right wing Grey Wolves. Trade unions became unequivocally divided along the political lines which were increasingly affecting the lives of ordinary people. In 1980 the general secretary of DISK (Türkler) was assassinated by right wing activists.

In 1979, the economic situation came under the scrutiny of the IMF but the austerity measures proposed by the IMF to remedy the situation were so unacceptable to Turkish politicians reared in the ideology of etatism and the closed-economy that they found it very difficult to implement the IMF Stabilisation Programme effectively. One condition of the programme was to level wage increases and to lower real wages. Other conditions were related to the adoption of export-orientation and reduced reliance on import-substitution, the establishment of money markets, and the encouragement of foreign investment.

In September 1980, civil disorder and open political struggles in the streets reached such a peak that the military intervened yet again. This coup differed from earlier ones, however, in that this time the military had a clear economic and political strategy which necessitated the restructuring of the state in order to implement the IMF programme. This restructuring stabilised the state by making it possible for industrial and financial capital, for the first time since the establishment of the Republic, to have the opportunity to gain monopolistic use of state power. This achievement ended the long period of political instability characterised by power struggles between fractions of capital. The mistakes of the 1971-73 military intervention were not to be repeated.

The Period Since 1980

Although instability in society and politics had been generated within the capitalist class, civil disorder was still publicly attributed to left wing activity (10).

The impact of the military intervention on Turkish society was total. Political parties were banned, politicians were forbidden to take part in politics in the future. Professional associations were closed down. Universities, schools, state organisations, etc., were all purged of so-called leftists and 'anarchists'. Kemalism was reinstated as the only ideology allowed in the country. Anything that was not in strict accordance with the stated objectives of the state, was deemed to be unacceptable and punishable. People who had files with the security forces were taken into custody by the police or the military without the benefit of a civilian trial. Migration from countryside was actively discouraged, and people were put on trains and sent back to their villages. Eastern provinces, where the majority of the population are Kurdish, are usually controlled more tightly than anywhere else in Turkey, and after the coup this control became even more strict. Systematic cleaning up operations in these areas went into full swing. New codes of behaviour and dressing were issued for public employees, etc.

People were told to accept tight monetarist policies and austerity measures and not to complain, because everything was done in the name of Atatürk and his Kemalist principles.

In its first communiqué, the National Security Council abolished the 1961 constitution and banned all the trade unions. The right for the trade unions to participate in collective bargaining and the right to strike were suspended until new legislation was passed. DISK leaders were taken into custody and put on trial, with the threat of death sentence hanging over them. Wages were frozen, and public servants were forbidden to take part in trade union activities. Remittances of workers in Europe were encouraged to be brought into the country and invested in projects which had the support of the state, either in the form of subsidies and tax concessions or as premium interest rates applicable only to foreign currency savings.

In 1980, the National Security Council decreed that a new process of collective bargaining would be undertaken by the Supreme Arbitration Council until legislation regulating trade union activity was prepared. The Supreme Arbitration Council adopted the view that the galloping inflation rate of the 1970s was mainly due to wage increases and, therefore, wages had to be restrained. The ensuing actions of the Council led to a decrease of real wages, so that in 1980 wages were worth only 56.7 per cent of the 1977 real wage level. This explanation of inflation was very popular with the employers and the government, although there was no relationship between the rate of inflation and increases in wages as wages are always determined politically and not by market forces.

The new constitution of 1982 was part of a broad restructuring of Turkish politics away from democracy in a form that would last. The constitution further limited trade union rights. Trade unions were banned from taking part in politics and from pursuing political ends. Article 14 of the constitution de facto excluded the working classes from taking part in politics. Article 51 laid conditions on the formation, the organisation, and the membership of trade unions. To be eligible for selection to high office in a trade union, a person must have been a working employee in that particular industrial sector for ten years. Article 52 prohibited trade unions from affiliating with political parties in order to promote their members' interests. This is clearly contrary to any established international agreement supported by the ILO and also against any convention of democratic politics.

Article 54 specifically curtails the right to strike and right to lock-out, and stipulates that strike actions and lock-outs cannot be used to damage social harmony and national wealth. This is again totally at variance with the established ILO policy on strike actions and lock-outs. The Supreme Arbitration Council was given the final authority to make decisions on disputes which must be accepted as binding.

Strike action was clearly seen by the authors of the 1982 constitution as a limited right, only appropriate in exceptional circumstances. This is a complete reversal of the democratic political framework laid down by the 1961 constitution, where strikes were seen as fundamental to trade unionism.

New legislation regarding the process of collective bargaining, Law 2821, and strikes and lock-outs, Law 2822, came into being in 1983. These laws imposed a new framework on working class organisation and action. Every conceivable obstacle to the development of a successful trade union can be found in these laws. Trade unions explicitly cannot act to serve working class interests. This is a major stipulation that underlines the spirit of the current legal framework in Turkey.

When DISK was banned and its leaders put in gaol, the vacuum they left was meant to be filled by other confederations (Türk-Is, MISK and Hak-Is) who were closed down together with DISK, but allowed to open later. Today, Türk-Is is the only trade union confederation that is accepted by the Turkish ruling classes and the Turkish state as representative of the Turkish working classes. The struggle to re-establish trade union rights has already started, and Türk-Is is seen as the first target to be transformed into a more representative organisation.

CONCLUSION

The final stage in the transformation of Turkish capitalism has been reached where monopoly/industrial and financial capital are in the process of becoming dominant fractions at the political and economic levels. The main contradiction of capitalism between the interests of capital and of labour is becoming clearer, and is now the one that will determine the future of the transformation process in Turkey. The ability of the dominant fractions of the ruling class to develop flexible structures and ideology which can meet some working class demands, and their ability to stabilise their monopoly of state power will determine the outcome of future class struggles in Turkey, hence the future of Turkish social formation. The working classes and working class organisations are battered and now very weak. These are not yet in a position to impose their political agenda on the ruling classes.

It is still very early to talk of a successful working class revival, or for that matter its shape or form. But workers cannot be repressed for ever, and the current political framework is only there to be challenged and broken. What the labour movement has to learn is that they operate under a framework initiated and controlled by the state. Any attempt to form organisations outside this framework will be in vain. The crisis of Turkish trade unionism today is rooted in a lack of experience in understanding the logic of capitalism. As a result, there is little experience of having to develop strategies suitable to concrete conditions which are in the process of change. Any attempt to stop the reproduction of capitalism will result in further disaster. Capitalism is already deeply rooted in the Turkish social formation and is dominant in all levels of social relationships of production. There is a need to understand its dynamic and develop consciousness, experience, and long-term political strategies within this framework. The real contradiction is not between American imperialism and the Turkish people, but it is between capital and labour as determined by the specificity of Turkish capitalism. If working class organisations, including trade unions, can contribute to the formation of this new capitalist order, their task is likely to be that much easier in the future. If they do not, then the future is likely to be that much harder. Revolution is not lurking just around the corner.

NOTES

(1) See chapters 2, 3 and 8 in H. Ramazanoglu (ed), Turkey in the World Capitalist System: A Study of Industrialisation, Power and Class, London, Gower, 1985.

(2) England was unique in the degree of separation of early industrial workers from the land. In Turkey, as elsewhere in the world, the continued attachment of urban workers to rural communities and agrarian production is complex and variable. For a more detailed discussion of this point see C. Ramazanoglu, 'Labour migration and the development of Turkish capitalism' in Ramazanoglu (ed.), op. cit., and G. Standing, 'Migration and modes of exploitation', WEP, 2-21/wp 72, Geneva, ILO (mimeo), 1979.

(3) This was a period of utmost importance in the history of the Ottoman empire. During this period, the Ottoman state and society were modernised and their structure reformed by a succession of laws. This process contributed to the further centralisation of administration and brought increased state participation in Ottoman society between 1839 and 1876. See S. Shaw and E. Shaw, History of the Ottoman Empire and Modern Turkey, vol. 2, Cambridge University Press, 1977.

(4) The Kemalist regime was a form of state that embodied six principles of Kemalism, which were etatism (see next footnote), republicanism, populism, revolutionism/reformism, secularism and nationalism. For a contradictory argument to the one presented here see S. Snurov and Y. Rozaliev, Turkiye'de Kapitalistlesme ve Sinif Kavgalari, Istanbul, Ant, 1970, chapters 1-6 (translated from the Russian).

(5) Etatism means that the state encouraged the development of capitalism by performing economic functions which were essential for the development of private capital and also that the state intervened in those spheres of economic activity where private capital was unable to play an active role. See my 'A political analysis of the emergence of Turkish capitalism, 1839-1950' in Ramazanoglu (ed.), op. cit., and F. Ahmad, 'The political economy of Kemalism' in A. Kazancigil and E. Ozbudun (eds.), Atatürk, Founder of a Modern State, London, Hurst, 1981.

(6) For full documentation of the Congress reports see G. Okcün, Turkiye Iktisat Kongresi, 1923 - Izmir: Haberler, Belgeler, Yorumlar, Ankara, Faculty of Political Science, 1970.

(7) For an analysis of the development of trade unionism at this period see K. Sülker, Turkiye'de Sendikacilik, Istanbul, 1966 and 100 Soruda Turkiye'de Isci Hareketleri, Istanbul, Gercek, 1973. Hale is also a useful source on this subject: W. Hale (ed.), Aspects of Modern Turkey, London, Bowker, 1976.

(8) This is a complicated theoretical issue that has been in the forefront of a great many debates. The Turkish left certainly devoted considerable energy to discussing this problem. It would be true to say that this view, as explained here, constituted the theoretical rationale for the actions of the majority of the left wing organisations in Turkey at the time. A major theoretical intervention in the debate was made by Bill Warren in his various works which, although much criticised since, clarified a number of important theoretical issues on this subject and opened up new areas of discussion. The main arguments can be found in B. Warren, Imperialism: Pioneer of Capitalism, London, Verso, 1980.

(9) This event was a turning point in the escalation of violence in society. The new level of violence was such that the left largely lost its broader political objectives in the need to survive state violence, and the wish to retaliate against right wing provocation.

(10) See my 'The state, the military and the development of capitalism in an open economy' in Ramazanoglu (ed.), op. cit., and also F. Ahmad, 'Military intervention and the crisis in Turkey' in MERIP Reports, no, 93, January 1981 (edited version reprinted in Ramazanoglu (ed.), op. cit.).

11 South Africa in crisis: the role of the black trade unions

MARK MITCHELL AND DAVE RUSSELL

INTRODUCTION (1)

There is no doubt that the formation in recent years of an authentic independent labour movement in South Africa has been a profoundly important development. Indeed for some commentators these 'new wave' unions currently present the most serious challenge yet to the South African state, overshadowing all other forms of black resistance (2). However the assessment of the political potential of the black unions advanced in this paper is more cautious. Industrial militancy and black trade union activity have certainly played an important part in the deepening crisis experienced by the Nationalist regime since the mid-1970s, but the actual strength and achievements of the new black unions appear so far to have been relatively limited.

This is not to say that the emerging unions have been successfully controlled and contained by the Botha Government's labour reforms. The black trade unions have gained much more from these reforms than was originally intended by the Government and the spread of industrial unrest is a clear sign of the inability of the South African state to co-opt and regulate the new unions. The reasons for this are fairly obvious. The absence of political rights for blacks in South Africa has prevented black unions from fulfilling the stabilising role that is often claimed for trade unions within 'normal capitalism' (3). Rather black unionisation has offered the African population an avenue for the development of the kind of legal organisations that are prohibited in the political sphere. In these circumstances trade union activity has become a central focus for black political discontent and, as industrial conflict has become increasingly politicised, so there has been a mounting tide of state repression against the unions. The result has been that the Nationalist Government's reforms have been made to appear increasingly hollow as more and more union leaders have been detained or forced underground (4).

SOUTH AFRICA IN CRISIS

The main features of the current crisis in South Africa are by now well known. Escalating state repression, mounting economic problems, unprecedented turmoil in the black townships and greatly increased political and industrial militancy have together created an unparalleled situation for the Nationalist Government. However it is important to emphasise that the essential ingredients of the present crisis, together with the underlying character of the state's response, have been identifiable for a decade or more. Throughout this period the government of P. W. Botha continued to present its diverse policies and practices as the coordinated elements of a 'total strategy' for survival, designed to overcome the multiple pressures threatening the system of white rule in South Africa (5). In practice the total strategy has not delivered the goods! Not only has it failed miserably to reproduce the political stability and economic growth of the 1960s; in addition certain key aspects of the strategy appear to have had the opposite effect to that envisaged by its architects. The result has been that, despite its controversial commitment to reform, the Government has been forced to rely more directly on coercion in order to maintain its rule. Each ratchet-like advance of state repression and violence has only served to undermine the prospects for generating significant support from sections of the non-white population. Instead South Africa has been plunged ever deeper into a spiralling economic and political crisis that the Nationalist regime appears powerless to resolve.

Looking back to the original formulation of the ill-fated 'total strategy', it should be noted that the growth of militancy and illegal unionisation amongst black workers was only one of a complex series of internal and external problems that were confronting South Africa's white rulers in the 1970s. Internally, problems of economic decline loomed large. Relatively high levels of inflation, a deterioration in the balance of payments and a lack of economic growth contrasted sharply with the boom years of the 1960s. The nature of South Africa's integration into the international economic system made it particularly vulnerable to the world economic slump of the mid-1970s and these economic difficulties were made more acute by the massive flight of capital from the Republic following the Soweto uprising of 1976 (6). This period was also marked by an increase in guerrilla activity by the African National Congress (ANC), with an intensification of their sabotage and bomb attacks. Externally, the collapse of white colonialism in the buffer states of Mozambique and Angola, together with the rising tide of guerrilla warfare in Namibia and Zimbabwe, shattered the regional security previously enjoyed by Pretoria. Faced with growing problems of regional and internal security, the idea of a massive 'total onslaught' on the nation from outside and inside its borders became a key motif within a new form of survival politics that was increasingly adopted by the Nationalist government from the mid-1970s onwards (7).

In these circumstances, the military became the main driving force behind Pretoria's strategy for survival. Operating from within a kind of siege mentality and strongly influenced by counter-revolutionary experiences elsewhere, military leaders sought to equip South Africa strategically, economically, politically and psychologically for 'total war' (8). Their 'total national strategy' argued for an integrated response to the various internal and external crises facing the country. In turn this emphasis on a totally coordinated effort had important repercussions for the internal organisation of the state system and the role of the military within it. According to one writer, there was "a fusion of military and political decision-making with soldiers a dominant element in the shaping of national security policy" (9). The development of the 'total strategy' should therefore be associated with the cultivation of a garrison state mentality, which has itself fostered in a mutually reinforcing way the power and influence of the military establishment (10). Elsewhere we have discussed at length the rise of a 'military-corporate' state in South Africa and the extensive militarisation of policy processes that was the outstanding feature of a tougher, more streamlined mode of crisis-management adopted by the ruling Afrikaner elite from the late 1970s onwards (11).

The ascendancy of the military - together with business representatives - into positions of power inside the state coincided with the demise of an Afrikanerised version of corporatism, in which the major organisations of the white labour movement had collaborated closely with the state and capital to sustain the apartheid system. It was the introduction of the labour reform programme in 1979 that marked the effective termination of the special relationship between the white working class and the Nationalist Government. The pressures that propelled the Afrikaner state towards this radical break with the past are by now well known. Firstly, high levels of economic growth during the 1960s had served paradoxically to increase the dependence of the South African economy on black labour. In particular the rapid growth and strategic importance of a more skilled black workforce enhanced the potential bargaining power of the black working class. At the same time the growing political marginality of the shrinking white working class undermined their ability to continue to preserve the statutory racial division of labour (12).

Secondly, the early 1970s saw the birth of a limited number of new democratic union organisations following the dormant period during the 1960s when black unionism was virtually non-existent. Strikes were illegal and the new unions were denied official bargaining rights but in spite of this, the 1970s saw a significant increase in the overall levels of strike activity. A number of different attempts were made to contain this growth of industrial militancy. A series of black 'parallel unions' was set up under the paternalistic control of existing white unions (13); a concerted attempt was made by some employers, with the encouragement of the state, to promote tame factory-based liaison committees to deal with the grievances of African workers (14); and many of the union organisers of these 'new wave' black unions were banned or imprisoned. Nevertheless the independent black union movement managed to enjoy a steady growth in strength and support throughout the 1970s. In spite of its fairly modest size, the Government was alarmed by its inability to stifle or eradicate a grass roots movement that was gradually expanding 'factory by factory' (15). It responded by setting up the Wiehahn Commission in June 1977, with a brief to investigate existing legislation in the labour relations field and to recommend ways of making it more effective. It was the report of this Commission, which completed its work in 1979, that was to provide the Nationalist Government with the basis for its subsequent strategy towards the new black unions (16).

The recommendations of the Wiehahn Commission have been widely interpreted as providing the basis for some of the most important reforms within the 'total strategy'. In effect, Wiehahn suggested the legalisation of black trade unions and an end to the system of job reservation. In making its recommendations, the Commission appeared to be supporting the idea that these unions should be coopted into the system via a two fold strategy. On the one hand this was to involve the incorporation of the black trade union movement into the tightly regulated system of industrial conciliation, by granting them access to the industry-wide Councils that negotiated minimum wage levels for all workers in a particular industry. In this way it was hoped to cut the ground from under the feet of the factory-based union movement. On the other hand, there was to be a concerted attempt to create a relatively privileged minority of black workers by increasing their access to training and better paid jobs, thus accentuating the divisions between 'insiders' and 'outsiders' within the black population.

In practice, the implementation of this transparent incorporation strategy has gone badly wrong, and it would now appear that many of the reforms designed to strengthen the regime may instead have served to intensify the crisis in South Africa. Although in large part this failure has been a consequence of the rising tide of black resistance, both on the factory floor and in the wider community, it is important to emphasise that the 'total strategy' itself was inherently contradictory. The faltering attempts by the Afrikaner state to engineer control-through-reform have failed because they were always subsidiary features within a programme that was unambiguously directed at the perpetuation of white minority rule. Given the growth of the garrison state in which everything has become increasingly subordinated to the security needs of the white regime, it was always highly unlikely that political and industrial conflict would be contained and controlled in a consensual manner. The main thrust of the 'total strategy' has been towards the creation of a more militarised society where order is valued more than change and where the conflict between the state and the masses has been accelerated rather than diminished.

The Wiehahn reforms themselves have served to amplify rather than to control industrial conflict in three important ways. Firstly, the concession of trade union rights was itself a most important gain for black workers. Above all it provided them with the opportunity for freedom of association effectively denied elsewhere under the apartheid regime. Subsequent improvements in wages and working conditions gained through collective action have increased the assertiveness and confidence of the black unions, which in turn have encouraged the further expansion of unionisation. We would therefore agree with Friedman's claim that "reforms which permit black organisation - no matter how controlled - are likely to do more to increase pressures for change than to diminish them" (17). Secondly it was always impossible to imagine that black trade unions would confine their demands to economic or industrial matters, as has been the case with unions in many democratic capitalist societies. In part this was because, as Adam has noted, "economic bargaining is inevitably politicised by the exclusion of black workers from equal citizenship rights" (18). But also the hand of the state has always been so extraordinarily visible within every aspect of

South African economic life, that trade unions have been almost irres-
istibly drawn into challenging state policies. Thirdly, the attempt to
institutionalise industrial conflict in South Africa was always likely
to be undermined by the emphasis given within the 'total strategy' to
the heavy policing of internal dissent and unrest. The focus on 'total
onslaught' and 'national security' has served to fuel the drive towards
greater state repression, with the result that union organisers and
activists have become one of the principle targets for the security
forces.

THE DEVELOPMENT OF BLACK TRADE UNIONS

The last fifteen years have seen a transformation both in the extent of
unionisation and in the level of industrial militancy amongst the black
working class in South Africa. The significance of this 'new wave' of
union activism first became apparent in 1973, when a series of strikes
erupted in the Durban area. In retrospect it is clear that this unprecedented outburst of militancy represented a turning point in the post-
war development of trade unionism in South Africa in two important
respects. In the first place, 1973 marked the beginning of a sustained
increase in the level of strike activity amongst blacks which, though
varying from year to year, has never since fallen back to the exception-
ally low level of the previous decade. During the 1960s state repression effectively emasculated the black trade union movement and this
produced a period of unparalleled industrial quiescence in which the
number of people involved in strike action was never greater than 2,000
in any one year, In contrast, 1973 saw nearly 100,000 workers take part
in strike activity and, although the intensity of industrial action
later declined following the attempt by the state to repress the union
movement, the number of strikes in any one year has never since fallen
below 14,000 (19).

Secondly, the aftermath of the Durban strikes saw the emergence of a
new type of unionism in the South African context, one that was based
upon effective shop floor organisation in the factory and regular involvement of the rank-and-file membership in union affairs. This contrasted with the long history of 'mass movement' unionism in South
Africa which had frequently concentrated on signing up as large a membership as possible in the pursuit of general economic or political
objectives. Such 'top-down' unions are particularly vulnerable to state
repression since the banning or imprisonment of a handful of key activists effectively decapitates the movement, rendering it totally ineffective. Consequently the history of South African trade unionism is
littered with examples of the rapid rise and fall of such organisations.
The 1970s too were not completely devoid of these tendencies and the
predictable bannings that followed both the Durban strikes and the
Soweto uprising of 1976 did significantly weaken the union movement
(20). Nevertheless during this period the foundations were laid for a
new 'bottom-up' system of union organisation based upon a network of
shop stewards accountable to their members at their places of work.
This form of organisation has proved to be a good deal more resilient in
the face of state repression (21).

The post-Wiehahn reforms introduced by the Nationalist government in
1979 and 1980 created a changed environment for black trade unions.
There was little dissent from the view that the government was adopting

a 'control-through-reform' approach to the new unions and that the Wiehahn proposals were a central part of the "total strategy for survival" advocated by government spokesmen. Nevertheless the granting of official black trade union rights for the first time in South Africa prompted a re-examination of the role and function of trade unions within the restructured apartheid state, and this brought to the surface a number of disagreements between different groupings within the black trade union movement. Three issues in particular were of major significance. Firstly, in the immediate aftermath of the Wiehahn report, there was the question of whether or not unions should register with the state in order to avail themselves of the limited benefits on offer. Secondly, there was the issue of whether these new unions should be designated as "non-racial" or "black" and in particular whether so-called 'white intellectuals' should be allowed to play a leading role within a union movement that was recruiting almost exclusively from amongst black African workers. Thirdly, as the political crisis intensified during the 1980s, the unions necessarily had to confront the question of whether or not to ally themselves with the wider struggles within black communities and this in turn prompted more general questions about the role of trade unions in politics.

Each of these issues gives important insights into the development of black trade unionism in the post-Wiehahn period and we shall discuss all three in some detail. However before doing so it is important to make two points, both of which serve to underline the fact that the positions taken by the different organisations have not in general been fixed or static. In the first place, since the political context within which the unions have been operating has been subject to dramatic and sudden changes, the various union positions on these issues has necessarily been subject to periodic reconsideration. The principled disagreements which occurred in 1985 have frequently been rendered irrelevant by the rapidly changing political environment. Secondly, it is important to recognise that there has been no necessary overlap between those organisations which agree - or disagree - on the different issues. In effect this has tended to produce a system of cross-cutting alliances which have formed and reformed between the various unions and union federations thus preventing the emergence of irreparable divisions. Although there are undoubtedly some major issues of principle involved, many of the disagreements have been over what are essentially tactical questions. In other words it is wrong to view the black union movement as divided into warring factions that are both organisationally and ideologically irreconcilable.

Registration or Non-Registration?

In line with its overall objectives of re-imposing control via reform, the post-Wiehahn proposals offered both advantages and disadvantages to the black unions. As far as the benefits were concerned, registration appeared to offer five advantages to black unions. Firstly, it allowed them to organise and recruit openly without fear of prosecution - providing of course that they did not infringe any of the other conditions of registration. Secondly, it gave them access to the official system of industrial councils, thus enabling them to participate in collective bargaining on an industry-wide level. Thirdly, it allowed black unions for the first time legally to call out their members on strike, but only after the elaborate conciliation machinery had been fully exhausted. Fourthly, it promised black unions access to a new Industrial Court which had been set up to adjudicate on unfair labour practices. Finally, it made it easier for unions to collect their members' subscriptions since registration enabled unions to win check off facilities - the automatic deduction of union subscriptions - from their employers.

On the other hand most of the black unions were well aware of the serious shortcomings contained in the proposals, four of which were particularly problematical. Firstly, the registration proposals excluded major categories of black workers, notably those employed in agriculture and domestic service, which automatically placed the majority of the black labour force, and in particular women workers, outside the framework of legal trade union organisation (22). Secondly, since their bargaining rights were to be exercised only through the Industrial Councils which were composed of industry-wide representatives of employers and unions, this effectively prevented the new factory-based unions from negotiating directly with management on a plant-by-plant basis over wages and conditions of work. Thirdly, unions were to be subjected to investigation by a new National Manpower Commission which was to scrutinise the constitutions, election arrangements and officials of all registered unions. Finally, a condition of registration was that unions should be non-political in the broadest sense in that they should have no links with political parties nor engage in political activities of any kind.

These costs and benefits made the choice over registration a very difficult one for black unions and not surprisingly there were significant differences of opinion over whether to register or not. Broadly it is possible to distinguish between three different tendencies amongst the 'new wave' black unions over the question of registration which can be labelled: non-registration, collaborative registration and conditional registration.

a) Non-registration Those organisations which rejected registration out of hand included: the South African Allied Workers' Union (SAAWU), the Food and Canning Unions (FCUs) (23) and the General Workers' Union (GWU). Their rejectionist stance coincided with the call by the exiled South African Congress of Trade Unions (SACTU) to boycott the registration proposals. There were two major arguments advanced by the boycotters for rejecting registration (24). In the first place, it was claimed that registration would be divisive of the African working class since it would lead to the incorporation of a minority of privileged black labour aristocrats at the expense of the under-privileged majority of African workers. Secondly, it was argued that, since the conditions attaching to registration tended to reinforce rather than undermine the denial of basic rights and freedoms, registration had to be rejected since it could only compromise the struggle to achieve these more fundamental goals (25). However despite their non-registration several of these unions have won recognition agreements with particular companies (26).

b) Collaborative registration Although several of the independent unions eventually decided to collaborate with the post-Wiehahn reforms, the initial reactions to the White Paper that followed the report were almost universally hostile (27). The reason for this was that the government had rejected one of the most important of the Wiehahn recommendations and was proposing to deny registered union rights to migrant workers and commuters (28). Faced with this proposal, the entire black trade union movement said that it would refuse to register since many of the new unions had recruited heavily from amongst these groups of workers. Even some of the conservative 'parallel' unions affiliated to the Trade Union Council of South Africa (TUCSA) rejected registration on these terms (29). From the Government point of view this situation was clearly untenable and at the end of October 1979, some weeks after the new regulations had come into effect, the Minister of Manpower extended union rights to migrants and commuters by proclamation.

This retreat by the Government had the effect of convincing those unions who had earlier adopted a more positive attitude to the Wiehahn proposals to apply for registration. They argued that the reforms in themselves offered real gains to black workers and that participation in the newly created system would provide a real opportunity to work from the inside to improve the situation further in the future. As well as the parallel TUCSA unions, the black unions affiliated to the so-called Black Consultative Committee of Trade Unions - soon to be renamed the Council of Unions of South Africa (CUSA) - also registered in this collaborative manner, including the all-important National Union of Mineworkers (NUM). The stated intention of the CUSA unions was to attempt to reform the system from within and from the outset they expressed reservations about particular aspects of the registration package. They were especially critical of the proposal that registered unions should negotiate only via the established system of Industrial Councils, arguing instead for workplace bargaining between management and unions. In this way they found common ground with other black unions which had opted either for non-registration or conditional registration. The desire for an alternative factory-based system of collective bargaining based upon formal recognition agreements was a common aim of most of the 'new wave' unions in spite of their differences over the registration issue.

c) Conditional registration A third group of black unions also sought to register under the new dispensation, but only after a much more profound internal debate and a more sober assessment of the likely costs than took place within the CUSA unions. The unions affiliated to the Federation of South African Trade Unions (FOSATU), including the Metal and Allied Workers' Union (MAWU), chose to register but only on condition that the government accede to further demands from the unions themselves. Thus unlike the CUSA unions, the FOSATU unions did not fall over themselves in the rush to register following the government's climb down on the issue of the recruitment of migrant workers. After discussing the question at length with some of the non-registration unions, they announced that they would conditionally apply for registration but on their own terms in an attempt to wring further concessions from the government. They demanded that FOSATU itself be registered as a non-racial organisation operating with a non-racial constitution. They also demanded the right to register unions with a racially mixed membership. Both of these demands were subsequently conceded by the Government. The differences with those unions opting for collaborative registration is clear. FOSATU's strategy of conditional registration, by squeezing additional compromises from the Nationalist regime, has served to improve the situation for all the black unions in South Africa.

So in effect, as Southall has noted, both registration and non-registration can be seen to have brought gains to the movement as a whole. Whilst those who boycotted the reforms can "take the credit for breaking the link between registration and recognition", those who chose to register can at least in part "claim to have used the registration process to cajole the state into making further concessions" (30). In addition it is worth noting that in 1981 the Government amended the legislation so as to extend some aspects of the post-Wiehahn reforms to the unregistered as well as to the registered unions. As a result differences over registration that appeared to be potentially divisive in 1979 and 1980 have become much less significant today.

BLACK EXCLUSIVISM OR NON-RACIALISM?

Over the past decade the 'new wave' unions have been divided over the question of whether or not they should be exclusively black - both in terms of their membership and leadership - or non-racial. These unions have therefore become embroiled in a variant of the 'class vs race' debate that divided the liberation movement in the 1950s and 1960s. One of the most obvious manifestations of this has been the institutional separation of FOSATU and CUSA. In part these differences can be explained by reference to the different historical origins of the two organisations. FOSATU's power base was in Natal, where a number of whites sympathetic to black unionisation had set up a system of workers' advice centres in the early 1970s. These were to become the nucleus of the 'new wave' unionism in Natal and were to play a crucial role in the 1973 strikes. The unions that emerged in the aftermath of the strikes formed themselves into the Trade Union Advisory Coordinating Council (TUACC) which then began to extend its influence into the Transvaal. The black consciousness movement, which in the 1970s rekindled the flame of black nationalism in South Africa, was never particularly strong in Natal and the adoption of the non-racial principle together with the employment of several white officials in the union hierarchies was never seriously challenged. In 1979 the TUACC joined with two motor workers' unions from the Cape with a mainly coloured membership to form FOSATU.

CUSA on the other hand, which was formed in 1980, emerged from the Johannesburg-based Black Consultative Committee of Trade Unions and was from the start much more influenced by the black consciousness movement. Membership of the CUSA unions was normally restricted to blacks, but in practice individual unions have recently adopted a more relaxed attitude to the question of members from other racial groups, whilst reserving their leadership posts exclusively for blacks. Current CUSA policy is "to build a non-racial, non-exploitative democratic society based on black leadership" (31). Thus while the FOSATU unions, with a number of whites occupying senior positions, argued that it was up to the members to choose their own leaders, black or white, the CUSA unions insisted upon the principle of black leadership because black workers comprised the overwhelming majority of the membership.

It is important to stress that within both federations there were different opinions on the issue of white involvement. In June 1984 a split developed in MAWU, the largest constituent union within FOSATU, in which the role played by so-called 'white intellectual bureaucrats' within the union was certainly one of the issues at stake. This led to the formation of the breakaway United Mining, Metal and Allied Workers of South Africa (UMMAWSA) (32). And towards the end of 1985 the NUM, the largest of the CUSA affiliates, left the federation and embraced the principle of non-racialism.

The more recently formed Azanian Confederation of Trade Unions (AZACTU) has adopted a much more militant black nationalist stance that strictly precludes white involvement. However the unions that make up AZACTU are generally held to have only a minimal presence on the shop floor and little in the way of permanent organisation. In reality AZACTU is little more than a labour front for the Azanian People's Organisation (AZAPO).

Since 1981 a number of meetings have been held to discuss the possible unification of the new black unions under one 'super-federation'. After much acrimonious debate a set of five principles were put forward as the basis for this new federation in 1984. These were: industrial unionism (one union for each industry); workers' control; representation on the basis of paid up membership; national cooperation through the new federation; and non-racialism (33). These were discussed at a conference in Soweto in June 1985 which brought together 200 delegates from 42 black unions. The AZACTU unions, together with some of the CUSA unions, could not accept the principle of non-racialism, though significantly the NUM - the largest independent union in South Africa and former affiliate to CUSA - was prepared to support the unity platform. Its subsequent resignation from CUSA and its affiliation to the new 'super-federation', the Congress of South African Trade Unions (COSATU) formed in November 1985, was a serious blow to the influence and future viability of CUSA and its constituent unions. In addition to the NUM, those joining COSATU included: the GWU, the SAAWU, the FCUs and the unions previously affiliated to FOSATU which was formally dissolved when the new confederation was founded. It is interesting to note however that in contrast to FOSATU whose general secretary was white, the leadership of COSATU is exclusively black. In view of this it seems likely that the continued tension between CUSA and the new confederation has more to do with inter-personal rivalries than with significant ideological differences (34).

In summary, the formation of COSATU on the basis of the principle of non-racialism, together with the emergence of a substantial group of competent black union leaders both inside and outside the new federation and its constituent unions, has served to undermine the black consciousness position. It is doubtful whether the AZACTU unions together with the rump of the CUSA unions will be able to mount a serious challenge to the hegemony of COSATU in the foreseeable future.

WORKERISM OR COMMUNITY POPULISM?

One of the major areas of debate between different sections of the black unions has been over the political role that should be played by these unions in the current crisis (35). Two broad strands of opinion can be distinguished. On the one hand the workerist unions have argued for priority to be given to the expansion of shop floor organisation. This does not imply that these unions are guilty of a narrow economism as some of their critics have maintained. All of the workerist-oriented unions recognise the central importance of political reforms and support the demand for a fundamental shift of political power in South Africa. However they argue that in the struggle to build a democratic society, the organised working class must play a leading role and that since at present the trade union movement is relatively weak, the primary task must be to expand its sphere of influence amongst the African working class rather than diluting its efforts in wider community struggles. Further, these unions insist upon a clear distinction between economic and political liberation, arguing that a small but growing section of the black population - in particular the African petty-bourgeoisie - has already achieved a high degree of economic liberation necessarily denied to black workers in South Africa. This workerist position was adopted by both pro-registration unions like those affiliated to FOSATU and by several of the anti-registration unions like the GWU and the FCUs.

On the other hand those unions committed to a strategy of community populism have argued that at the present time the specificity of working class interests should be subsumed within a more all-embracing national democratic struggle. Trade unions, though an important vehicle for the expression of working class interests, cannot claim to represent the whole of the African working class since this class is itself deeply fractionalised. In particular, by concentrating on increasing the levels of union membership and expanding the number of recognition agreements, the interests of non-unionised workers - many of them women - especially in agriculture and domestic service, are inevitably downgraded. Further, this approach must necessarily fail to address the needs of the mass of unemployed blacks in the homelands who increasingly comprise a surplus population peripheral to the needs of the capitalist economy. For these reasons, some of the black unions such as the SAAWU have been prepared to forgo workplace organisation in favour of establishing broader roots in the community. Others such as the CUSA unions have sought to combine a close identification with populist political protest together with the recruitment of workers at their places of employment. Again there are both pro- and anti-registration unions amongst those who favour the strategy of community populism.

The issue of workerism or populism came to a head with the formation of the National Forum (NF) and the United Democratic Front (UDF) in 1983 (36). Some thirteen separate unions applied to join the UDF, the most important of which were the SAAWU and the General and Allied Workers' Union (GAWU). CUSA also affiliated to the UDF having participated in the NF earlier in the year, and continues to maintain close links with both bodies. In some unions differences arose between national and regional levels and the affiliation to the UDF of the Western Cape region of the Media Workers' Association of South Africa (MWASA), despite the opposition of its national organisation, later precipitated a split in the MWASA. Predictably the AZACTU unions have rejected overtures from the UDF in favour of participation in the NF.

The workerist-oriented unions have not surprisingly rejected the idea of any formal links with the UDF. At the same time FOSATU, the CFUs and the GWU have all issued statements supporting the UDF and encouraging their members to participate in its campaigns. Formal affiliation has been ruled out however because of ideological and organisational misgivings about the UDF (37). In the first place, the workerist trade unions have insisted that unions are working class organisations, able to attract workers with differing political opinions to their ranks precisely because they are all workers who have a common interest in the improvement of their wages and conditions of work. In contrast the UDF is seen as an alliance of multi-class interests formed to achieve political goals. Joe Foster, former general secretary of FOSATU, has stated quite openly that, in the interests of unity, they were unable to affiliate since a section of their membership was openly hostile to the politics of the UDF (38). Secondly, the workerist unions have also expressed concern about the chaotic and unrepresentative character of the UDF. In particular they are worried about the wisdom of affiliating to a political organisation that includes both democratic mass-based organisations like trade unions alongside much smaller groups of community activists that often lack any internal system of democratic accountability. Without a more representative structure the UDF is unable, it is argued, to reflect the strength and significance of the black trade union movement.

Although there have been serious disagreements between the workerist unions and the UDF, the intensification of the crisis in 1985 and 1986 has had the overall effect of tending to unify rather than divide the union movement. The root cause of this is the existence in South Africa of a number of factors that together have resulted in the seemingly irreversible politicisation of all black unions irrespective of their workerist or populist orientation.

Firstly, the inability of the state to disengage itself from industrial affairs has meant that politics and labour relations have always been deeply intertwined in South Africa. Despite its declared intention to 'roll back' state economic intervention, this has not occurred to any significant degree and the ever-present hand of the state has created a powerful thrust towards the politicisation of 'new wave' unionism. A good example of the 'politicisation effect' took place in 1981 when FOSATU and a number of other unions organised a series of strikes against a government bill that proposed to restrict black workers' rights to draw on their pension funds to support themselves during periods of industrial action.

Secondly, the fact that black unions have always had to live with the daily threat of state repression in the form of the banning, imprisonment and general harassment of their union activists has inevitably served to politicise black trade union struggles. In February 1982 for example following the death in police custody of Neil Aggett, a white organiser for the FCUs, a nationwide protest was held in which workers were called on to "down tools" for half and hour. Over 100,000 workers took part, the majority of them in unions affiliated to FOSATU.

Thirdly, since blacks have been denied access to the normal channels of political representation and have seen their major political parties suppressed and driven underground, it is not surprising that trade unions have come to provide an alternative avenue for the expression of black political aspirations. In recent years involvement in union affairs has been the principle means by which blacks have been able to create a degree of political space for themselves and consequently black unions have been an important training ground for a new generation of black activists. In the words of one writer black unions are "independent schools of democracy where substantial worker leadership has developed with the potential to play a central role in changing South Africa" (39).

Fourthly, the determination of the Nationalist Government to press ahead with its Bantustan policy has also had profound consequences for many of the black unions. Those which have recruited heavily from amongst commuters, such as the SAAWU which has as its main constituency the Mdantsane township in the Ciskei, have inevitably been drawn into a political confrontation with the Government over the question of homeland 'independence'. More generally, the centrality of the Bantustan policy within the overall system of influx control over migrant labour has meant that the homelands issue is of fundamental importance to those unions such as MAWU and the NUM who recruit heavily from amongst migrant workers.

Finally, as the crisis has intensified and more and more black communities have been forced to endure the blunt instruments of state repression, so inevitably even the workerist unions have found themselves having to adopt a more overtly political stance. In November 1984 FOSATU and CUSA combined with the UDF to organise a two-day strike in the Transvaal to protest against repression in the black townships. More recently both COSATU and the NUM have threatened industrial action if the current State of Emergency is not quickly rescinded. At the time of writing (June 1986), as the mailed fist of the militarised South African state comes crashing down upon workerist and populist unions alike, it is questionable whether the differences and divisions of the last few years are any longer of any great significance.

THE LIMITATIONS OF THE BLACK TRADE UNION MOVEMENT

Any assessment of the 'new wave' unionism must recognise that it has made enormous advances in a relatively short period of time. Indeed given its moribund condition at the end of the 1960s the present strength and vitality of the black trade union movement in South Africa represents a remarkable achievement. High levels of growth in black unionisation, strike activity at an all-time record, and an increasing number of recognition agreements with employers all point to the relative success of the movement in the post-Wiehahn period. One of the most significant features of this advance has been the strength of many of the new unions at the factory level and some have extended their activities beyond the factory gates, helping to coordinate a variety of protest campaigns in the black townships. Both in the workplace and in the community these unions have provided a major focus for the political aspirations of the black population of South Africa. Nevertheless any assessment of the significance of the black trade union movement must take account of a number of factors that at present serve to restrict and limit its potential political impact.

a) The problem of relative weakness In the first place, it is important to recognise that black unionisation is still relatively weak and underdeveloped. Although the black unions have grown rapidly since 1979 their membership size remains modest. Combining together the membership of both the traditional and the new unions, South Africa has a total union membership of approximately 1.5 million workers out of an economically active population of at least 10 million people (40). A large majority of black workers remain unorganised and a considerable number, especially women workers in domestic service, will prove very difficult to unionise in the future because of the nature of their employment. At around 15 per cent South African union density is significantly lower than in developed capitalist countries, even those like the United States and Japan whose labour movements are usually considered to be weak (41). In addition many of South Africa's trade unions are quite small compared to some of the unions in Western Europe and even COSATU has only around 450,000 signed up members - less than five per cent of

South Africa's potential workforce (42).

Similarly when viewed from a comparative perspective the level of strike activity in South Africa appears quite low (43). Although in recent years the strike figures have been boosted by a number of politically motivated national stoppages, the short small-scale single-factory dispute is more typically representative of union militancy. Partly this is the result of the organisational structure of the unions but it is also due to a lack of the resources needed to sustain industrial action for longer periods. In general strikes are still difficult and often costly for workers in a country where "the dice are loaded against strikers and more strikes have ended quickly in total defeat for workers" (44). South Africa's many migrant workers are especially vulnerable when they become involved in industrial disputes. The risk of dismissal and swift return to their homeland or country of origin is a powerful disincentive to strike action for these workers and this continues seriously to weaken the bargaining power of black unions. Although some of these unions have been quite successful in recruiting migrant workers, the tightening controls over migrant labour together with the worsening plight of the reserve army in the bantustans is bound to have a detrimental effect on these workers and their unions (45).

b) The problem of black unemployment The strength and bargaining power of the black unions has also been adversely affected by the soaring level of black unemployment which in real terms is now variously estimated to be running at between one quarter and one third of the economically active black population (46). There is no doubt that black unemployment has been made considerably worse by the widespread retrenchment of black workers during the economic recession that has gripped South Africa since 1981 (47). However the underlying upward trend in black unemployment long predates the present crisis and has been caused by the structural tendency towards capital intensification and the modernisation of production methods, especially in the mining and manufacturing sectors of the economy (48). Even during the 1978-81 period when the economy began to expand the rate of black unemployment continued to rise, due in part to a steady increase in the supply of black labour (49). Long term trends point to a widening structural gap between an increasing number of entrants into the labour market on the one hand and the limited ability of the South African economy to provide jobs for the expanding population on the other.

More recently the problem of unemployment has been exacerbated both by the Government's adoption of monetarist-influenced economic policies and by the extra-economic difficulties brought on by the escalating political unrest. With the economic recession worsening the Government turned to new economic management techniques familiar to people in Britain. Faced with persistently high levels of inflation, rising public expenditure, plummeting gold prices, a sinking rand and an increasing balance of payments deficit, the Nationalist regime introduced a tough deflationary package that was bound to push up unemployment still further. This consisted of cuts in public expenditure, extremely high interest rates, tight credit controls and various restrictive fiscal measures (50).

Predictably these 'monetarist' policies have not in fact resolved the economic crisis. Furthermore the political turmoil of the past two years has meant that the battle against inflation has increasingly become of secondary importance. Panicked by growing civil unrest, the Government announced early in 1986 a R1.2 billion reflationary package in response to the domestic political pressures (51). However this policy 'U-turn' seems unlikely to halt an economic slide that has been accelerated by the dramatic fall in the value of the rand and by a critical loss of international business confidence in the South African economy. The future impact of these factors together with the likelihood of further disinvestment and the imposition of economic sanctions of one form or another can only worsen the problem of black unemployment. In these circumstances, given their limited ability to protect jobs and improve the wages and working conditions of their members, it is not surprising that more and more of the black unions have turned to more overt forms of political activity.

c) The problem of disunity The strength and effectiveness of the black trade union movement is also significantly affected by the internal divisions and rivalries that have already been discussed in detail. The formation of COSATU, though undoubtedly a great step forward in the creation of an effective united union movement, may only have served to contain rather than to solve some of these basic divisions. The ideological differences that characterise the politics of black trade unionism in South Africa today ensure that COSATU's task of binding together the 'unity unions' will be a difficult if not insurmountable one. Certainly there is little prospect in the foreseeable future of COSATU becoming a strong centralised peak association of the kind that represents the labour movement in some Western European countries.

However the attempt to unify the black union movement involves much more than the reconciliation of political and ideological differences. It demands the rationalisation of an immensely complex and diverse trade union system characterised by regional differences and inter-union rivalries. The nascent black trade union movement has developed unevenly, with several regionally-based general unions and a multitude of small industrial unions, and this had undoubtedly hindered attempts to build a greater degree of unity. The formation of COSATU can only be the first step towards easing some of these problems.

d) The problem of repression Finally it should be remembered that the greatest difficulties confronting the fledgling black unions are those that arise from the hostile environment in which they operate. The impossible task of developing a genuinely free trade union movement under South African conditions has recently become even more apparent with the mass arrests of trade union officials under the State of Emergency. The detention of nearly 1,000 trade unionists, including the general secretary of COSATU together with more than seventy of the federation's key leaders, suggests that organised labour has now become the prime target for state repression (52). At the same time it is significant that no action has so far been taken against the United Workers' Union of South Africa (UWUSA), the anti-sanctions union launched in May 1986 by Chief Buthelezi's Inkatha organisation. The drive against COSATU by the security forces has led to fears that the threat of an increasingly politicised black trade union movement has led Pretoria to turn away from its cooptation strategy towards a new aggressive policy of 'decapitation' (53). An onslaught of this kind against the leadership of the black unions could possibly create a leadership vacuum that would prove difficult to fill. It could also push many union activists into the kind of underground unionism that the Wiehahn Commission was so anxious to avoid.

CONCLUSION

The growing strength and confidence of the new black trade unions has played an important role in the intensification of the crisis that currently besets the white regime in South Africa. Nevertheless it is premature to claim that these unions have the power to bring about the final demise of apartheid. Nor should they be seen as a catalyst in some long-awaited transition towards non-racial or 'normal' capitalism (54). Rather the black unions are one of the principle reasons for the current political impasse in South Africa, an impasse brought about through the inability of the Nationalist Government to re-impose political control from above and the inability of the African majority to seize political power from below.

The Botha Government has consistently tried to present its individual policies as part and parcel of a well-designed masterplan for white survival. Nevertheless it has increasingly failed in its attempts to contain and control the rising tide of black resistance in which the political and industrial militancy of the black trade unions has been a central feature. Indeed it would now appear that it is the labour reforms that have rebounded most severely on a Government whose controversial policies have now been reduced to a total shambles. In the wake of the undoubted failure of the control-through-reform strategy, the black unions once again have had to suffer the full force of the authoritarian side of the Government's survival strategy. The question now must be whether the unions can survive a sustained state offensive against them.

We believe that there are a number of factors that favour the survival of black unions as a significant political and industrial force in South Africa for the foreseeable future. Firstly, the black trade union movement today is far stronger and better organised than it was in previous periods when it was less able to resist attacks on its leadership. The strength and vitality of shop-floor organisation in many unions suggests that the present movement has a greater capacity to withstand such assaults than in the past. Secondly, the attitudes of employers are not uniformly hostile to the new union movement and a number of individual corporations and groups of companies together with organisations like the Federated Chambers of Industry (FCI) may deem it expedient to oppose any attempt to crush the unions (55). Certainly many companies were strongly supportive of the incorporation strategy embodied in the post-Wiehahn reforms and are fearful of a return to the illegal union militancy of the 1970s. Thirdly, it is likely that there will be concerted 'verligte' opposition both from inside and outside the ruling National Party - including some elements within the military - to any further escalation of the current political crisis through a full-frontal attack on union organisers and activists. There have been many indications over the past few months that a growing minority of whites are opposed to President Botha's authoritarian attempt to re-impose control through an intensification of state repression (56).

As the old Afrikaner monolith begins to crumble, the divisions that are daily more evident within white politics over future strategy contrast sharply with the growing convergence of the different factions within the black trade union movement. Only UWUSA, Chief Buthelezi's recently formed pro-capitalist rival to COSATU, breaks ranks with the solidarity shown by virtually the entire black trade union movement in its opposition to the system of racial capitalism in South Africa. In spite of the fact that these unions are not yet strong enough to take on the leading role within the black resistance movement it is none the less certain that they will be a vital factor in the struggle to over-throw white rule.

NOTES

(1) There is no single designation that satisfactorily describes the trade unions that are the subject of this paper. Although their membership is overwhelmingly drawn from the African workforce, there are a number of coloured and some Indian workers within their ranks. Whites have also occupied senior positions within some of the black unions and as we shall see below, the question of whether these unions should be formally constituted as 'non-racial' or 'black' has been an important point of debate within the black trade union movement. Other writers have preferred to describe these unions as "independent" or "democratic" unions in order to distinguish them from the more conservative black unions that were established with official Government blessing under the control of the Trade Union Council of South Africa (TUCSA) in the 1970s. On balance we prefer the term "black trade unions" and have used it throughout this paper to refer to the non-TUCSA unions that recruit the vast majority of their members from the African population irrespective of whether they are formally 'non-racial' or 'black'.

(2) See for example: B. Fine and L. Welch, A Question of Solidarity: Independent Trade Unions in South Africa, London, Socialist Forum for Southern African Solidarity, 1982; H. Adam, 'South Africa's search for legitimacy' in Telos, no. 59, 1984; and S. Friedman 'Political implications of industrial unrest in South Africa' in D. Hindson (ed.), Working Papers in Southern African Studies, vol. 3, Johannesburg, Raven Press, 1983.

(3) See Adam op. cit. and Friedman op. cit.

(4) At the time of writing - July 1986 - the mass arrests under the current State of Emergency have left nearly 1,000 trade unionists in detention. Many others went underground when the emergency was declared on 12 June. See D. van der Vat and A. White, 'The sjambok falls on the unions' in The Guardian, 2 July 1986.

(5) For a discussion of the component parts of the total strategy see: M. Mitchell and D. Russell, 'Militarisation and the South African state' in C. Creighton and M. Shaw (eds.), The Sociology of War and Peace, London, Macmillan, 1987 (forthcoming); P. Frankel Pretoria's Praetorians: Civil Military Relations in South Africa, Cambridge University Press, 1984; S. Jenkins, 'The tribal glue' in The Econ-omist, 21 June 1980; and R. Davies and D. O'Meara, 'The state of analysis of the Southern African region: issues raised by South African strategy' in Review of African Political Economy, no. 29, 1984.

(6) It is sometimes argued that South Africa is a relatively backward capitalist country occupying a peripheral position within the world capitalist order and that this makes it especially vulnerable to international recessions. See: M. Bienefeld and D. Innes, 'Capital accumulation and South Africa' in Review of African Political

Economy, no. 7, 1976; M. Legassick, 'South Africa in crisis: what route to democracy?' in African Affairs, no. 84, 1985; and S. Gelb and D. Innes, 'Economic crisis in South Africa: monetarism's double bind' in Work in Progress, no. 36, 1985.

(7) See H. Adam, 'Survival politics: Afrikanerdom in search of a new ideology' in Journal of Modern African Studies, vol. 16, no. 4, 1978.

(8) Frankel argues that in formulating the total strategy, South Africa's military leaders have used the counter-revolutionary experiences of the United States in Vietnam, the British in Malaya and the French in both Algeria and Indo-China. At the same time he claims that "the ideological and strategic spirit of the South African military is peculiarly Francophile in character", with the writings of the French general André Beaufre especially influential: op. cit., p. 46.

(9) Ibid. p. 30.

(10) Ibid. Chapter 7.

(11) See M. Mitchell and D. Russell, op. cit.

(12) See K. Jochelson, 'You name it, we got it: unions and right wing politics' in Work in Progress, no.37, 1985.

(13) See note 29 below for a brief explanation of the term 'parallel union'.

(14) Liaison committees are a form of works council set up by the employer as a substitute for genuine forms of trade union representation.

(15) By 1977 it was officially reported that there were twenty-seven unions with African members representing between 55,000 and 70,000 workers. Figures quotes in Friedman op. cit., p. 129.

(16) For an outline of the main recommendations of the Wiehahn Commission see W. Vose, 'Wiehahn and Riekert revisited: a review of the prevailing black labour conditions in South Africa' in International Labour Review, vol. 124, no. 4, 1985.

(17) Op. cit., p. 145.

(18) H. Adam, 'South Africa's search for legitimacy', op. cit., p. 60.

(19) The figures are those of the National Manpower Commission, quoted in R. and L. Lambert, 'State reform and working class resistance, 1982' in South Africa Review One: Same Foundations, New Facades, Johannesburg, Raven Press 1983, p. 220.

(20) It was the post-Soweto repression that helped to bring about the much lower levels of union militancy in 1977 and 1978. See ibid. In November 1976 twenty-eight organisers and activists from the new unions were banned. See M. Murphy, Trade Unions in South Africa, London, Workers' Educational Association 1984, p. 14.

(21) Even the reported detention of around 1,000 union activists under the current State of Emergency did not prevent a much publicised meeting of the Confederation of South African Trade Unions (COSATU) at which an ultimatum was issued to the Government in an attempt to secure an end to the repressive actions against trade unions. Neither did it prevent the organisation of an effective work to rule campaign at several gold and diamond mines. It is estimated that there are around 6,000 black shop stewards in South Africa who provide the basis of the shop floor union organisation. See M. Murphy, ibid., pp. 21-22.

(22) In so far as the Wiehahn proposals confer limited privileges on particular categories of black male employees who constitute a minority of the black population, they can be seen as one part of the Government's more general strategy to 'divide and rule' the

non-whites in South Africa. See M. Mitchell and D. Russell, 'Restructuring apartheid', a paper read to the Annual Conference of the British Sociological Association, University College Cardiff, April 1983.

(23) The Food and Canning Unions comprise both the African Food and Canning Workers' Union and the Food and Canning Workers' Union that largely function as a single union. See R. Davies, D. O'Meara and S. Dlamini The Struggle for South Africa, vol. 2, London, Zed Books, 1984, pp. 342-344.

(24) See B. Fine, F. de Clerq and D. Innes, 'Trade unions and the state in South Africa: the question of legality' in Capital and Class, vol. 15, 1981, pp. 99-100.

(25) For a critique of this position see ibid.

(26) Barlow Rand, the biggest industrial conglomerate in South Africa, issued a statement towards the end of 1980 saying that it might be necessary to negotiate with unregistered unions. See S. Friedman, op. cit., p. 140.

(27) For a good discussion of the problems of translating the Wiehahn proposals into concrete legislation, see ibid., pp. 134-135.

(28) Commuters are African workers who reside in a so-called black homeland but travel to work each day to a designated white area in the Republic.

(29) TUCSA was for a long time the largest of the trade union federations in the Republic. Although for years it excluded blacks in favour of white, coloured and Indian workers, from 1973 onwards it began to promote a system of 'parallel' unions for Africans under the direct paternalistic control of an existing non-African union. Black workers were then enrolled by the union leaders fixing closed shop agreements with employers. See C. Cooper, 'The established trade union movement' in South Africa Review One, op. cit., pp. 208-209. The attitude of the TUCSA Unions towards the independent black unions has generally been hostile, so much so that the 1983 TUCSA conference approved a motion calling for all non-registered unions to be banned! See E. Webster, 'New force on the shop floor' in South Africa Review Two, Johannesburg, Raven Press, 1985, p. 84. In recent years TUCSA has been losing members heavily, with a reported drop in membership of over 200,000 between 1983 and 1985. See Annual Report on Labour Relations in South Africa 1985-86, Johannesburg, Andrew Levy and Associates, p. 8. This Report concludes that "it is now abundantly clear that TUCSA has no credibility amongst blacks".

(30) R. Southall in a review article entitled 'South African labour studies' in South African Labour Bulletin, vol. 9, no. 7, 1984, p. 107.

(31) Quoted in Annual Report on Labour Relations in South Africa 1985-86, op. cit., p. 38.

(32) For a discussion of the issues involved in this split see: I. Obery and M. Swilling, 'MAWU and UMMAWSA: fight for the factories' in Work in Progress, no. 33, 1984.

(33) See: Annual Report on Labour Relations in South Africa 1985-86, op. cit., p. 35.

(34) "CUSA's decision to stay out would seem to have a great deal more to do with long-standing antagonisms between some of its longer-serving leaders and the older COSATU unions than with any cosmic ideological rift." Industrial Relations Data, vol. 5, no. 6, 1986, Johannesburg, Andrew Levy and Associates, p. 8.

(35) For a discussion of the different political tendencies within the

black labour movement see: Annual Report on Labour Relations in South Africa 1985-86, op. cit., pp. 32-34; H. Barrell, 'The United Democratic Front and the National Forum: their emergence, composition and trends' in South Africa Review Two, op. cit., especially pp. 7-9; and M. Murphy, op. cit., especially pp. 20-23.

(36) The National Forum was not intended to be a permanent body but as its name suggests a consultative gathering of approximately 200 organisations of various kinds more or less bound together by a common commitment to black nationalism. The organisational thrust for the NF was provided by AZAPO. The UDF was born out of the election boycott campaigns of the early 1980s. It is an ad hoc coalition of community groups of various kinds - perhaps as many as 650 are currently affiliated - committed to the dismantling of apartheid. It subscribes to the Principles contained in the 1955 Freedom Charter drawn up by the African National Congress. For a brief discussion of both the NF and the UDF see H. Barrell op. cit.

(37) For a clear statement of these misgivings, see the interview with David Lewis, former general secretary of the GWU, 'General Workers' Union and the UDF' in Work in Progress, no. 29, 1983. For a statement of the opposing populist standpoint by one of the leaders of the SAAWU, see S. Njikelana, 'The unions and the Front: a reply to David Lewis' in South African Labour Bulletin, vol. 9, no. 7, 1984.

(38) Reported in H. Barrell, op. cit., p. 14. The FOSATU unions with their base in Natal had inevitably recruited members who were also involved with Chief Buthelezi's Inkatha movement. The hostility between the UDF and Inkatha is well known.

(39) E. Webster, op. cit., p. 88.

(40) Unlike official Government statistics this figure includes the ever-increasing number of workers in the 'independent' bantustans or so-called "TBVC countries" of the Transkei, Bophuthatswana, Venda and the Ciskei.

(41) Webster compares the figure for union density in South Africa - "the lowest percentage of workers unionised in the developed capitalist world" - with the figures for Sweden (83 per cent), the UK (50 per cent), West Germany (38 per cent), Japan (33 per cent) and the USA (20 per cent). Our figure of 15 per cent union density in South Africa is an estimate for 1986 and compares with Webster's 1983 figure of 12 per cent. See E. Webster, op cit, p. 80.

(42) Reliable figures on COSATU's membership are difficult to obtain. This figure is an estimate given in the Annual Report on Labour Relations in South Africa 1985-86, op. cit., p. 35. Other estimates put the figure closer to 500,000.

(43) According to Webster in 1981-82 ,Sweden had the highest number of working days lost per annum per 1,000 workers, with 105 days lost. The corresponding figures for the UK, the USA and South Africa were 45, 32 and 26 respectively. Op. cit., p. 81.

(44) S. Friedman, op. cit., p. 137.

(45) It should be remembered that foreign migrant workers are forbidden to join the new unions.

(46) Vose estimates that the long-term rate of black unemployment is 25 per cent: op. cit., p. 459. Other estimates suggest that the real level of black unemployment is closer to one third of the economically active black population. For example R. Davies, D. O'Meara and S. Dlamini state the black unemployment stood at three million at the end of 1982: op. cit., vol. 1, p. 55. The Government's own figures suggest a much lower rate of unemployment - 8.1 per cent in

September 1983. See J. Keenan, 'The recession and the African working class' in South Africa Review Two, op. cit., p. 136, for a critique of these official statistics.

(47) See G. Jaffe, 'The retrenchment process' in South Africa Review Two, op. cit.

(48) This is argued by R. Davies, D. O'Meara and S. Dlamini, op. cit., vol. 1, p. 55, and by J. Keenan, op. cit., p. 138.

(49) J. Keenan, ibid.

(50) See S. Gelb and D. Innes, op. cit., for a useful discussion both of the causes and of the content of the monetarist policies that the South African Government has used to attempt to resolve its economic crisis.

(51) Reported in C. Huhne, 'Hurting them may not hurt us' in The Guardian, 26 June 1986.

(52) D. van der Vat and A. White, op. cit.

(53) Ibid.

(54) The idea of non-racial or 'normal' capitalism is taken from R. Davies and D. O'Meara, op. cit., p. 65.

(55) The Federated Chambers of Industry is one of several organisations of industrial capital mainly representing domestic English-speaking employers. As a strong supporter of the 'total strategy' it argued strongly for labour reforms and for the integration of the new black unions into the established industrial relations system through the development of limited plant level bargaining. See R. Davies, D. O'Meara and S. Dlamini, op. cit., vol. 1, pp. 108-110.

(56) The much publicised visit by a group of prominent white businessmen to talk to the ANC is a good example of this 'verligte' tendency within white politics.